Re-Membering and Re-Imagining

Re-Membering and Re-Imagining

Nancy J. Berneking
and Pamela Carter Joern,
Editors

The Pilgrim Press
Cleveland, Ohio

The Pilgrim Press, Cleveland, Ohio 44115

Grateful acknowledgment is made for permission to reprint all or portions of the following material. Two poems, "Sophia's Lace" and "Fallout" by Nancy M. Fitzgerald, originally published in the *Journal of Feminist Studies in Religion,* vol. 11, no. 1, spring 1995. Reprinted with permission of the *Journal of Feminist Studies in Religion.* "A Time of Hope—A Time of Threat," originally prepared for a news conference on 22 February 1994. Reprinted with permission of Beryl Ingram-Ward on behalf of the Nine of Us: J. Ann Craig, Heather Murray Elkins, Ruth Harris, Peggy Halsey, Beryl Ingram-Ward, Susan Morrison, Pat Patterson, Jeanne Audrey Powers, Barbara Troxell. "Milk and Honey Ritual," by Hilda A. Kuester, originally written for the 1993 Re-Imagining Conference. Copyright © 1993 by Hilda Kuester. Reprinted with permission of the author. "Stay" by Carol Maillard. Copyright © 1993 by Carol Maillard. Lyrics reprinted with permission of the author and 4Jagadish Music. A portion of "Re-Imagining God," by Ingeline Nielsen, published in August 1994 in "Ascent," newsletter of Church of the Ascension, Hillside, Bulawayo, Zimbabwe. Here published as "Naming God" and reprinted with permission of Rector Noel Scott. The Re-Imagining logo used with permission of the Re-Imagining Community Coordinating Council. "Heresy," by Jeanette Stokes, originally published in "South of the Garden," the newsletter of the Resource Center for Women and Ministry in the South. Reprinted with permission of the Resource Center for Women and Ministry in the South, Durham, North Carolina. A portion of "After the Fact," by Martha D. Ward, originally published in *Sarah's Circular Journal,* vol. VII, June 1994, an annual publication of the Iowa Women in Ministry, an affiliate organization of the Iowa Conference of the United Methodist Church. Here published as "After the Fact" and reprinted with permission of *Sarah's Circular Journal.*

Biblical quotations are from the New Revised Standard Version of the Bible, © 1989 by the Division of Christian Education of the National Council of the Churches of Christ in the U.S.A., and are used by permission

Library of Congress Cataloging-in-Publication Data

Re-Membering and Re-Imagining / Nancy J. Berneking and Pamela Carter
    Joern, editors.
        p.   cm.
    Includes bibliographical references and index.
    ISBN 0-8298-1074-9
    1. Re-Imagining Conference (Minneapolis, Minn. : 1993)
    2. Feminist theology—Congresses.   I. Berneking, Nancy J., 1943–
II. Joern, Pamela Carter, 1948–
BT83.55.R4   1995
230'.082—dc20   95-16811
                                                         CIP

For our mothers

and grandmothers

Contents

Part Three: *Lamenting*

Part Four: *Rejoicing*

Part Five: *Going On*

Preface

Now and again Minneapolis is walloped by a severe winter storm with snows so heavy that one can only sit back in amazement, watch the inches pile up, and try to cope with the growing feeling of isolation. In the stormy aftermath of the Re-Imagining Conference, a global theological colloquium held in Minneapolis in November 1993, reaction was similar. Participants and planners were amazed by the fury of the storm as they watched rumors, innuendoes, charges, and countercharges deepen, and they felt increasingly isolated by a debate that largely ignored those who attended or were most responsible for creating the event.

But as the story of the controversy played itself out in column inches in religious tabloids and gigabytes on the Internet, different stories were making their way to Minneapolis. Like the persistent letter carrier who somehow makes it through a blizzard, these stories arrived unexpectedly and attested to their writers' conviction that truth must be heard. The stories spoke of transformation, affirmation, relief, and sheer joy. They were personal and holy. Sometimes angry, sometimes funny, the stories came as letters, poems, short typewritten notes, long handwritten statements. They filled hearts and notebooks.

As the rhetoric surrounding the conference reached a peak, some were calling it the Second Reformation, while others labeled it theologically aberrant. In either case, it became important to find a way to preserve the fragile, unpublished stories of those whose firsthand accounts should create the historical record of such an event. The idea of remembering the re-membering that happened at Re-Imagining developed into this book.

Since one of the premises of the conference was that everyone is capable of doing theological work, it was important to make this book one in which everyone could have a voice—not only the academically trained presenters. A letter went to all participants, inviting them to write their stories to add to those that had come unsolicited. In song, in poetry, in satire, in prose, in dialogue, in list, in drama, in letter the stories came. So many wonderful stories came in that we could only include a sample in the book, but we did try to select stories from a diversity of voices.

The youngest storyteller is eight, the oldest over eighty. They are mostly female, but the small number of male voices reflects the conference itself. Some are clergy, some are lay, some are lesbian, some are straight. We hear voices from the community of people with disabilities and from communities of color, from people whose lives revolve around church, and from people who no longer feel safe there. The storytellers come from nearly half of the states in the United States as well as a number of other countries. The diversity of faith groups is similar to the representation at the conference itself: many voices are Presbyterian, United Methodist, and Roman Catholic; fewer voices are American Baptist, Lutheran, United Church of Christ, evangelical, and Episcopalian. We also hear from those who are Waldensian or Disciples of Christ, Mennonite or Moravian, Church of England or Metropolitan Community Churches, among others. Included with stories of participants, presenters, and planners are stories submitted by some who did not attend the conference but were nevertheless affected by it.

When ninety-five people write about an event from their unique perspectives, intersections of stories—stories of the same moment unknowingly and independently written—can occur. Several such intersections are found in these stories. For example, the story of an announcement by women of the Church of the Brethren, renaming their denomination, is told by a church member and by nonmember observers; a Saturday morning call for solidarity with lesbian and bisexual women is told from the perspectives of the speaker, a conference planner, an admiring straight woman, and a man who lost his job because of it. Other intersections are those of people who sat at table together and changed one another, of people who came from the same church not knowing the other's shared interests, of people who renewed friendships though living a continent apart, of people who never met but shared a conference ticket.

Any time people come together as a community to worship God, it should be an evocative experience—one that calls forth the power of memory and imagination. It should be a work of the whole people of God who have come together, in which each person is invited to savor the gathering, to listen for and find God in the stories of lived experiences, to voice the prayers of lamenting, to raise the prayers of rejoicing, and to go out into the world to carry on the work of the gospel. The Re-Imagining Conference was designed to do just that.

The stories in this book are meant to be evocative as well, to call forth your memory and imagination. The book is divided into five sections—Gathering, Finding God, Lamenting, Rejoicing, and Going on—full of possibilities for re-membering and re-imagining.

You bring your own story to this book, and many of the stories in it will spark your memories of encounters with church, good and bad. Remembering—acknowledging, owning, and valuing the past that cannot be taken away—allows us to begin to re-member and to feel safe re-imagining the future.

Imagination, one of the gifts of a wildly imaginative Creator, helps us reach beyond the boundaries of what we know to embrace the possibilities of exploration. We are invited by the gospel to do that exploring within a community of differences, trusting that the community's process will lead to wisdom. The stories of the community of people who attended the Re-Imagining Conference call us to imagine what church can be. Evoking stories, listening and speaking, calling and recalling, re-membering and re-imagining will all be necessary to build a community of faith where justice finds a home. Listen to the stories.

Nancy J. Berneking

Introduction

In November 1993 a global ecumenical event was held in Minneapolis: the Re-Imagining Conference. It sparked enthusiasm and controversy; most people who were there loved it, some people who read about it were outraged.

The idea for the event came out of the Presbyterian Church (U.S.A.) as part of their effort to promote the World Council of Churches' Ecumenical Decade: Churches in Solidarity with Women. Decade projects were happening all over the world, but no major effort had yet been accomplished in the United States. The Women's Ministry Unit of the Presbyterian Church (U.S.A.) conceived the dream of a global theological colloquium; and Mary Ann Lundy, then head of the unit, shared the dream with the Reverend Sally L. Hill, a friend and colleague.

Sally Hill served as a liaison staff member for three councils of churches —Saint Paul Area, Greater Minneapolis, and Minnesota—and had already gathered a committee of denominationally appointed representatives to consider the needs of women in churches. The Minnesota committee agreed to the idea of a conference. Presbyterian money would provide the seed, but a great deal more money would have to be raised before the project was completed. Over the next four years, Sally Hill and a group of nearly 150 volunteers pulled together an event that was bolder and broader than anyone originally conceived.

The purpose was to bring together female theologians, clergy, and lay people to do theological work born out of women's experience. The conference, held at the Minneapolis Convention Center, ran from Thursday evening through Sunday morning, 4–7 November. There were thirty-four presenters, all women, in major plenaries and arts leadership and a host of women presenting on a wide range of topics in a period of afternoon options. Approximately two thousand people attended, representing forty-nine states and twenty-seven countries. Women outnumbered men twenty to one. Two-thirds of the participants were lay people, the rest clergy. With very few exceptions, they were church members, from nearly forty different denominations.

Within days after the closing ritual of the conference, conservative factions of some denominations mobilized an effort to denounce the conference. Mailings were sent encouraging churches to withhold funds from denominational activities and call for the resignation of church leaders and the censure of future feminist/womanist/*mujerista* activities.

What was it about this conference that made it stand out? Why did the

Re-Imagining story achieve such fame and notoriety that *Christian Century*[1] listed it among the top religion stories of the year?

Although it was no doubt inspiring to have so many diverse ideas expressed in one time and place, the theological explorations presented at Re-Imagining were not new. Most of the major presenters had written books or articles that had been circulating, at least within the academy, for a number of years. Many of these works were on required-reading lists at seminaries around the country.

Some suggested that the design of the conference made it unique. Great attention was given to implementing ideologies on a practical level. To emphasize the organizers' conviction that theological work is *everybody's* work and not just the province of experts, participants were seated at round tables and invited to discuss issues among themselves. The name Re-Imagining was chosen to reflect a conviction that theological work is artistic work. The arts were interwoven through music, dance, visual art, and drama. Participants were encouraged to draw at their tables, to join in the dance, and to lift their voices in song. All of these activities were integrated so that meals, discussion, song, dance, and speeches flowed one into another. As much as possible, these various activities occurred within the same space to emphasize that all of life and all our activities are sacred. The execution of these details was superb at Re-Imagining, but other women's conferences over the years have stressed inclusivity, participation, and wholeness.

Some conjectured that what made this conference different, and particularly difficult for conservatives to ignore, was that much of what occurred was set within a worship context. Some conservative literature suggested that people do not exercise their critical faculties during worship, that a participant may feel free to disagree with a speech but that there is an implicit acquiescence to worship. There were charges of coercion, even the suggestion that strategically placed movement leaders operated as monitors. However, deliberate attention was given both orally and through the program booklet to encourage individuals to take responsibility for their level of participation. Certainly the Re-Imagining ritual team sought to express emerging theological concepts, particularly the notion of using women's experience as the basis for theological exploration. New rituals were created for the Re-Imagining event, but the idea of new ritual has been circulating as an outgrowth of the liturgical reform movement of the last several decades. Furthermore, women's spirituality conferences have commonly offered worship, and prayer and song have long stood alongside analysis and debate.

Perhaps what made the Re-Imagining Conference special—and threatening—is that it was supported and sanctioned by the institutional church. Although even the largest denominational grants were small when compared to the total budget, and the money given by several supporting denominations was minuscule, support was present. Denominational offices were a key factor in helping to secure the names of presenters from around the world. Denominational publications promoted the conference as part of the Ecumenical Decade: Churches in Solidarity with Women. Additionally, the three local councils of churches in Minnesota allowed a staff person to allocate a major portion of her time to developing the event.

This institutional support had three practical outcomes. First, it opened up participation beyond the academy, and beyond dedicated feminists, to invite women in the pew. Second, feminist/womanist/*mujerista* church leaders and theologians sensed that women's time had finally come. After a history of marginalization and invisibility, of oppression and outright persecution, perhaps the institutional church was ready to extend recognition and respect to *all* its members. Third, it ignited the fear and fury of the religious right. Suddenly, what had been a dangerous but marginalized movement was encroaching on home territory—and many conservatives rose up to stop it.

In the face of the religious right's threats to withhold funds and withdraw memberships, some denominations backed down. With varying degrees of attempted diplomacy, church officials sought to distance themselves from the actual event while declaring their support of women. This tactic didn't work. Conservative groups demanded concrete actions, and Re-Imagining supporters felt betrayed. Many institutions focused on keeping individual denominations intact and missed the opportunity for any real learning that might have resulted from the conference.

The story, of course, has not ended. The spirit of Re-Imagining continues through the newly organized Re-Imagining Community. The call for theological reform is broadcast by long-standing organizations and newly formed groups both within and outside the institutional church. Although the gap between women's concerns and the institutional church may appear temporarily widened and the bridge somewhat tentative, the Re-Imagining Conference took place—institutionally sanctioned and a good thing in the lives of many people—and that can never be taken away.

The stories in this book speak for themselves. They are loving, or in some cases challenging, remembrances. They build a history to remind us of common bonds, invite new participation, and enter our lives through grieving and celebration. We remember, literally, to re-member: to remind ourselves, once again, that we are members of a connected human community.

We offer this collection as an invitation. It is our great hope that this book of stories will evoke your memory and your imagination.

Pamela Carter Joern

PART ONE

Gathering

We gather as a community. All of us bring the stories of our lives to this time.

Though some stories may have intersected in the past, and many stories may

have elements in common, no two stories are alike. Our stories extend to the

past as far as we can remember and beyond, and our stories show the effects of

the most recent days and hours. But we gather, seeking to become a commu-

nity for a time, and so we must honor the stories we bring

of re-membering . . .

and re-imagining . . .

In the Beginning

MARY ANN W. LUNDY

We walked into the Minneapolis Convention Center on 4 November with excitement. Most of the nineteen of us from the Women's Ministry Unit of the Presbyterian Church (U.S.A.) were here among old friends and colleagues. We were finding each other across differences of age, culture, race, and denomination. Tears filled our eyes, tears of delight. We were overwhelmed and awed, for our dream of a global theological colloquium, as we had called it, had originated in our unit, and now it was happening: the Re-Imagining Conference.

In 1988 the Presbyterian church had instituted the Bicentennial Fund, a capital fund drive seeking $125 million for programs at every level of the church. These new monies were to be used to expand our programs and projects and to enable us as a denomination to be more responsive to the needs of those around us in the 1990s. All nine of the denomination's ministry units were to submit proposals to the prospectus committee, which would approve projects and funding levels. We were encouraged to "dream dreams" and to "be creative" as we shaped our proposals. Seven of the Women's Ministry Unit's projects were approved, most of them in observance of the Ecumenical Decade: Churches in Solidarity with Women (1988–1998).

The World Council of Churches had started the Ecumenical Decade in order to involve churches in the concerns of women, after realizing that the recent United Nations Decade for Women had had little impact on churches worldwide. There were several conversations among women leaders about a "Presbyterian gift" to the Ecumenical Decade's observance in the United States. What were we Presbyterians uniquely suited to contribute? It didn't take us long to come up with an idea: our historical interest in and articulation of theology. We had always been committed to an educated clergy as "a people of the book," the head-trippers. It was Presbyterians who had most often declared that if a subject is controversial, we study it, and then we know how to act on it. In addition, we wanted to do something with a global dimension since one goal of the Women's Ministry Unit was to do all our work in a global context—to seek to be in solidarity with women around the world.

So our proposal for a colloquium was born and approved for funding. Our original idea was for a small conference of two to three hundred people in dialogue with invited theologians. They would be videotaped, and texts

3

would be made available with study materials for use by local women's groups. We wavered on whether the conference itself would be ecumenical or for Presbyterians only, but our strong commitment was that any event would be dialogical: that the participants and leaders would have conversation, that the format would be in the round, and that there would be time for interaction among women from many parts of the world. We thought of round tables of people gathered as families, where women and men of various cultures could develop relationships as they responded to conference presenters.

During this time, the United States Committee for the Ecumenical Decade was organized. I had been elected co-chair, along with Bishop Forrest Stith, a United Methodist. One of the early considerations was whether this committee would sponsor major programs and projects or serve as a clearing-house for locally sponsored events. The conclusion of that ecumenical group was that if it doesn't happen locally, it doesn't make an impact. So we decided that we would support local ecumenical groups as they planned their own events, programs, and projects.

Meanwhile, we Presbyterians were thinking about how we could plan a major event in light of operating budget cuts and a staff overwhelmed by ongoing work. Having our colloquium planned locally made a lot of sense to us, and so we looked to those committees forming around the country for a group with whom we could work in partnership. We wanted a committee broadly representative of the ecumenical community, one that was well organized and that had a global perspective.

We found our local group in the Twin Cities Decade committee. It had been formed by the councils of churches with Roman Catholic participation and was already holding hearings in churches around Minnesota to determine the needs of women. With proposal in hand, I met with Sally Hill, a long-time friend and Presbyterian clergywoman, who was on the staff of the Twin Cities Metropolitan Church Commission of the councils of churches and who had been named to staff the Twin Cities Decade committee. Sally was enthusiastic about our proposal from the beginning and took it to her committee, which eagerly began to plan.

Though we did not write a contract outlining the partnership and the expectations for the event, Sally and I were both aware that the stipulations for the colloquium in the original Presbyterian proposal would need to be accountable to the Bicentennial Fund process. The colloquium had been proposed for 1992, but it soon became evident that we would not be ready by then. In addition, churches were not giving to the Bicentennial Fund at the rate originally projected. Thus everything was behind schedule.

By 1990 it was clear that a decision had to be made about whether to go ahead with the conference. The planning was proceeding, but international theologians had to be invited at least two years ahead, and funds needed to be in hand to cover their expenses. Nancy Thornton McKenzie, chairperson of the unit committee, and I sent a letter to the committee authorized to approve advances for projects that could not be begun or would have to be canceled without funding. Though our unit's original funding request had been for $175,000, I went before the committee to plead our case and was given immediate authorization for $66,000 to be used to bring at least twenty-two speakers for the conference. We were off and running!

At a retreat at the Minnesota Church Center, I joined a small group from the Twin Cities planning committee for dinner and the evening meeting. We met in the cafeteria, outlining our work on a portable blackboard. We began to discuss a title for the event. Sally was writing as we talked of several possibilities: "images," "image," "imaging," "re-imaging." But Sally wrote *re-imagining* by mistake. We laughed and discussed it at some length, and we said we liked it better. We did not make a firm decision that evening, but the title seemed to stick.

Little did we realize that first evening how descriptive, how perceptive, and how profound the theological process of re-imagining is. *Re-imagining* has become a household word[1] in American theological circles—the work of the Spirit once again!

As the planning continued, the efforts to publicize the event and monitor its development were under way as well. Presbyterian women distributed ten thousand brochures and informed all major women's networks. It became common for women to leave space in their luggage for brochures as they attended meetings all over the world. Some of the planners in the Twin Cities had difficulty believing that two thousand people would come, but those of us who were watching the event take shape from afar grew more and more excited. I could not attend regular monthly meetings of the Twin Cities planning committee, but I received minutes of all the meetings and sent a quarterly update to the ministry unit committee. A more extensive progress report was made at each unit committee meeting. In addition, a Presbyterian Church (U.S.A.) Decade committee had been formed of women and men from across the church. They, too, monitored the progress through written reports during the three years of planning.

And then, at last, the Re-Imagining Conference. Throughout the conference, it was my conviction and that of the ministry unit committee that what we experienced in those few days had not happened quite that way before and might never happen in that way again, but would be with us always, giving new energy, new dimensions to our lives. We were so proud to have been a small part in dreaming the beginning dream for a new reality for women of faith.

Mary Ann W. Lundy is serving a four-year term as deputy general secretary of the World Council of Churches in Geneva, Switzerland. She is a 1995 recipient of the Distinguished Alumni-ae Award of Union Theological Seminary in New York.

Nightmare and Miracle on Twelfth Avenue and Fifth Street

PATRICIA SCHUCKERT

It was Halloween weekend, a gray Saturday morning. I gathered all the things I needed for the last dance rehearsal for the Re-Imagining Conference before Carla De Sola arrived. I made a checklist: fifty-five pizza rounds to practice the bread dance, more than thirty rehearsal tapes and the recorder to dub them, rehearsal notes to be duplicated, notebook with the year's process and all choreographic notes, nametags, check-in sheets—you get the picture—and personal things: dance shoes, rehearsal clothes, professional calendar, purse, dress clothes for a church service after rehearsal, and so forth. My life and identity were in that bag.

Grateful for a station wagon, I headed for the copy shop: fifty-five copies of the rituals for the four days, rehearsal order, layout of the conference space, each dancer's position, partners for the opening song, and places for "Babylon." I thought to myself: finally everyone will have a sense of orientation and partnership in this adventure.

Next, pick up keys, set up, and get the synthesizer from Newman down the street. I pulled up alongside Saint Lawrence rectory, twenty feet from the front door. I didn't lock the door; the car was in plain sight. I rang the doorbell and turned to people-watch as I waited: an elderly woman down the street leaned into the wind, a young couple heading the other direction huddled together, a mother and child crossed the intersection, and a tall young man wearing a blue backpack came toward me with his hood pulled tight around his head. (Unless the weather changes, I reflected, Halloween is not going to be much fun for the little ones.) The door opened, and I asked for the keys. They were right there. I thanked the young woman and turned to go back to my car. But where did I park it? I thought it was on Twelfth Avenue. I spun to make sure that I wasn't on overload and had forgotten where I parked it. No—it was gone! I ran to the street; it was truly gone, and everything for the rehearsal with it.

I went back to the rectory, reported the theft, then headed over to the rehearsal space. The show must go on. It was there that the nightmare began to become a miracle. In the twenty minutes before rehearsal, my co-chairs, Susan and Trisha, took over check-in; someone else picked up the synthesizer;

7

another called her spouse to buy and bring more tapes; on and on as I talked with police.

We started on time, and as I told my story the support in the room became palpable—a deeply felt connection from the hearts of those beautiful women. Their concern spilled over into rehearsal, with each wanting to know how she could help. Sue dug into her storehouse to find copies of the ritual, music, space diagram, names, and phone numbers. May recontacted everyone about costumes. Susan and Trisha helped rebuild all the movement notes. Amy spun off the rehearsal tapes and collected names and addresses. Karen slowed me down enough to make a list of lost items and to cancel credit cards. Jean located all the tables where dancers had been assigned so that I could reconstruct the partnering and space arrangements. And so it went throughout the week. It even flowed over into the folks at my church who found me transportation until my car was located, and who went to the impound lot at 11:00 P.M. to claim it. It was totally cleaned out—even the smallest scraps of paper.

I'm told the conference ritual didn't show the stress and distress of my week, thanks to the gifted support of so many marvelous women, who became community to me and to each other.

After the conference, Amy sent out copies of my address with a note about offering some financial support. Carrie mentioned my experience at a celebration ritual after the conference. I later learned that people who didn't even know me prayed for me in their congregations the next Sunday. The collection of love and support that came in notes of appreciation were and continue to be most powerful, and the financial gifts almost covered all my deductibles. I still find myself filled to overflowing with awe and heartfelt gratitude.

Patricia Schuckert, MPS, is a Roman Catholic, living in Minneapolis, where she has a private practice as a body educator and therapist. She also works as a sacred dancer, choreographer, and ritual artist, and her work includes the 1993 and 1994 Re-Imagining Conferences. Her interest is in the integration of body, mind, and spirit, and the embodiment of the arts. She loves to watch life unfold.

A Musical Tapestry

GLORIA A. TAYLOR-JAMES

It wasn't until the moment we saw the dancers move to Denean's "As One We Walk This Earth Together" that the performance anxiety faded and the spirit of service arose. Until then, the music participants' Re-Imagining did not resemble the dream at all.

As we researched and gathered music for the conference, we asked hard questions. When an invitation is issued to other cultures and efforts are made to include elements expressing those cultures, what happens when the invitation is not eagerly accepted? Should we go forward with the plan, or would we be perceived as exploiting the richness of a culture?

Knocking on the door of hard questions like these, we forged ahead with a commitment to inclusiveness. While efforts were made to represent the ethnicity of all women—we wanted to have ethnic choral groups which would start on Thursday in corners of self-identity and become a tapestry of unity when we closed on Sunday—the stark reality was that many women, particularly women of color, have a difficult time conceptualizing the feminine side of the deity. Even though we are quick to acknowledge those attributes within our God—love, care, and compassion—that typically are defined as feminine, the gendering of God struck some immensely sour chords. As I attempted to recruit women for the "dream team" from within my own African American culture, I found myself warning that they would need to have a comfort level with the pronoun *She* associated with God. In retrospect, it was never an issue. The beauty of the music, dance, and artistry brought forward such a sense of warmth, gifts, service, and life force that the political agenda stood still. I attended all four days, and I remain completely baffled by the media reports of the event. I saw none of what was reported.

During the research, I was reticent about throwing my heritage into the pot for fear of low participation. Our African American songs are rich. Our African American presence is what interprets that richness—as within the genius of every other culture.

One of the more inspiring aspects of the research teams centered around reflective reminiscing about songs of our culture. "Hush, Somebody's Callin' Mah Name" brought to me a vivid image of an older African American woman sitting on her front porch in a rocking chair on a warm summer's evening,

9

singing, humming, crying, laughing to herself. That was the beauty of the research. We not only looked at the elements of inclusiveness, singability, encouragement, and celebration of female strength and solidity, but we warmed ourselves in the history each suggested song brought forward.

Beyond ethnic inclusiveness, there was the logistical nightmare of actualizing the dream of a four-corner stereo choral sound with four conductors. The single rehearsal in the space on Thursday was a rude awakening. But we were at the starting gate, and we could not turn back. Group I ahead of Group II. Group III dancing on the platform. Even these wrinkles smoothed over as the program started and the ritual began.

Then there was Jo Morris, the conference songleader. What an electric moment of working! Such spontaneity! Along with Jo, a number of us formed the music-stretches team. It was amazing how each team singer showed unique glitches of spontaneity. Each had something so different to offer, and Jo invited each of those spirits to come forward and utter joyful noises. We had a great time sharing and spreading that joy throughout the conference.

Over the entire course of Re-Imagining, the richness never faded. The closing service proved to be as powerful and inspiring as the first. At the first singing of Cathy Tisel Nelson's "What You Hold," we—all singers—recognized the beauty of such a wonderful and thought-provoking piece. It had been woven such that the culmination of the conference events seemed to filter through that song. As I tried to concentrate on the monitors for sound cues and on the other directors for light cues, tears just welled up and flowed uninterrupted. I seemed to have vivid reflections of every thought during the conference. The wonderful dream of weaving together a tapestry had been realized.

Gloria A. Taylor-James is an African American music minister, who has served as a music minister for Baptist, Catholic, and Methodist churches over the past twenty years.

Preparing to Leap

NANCY M. FITZGERALD

During the summer before the Re-Imagining Conference, I read and studied Elizabeth Johnson's *She Who Is*. Johnson, with her careful scholarship, convinced me of the existence of female spirit in the creation story. But being convinced rationally was just a start. I needed to know through the many layers of my soul; I needed a leap of faith. I went to Re-Imagining looking for a community of worshipers who were struggling to do the same work. I left exalted.

Sophia's Lace

It is summer on the hilltop.
Breezes fold field flowers.
Creamy white clusters of
Queen Anne's Lace
enfold me in their lacy space.

Gracious God Sophia,
Partner in Creation,
Tree of life, hidden treasure,
born before these hills,
before the brimming springs,
before the lakes,
breathe on me.

My imagination's been becalmed.
Breeze through my being,
blow through my mind,
like a billowing spinnaker.
Show me how to tack, to
zigzag through the mystery
to run before the wind
and name it you.

I have new truth
I need new faith.

It's time to see your hand
in wind and Queen Anne's Lace.

Fallout

On August first the moon is full.
It shines a shimmery streak
across the rippled water,
and beams bright white down
on this hilltop.
The cat looks up surprised as
I turn up the music and
step out to dance.
"This whole world keeps spinnin' 'round."
I move across the deck in Texas Two Step,
line dance without the line,
switch to pirouettes and arabesques.
My shadow leaps and lunges
staring now, alone in
her own brilliance.

The sky's a candelabra.
Ursa Major drips, Cassiopeia
billows sparks across the sky,
the waxy moon burns bright.

I turn the music down,
reach heavenward and stop—
released into believing.
All creatures of the earth
are made of fallout from the stars.

Nancy M. Fitzgerald is a poet living in Duluth, Minnesota, with her husband. She is co-chair of women's studies and teaches writing at the College of Saint Scholastica. Her chapbook An Inward Turning Out *was recently published by Poetry Harbor. She is a member of the United Church of Christ.*

Looking over the Edge

NORMA SOMMERDORF

Letters began to come in from remote places. Some had the beautiful hand-writing of the other side of the world. Others arrived addressed in the fine script of European training. Requests for tickets came from women who were lecturing on one continent but had to be reached on another because their schedules and expertise kept them traveling. These stimulating and scholarly women were coming to Minnesota to address the Re-Imagining Conference. In this way a small, woman-owned travel agency in Saint Paul became part of the exciting effort to bring women together from many parts of the world to re-imagine God and the world we live in today.

It was to become a global meeting of ideas and theological thought. Funding from many denominations made it possible to bring speakers who added the yeast to the dough of this conference. Those who presented lectures and workshops came from Sri Lanka and Korea, from Ghana and Zimbabwe, from Palestine and Jordan. Registrations flowed in from all continents and from most mainline denominations. Theological students came from South America and South Korea, from Newfoundland and New Zealand. People from every part of the world applied for scholarships, and additional funds were found to grant most requests. This alone was a refreshing experience. What woman associated with the church is not accustomed to low budgets and discouraged volunteers? To negative thinking and rigid reaction from the congregation or the church staff? To lack of money to do it right? The prevailing Re-Imagining attitude was that all things were possible: room for more to come and funds to make it happen.

Anticipation and hope for a precedent-setting, exhilarating experience were part of every planning session. The larger community, the wider circle of sisterhood was coming together. But this vision of what tomorrow could be—a world of oneness, of hope, of united purpose—at last drew so many registrations that by the time of the first session, hundreds of people had been turned away. The space selected years before, the Minneapolis Convention Center, could hold no more.

We sat together in table groups of ten, wanting to know one another, bewildered that there was not time. "Too white and too middle-class," was the reaction of one who sat down with her tablemates. She soon learned of the diversity among their similarities: a woman in the midst of chemotherapy, a former nun, a nineteen-year-old from northeastern Canada, a recent widow, a lesbian, a church leader. We wondered and thought together, thirsty for more, but some still bemoaned the small number of persons of color in the audience.

After bringing presenters from all parts of the world, participants could hear only a few of them. Every afternoon we had to choose between four simultaneous sessions, each with three diverse presenters. Each speaker raised questions; eager minds in the audience asked more questions, sometimes giving voice to thoughts not shared before. What was the world of the Old Testament like? How did these women assert themselves? Why are there so many seldom-mentioned women in the Bible? The women of Jesus' day, of Paul's acquaintance: who were they, and what did they think? What has happened to the church throughout history? How much does the church reflect its time rather than going back to ancient teachings? How much did the Victorian Era surround and influence the church that we are part of today? Many assumptions were open for examination. Questions and more questions. Not fear, but freedom. It was the beginning of the re-imagining process.

After years of questioning and doubt, many of us reach a plateau where we feel comfortable. It's a place where we no longer reexamine every thought and idea. We come to accept ourselves and the ways our minds work. But once in a while we look over the edge of that plateau. It's as though we live on a spinning plate; occasionally we spin to the edge of the plate and look over with a sense of fear and excitement. We have a fear of falling into the unknown, of leaving the security of the comfortable. Re-Imagining was like that. It was a time to reflect and reexamine thoughts and attitudes that living in our present age and place has deposited into our consciousness. It opened minds and feelings to a wider sphere. It gave us a sense of oneness. It was a rich experience among many other like-minded seekers. As we returned to the places in the world we each call home, minds soared with new ways of looking at age-old, often ignored stories.

Norma Sommerdorf is a Minnesota travel agent and an American Baptist.

Flat-heeled Shoes and Blue Jeans

MARION LOGAN

I checked my bank account then called my clergyman son in Toronto to ask if he wanted to attend a conference of the Ecumenical Decade: Churches in Solidarity with Women in the States. He exuberantly replied, "I'm going—to help coordinate ten other United Church of Canada young people!" I realized at that moment that my lifelong personal vision for wholeness and equality for women had become a part of my son's life.

Throughout Paul's growing-up years, his dad and I had provided opportunities for him and his two brothers to sample experiences we thought they should have—the symphony, museums, Stratford Shakespeare plays, camping trips to northern Ontario—but not hockey or football games. They paid their own way to any games where violence and extreme competitiveness ruled.

Paul grew up with a mother who spent much of her married life trying to break out of the wall or climb over the restrictions that narrowly defined women's lives in the 1950s and 1960s. Those were the days when family life was glorified, and every good church family trotted off to worship each Sunday, the mother dressed up in white gloves and a lovely flowered hat and the sons wearing gray flannel pants, white shirts with bow ties, and navy blazers. Paul and I both dumped some of the middle-class trappings at the same time. I went to flat-heeled shoes, comfortable and safe. He now preaches with blue jeans and running shoes showing beneath his alb. He jokes that he grew up with inclusive language and feminist liberation theology before they were named as such.

As I have extended my church experiences and spiritual horizons by global traveling to visit Methodist church women, particularly in South Africa, Paul has developed his spirituality through visits of his own. He went to Korea during the student uprisings in 1986, participated in the Roman Catholic Taizé Centre with prolonged periods of contemplative silence, met church activists in South Africa who took daily risks working to end apartheid, visited Muslim Morocco, and experienced the gentle Buddhist monks in India. The connections between and the causes of global poverty, enmity, and oppression, as well as gender inequalities, became clear to both of us. And now we would both travel to Minnesota to re-imagine other ways of further extending our spiritual horizons.

What a good feeling it was to be able to make eye contact with Paul across the several tables that separated us at Re-Imagining. To watch him sit quietly and listen deeply to the pain of the women at his table group, to know that he also was able to celebrate the liberating words of the theological speakers, was a unique experience for this mother.

Re-Imagining was a Pentecost moment for me. I know that it has also been a transforming time (electrifying jolt) in many church denominations. This transformation is just as institutionally painful as my own journey of transformation has been. As Paul grew up, he often experienced—sometimes in negative ways—my frustrations, anger, and confusion. How thankful I am that my son and other feminist men who remain in the church understand and are able to give voice to the need for change that must take place if women and men are to live in harmony.

Marion Logan sometimes found it difficult being a woman in a family with a husband and three sons; her reality was different. She recently retired as a college teacher. She also has worked for the YWCA and at the women's desk of the United Church of Canada. In 1994 she received an honorary doctor of divinity degree for her contributions to the women's movement in her church and for her international work.

Speaking of Theology

JUDITH ALLEN KIM

The minutes in my Ecumenical Decade folder begin in January of 1990, and I wasn't even in the first round of planners. It was a simple act of faith when we paid a deposit on the Minneapolis Convention Center for November of 1993. It seemed that we had forever to do the planning, that the date was so far away that it would never come.

As a member of the program committee, I remember the early brainstorming about which speakers to invite. In seminary I had not read many female theologians, but it was easy to begin the lists with those we had studied and were eager to hear more from. Most of these women were white and North American. But a major part of our plan was to have a multicultural and multiracial gathering, so we needed to expand our list of possible speakers.

Early in the process, we also decided not to invite only well-known feminist theologians, but to give some rising stars a chance to be heard. We received suggestions of names from women's program leaders of many denominations. Soon I didn't know most of the names on the list. We were challenged to learn pronunciations of unfamiliar names and biographies of amazing women. I trusted the process by which we sought names, especially when a recommendation came from more than one source.

When the Re-Imaginers convened in Minneapolis that blustery week in November 1993 we heard a number of North Americans. Both Letty Russell and Sally McFague were unavailable for our conference, but Beverley Wildung Harrison and Jacquelyn Grant came to stretch us. We were also challenged by Aruna Gnanadason, Sister José Hobday, Chung Hyun Kyung, Nalini Jayusuria, Mercy Amba Oduyoye, Kwok Pui-Lan, Elsa Tamez, and many others.

I arrived with questions and went away with even more questions. I came with a heart ready to re-imagine, and I was not disappointed.

Judith Allen Kim is an interim associate pastor serving a Presbyterian church in suburban Minneapolis. Before attending United Theological Seminary of the Twin Cities, she was a teacher and a community and church volunteer. She is amicably divorced and the mother of four fabulous young adults. She once received a phone call from her fifth-grade son's church school teacher letting her know that her child had begun a descriptive essay with the words "God is a loving dude or dudette."

17

Creating the Sophia Ritual

HILDA A. KUESTER

I wrote the Sophia ritual that was quoted over and over by the press and critics. I wrote it in one sitting. It was as if I'd been waiting all my life to have a public opportunity to thank the Creator for sexuality, sensuality, and physicality. It was my chance to express with abandon my joy and pride in being a woman. Obviously I struck a chord in the women at the conference. That Sunday morning when the words were read, a wave of electricity went through the crowd, and women hooted and hollered in celebration of a silence broken. Since that day, women have frequently asked my permission to use the ritual or to quote the text in their own writings.

My mother taught me to be proud of being a woman. She celebrated my first menses by announcing to female relatives, "She's a woman now!" As an adolescent in the 1970s, my society began to affirm human sexuality. However, I soon learned that affirming women's sexuality was dangerous. Courts blamed women's sexuality for the phenomenon of rape. Men had a love/hate relationship with sexually expressive women. That realization eventually inspired my doctoral dissertation on feminist theology and woman battering.

It was no surprise to me that the sexual content of my liturgy terrified, mesmerized, and angered the establishment. Fear of women's sexuality and power hasn't diminished much in my lifetime. In fact, religious fundamentalism in various cultures is trying to turn back the clock. I was sorry for the way misinterpretations of this liturgy and other conference events hurt my colleagues. I celebrate, however, the way the backlash helped us quickly organize to continue the work begun at Re-Imagining.

Creating rituals for the conference and then participating had a profound impact on me. One dramatic result of my experience is that I am beginning to hold a feminine image as my primary image of God. This was largely the result of discovering, as I wrote, all the richness in a fully developed, gender-specific image of God as Sophia. The pattern in many of our churches is to slip in a female name or image for God and then immediately return to nonsexist and neuter language for the deity. Seeing what flowed from my pen when Sophia was invoked, described, and praised created an inner shift. Unconsciously and spontaneously, my thoughts and language moved away from a neuter divinity to a feminine God with whom I connect in a very deep, primitive, and natural way.

Milk and Honey Ritual[2]

Blessing over Milk and Honey

> *Our mother Sophia, we are women in your image:*
> *With the hot blood of our wombs we give form to new life.*
> *With the courage of our convictions we pour out our life blood for justice.*

> Sophia-God, Creator-God,
> let your milk and honey pour out,
> showering us with your nourishment.

> *Our mother Sophia, we are women in your image:*
> *With the milk of our breasts we suckle the children;*
> *With the knowledge of our hearts we feed humanity.*

> Sophia-God, Creator-God,
> let your milk and honey pour out,
> showering us with your nourishment.

> *Our sweet Sophia, we are women in your image:*
> *With nectar between our thighs we invite a lover, we birth a child;*
> *With our warm body fluids we remind the world of its pleasures and*
> *   sensations.*

> Sophia-God, Creator-God,
> let your milk and honey pour out,
> showering us with your nourishment.

> *Our guide, Sophia, we are women in your image:*
> *With our moist mouths we kiss away a tear, we smile encouragement.*
> *With the honey of wisdom in our mouths, we prophesy a full humanity to all*
> *   the peoples.*

> Sophia-God, Creator-God,
> let your milk and honey pour out,
> showering us with your nourishment.

Thanksgiving for the Shared Milk and Honey

> *Sophia, we celebrate your life-giving energy which pulses through our veins,*
> *We celebrate women attempting to preserve life while surrounded by war,*
> *   famine and disease.*

We celebrate women's willingness to pour out their lifeblood for others; to celebrate, to fight, and to protect both what they believe in and those whom they love.

We celebrate your wisdom poured out upon women for eons.

We celebrate our unique perspectives, intelligence, intuitions, and processes.

We celebrate our mentors, our guides, our spiritual mothers, our models.

We celebrate the nourishment of your milk and honey.

Your abundance drips through your fingers onto us and we in turn feed others.

Through the sharing of this holy manna we enter into community which strengthens and renews us for the struggle.

We celebrate the sensual life you give us.

We celebrate the sweat that pours from us during our labors.

We celebrate the fingertips vibrating upon the skin of a love.

We celebrate the tongue which licks a wound or wets our lips.

We celebrate our bodiliness, our physicality, the sensations of pleasure, our oneness with earth and water.

The Reverend Dr. Hilda Kuester is a Disciples pastor and a marriage and family therapist working at a United Church of Christ church in the Twin Cities. She has served as a senior, associate, and interim pastor during the last fifteen years. Her doctoral dissertation in 1989 was on "Feminist Theology and Violence against Women." Her Sophia ritual is one of many creative worship texts she has written.

Kairos Moments

LOU SCHOEN

The *kairos* moments that shape our lives derive from events and relationships, words and actions, negative and positive experiences. A relationship with Jeanette Piccard in the Episcopal Society for Cultural and Racial Unity during the 1960s led to one such moment for me. In July 1974, when she was among eleven deacons ordained irregularly to the priesthood, I was inspired to get involved in the movement to ordain women as priests rather than leave a church that had voted three times not to ordain women. Thus I came to be at a hearing of a committee studying this issue and heard a Texas priest, who later became a bishop, testify that the crosslike shape of male sexual organs symbolizes the divine command for an exclusively masculine priesthood.

His perspective symbolized, for me, the dominant-white-male mentality which denies emotion and true spirituality, which disguises as justifiable anger its fear of power-loss, and which tries to brush off as mere "political correctness" active opposition to various forms of oppression. This mentality has shaped the oppressive systems that contradict the ideals of Western political democracies and, in the church, belie both the letter and the spirit of the gospel.

For me, the toughest question posed by Re-Imagining is: how does a responsible male rethink his identity and help transform male socialization in relation to Judeo-Christian teachings, to men's roles in the church and the family, and to our function in society? From home to church to politics to business to entertainment, traditional male role models have relied on projections of physical size and strength for credibility. How can we change the cultural expectation that we will seek to dominate women? I believe we must honestly acknowledge the power we hold in social and institutional life and seek out ways to share it.

Liberation theology teaches that change comes through praxis: interactive reflection and action. Men are typically socialized to act without reflection. I was prodded to reflection by pacifist parents; by a Methodist Sunday school teacher who taught that masculine God language was generic, not gender specific; by the historic 1972 federal equal opportunity decree against the Bell System, which I then served as a middle manager; by Jeanette Piccard; and even by a business failure that led me to enter seminary late in my fifth decade. Reflection has pressed me to acknowledge that my authentic ministry must be to other males if I am true to Christ's calling to be an agent of change in the church and society.

Men not exposed in their early years to a love for peace and justice—or to an understanding of these qualities as central to faith or of faith as central to life—are tough nuts to crack. The angry white male whose 1994 rebellion Gingriched the United States House of Representatives and Helmed the Senate reflects a form of insanity. I suspect that this insanity is not unlike that which Jesus had in mind when, while challenging disciples to keep working for healing, he acknowledged, "This kind [of demon] can come out only through prayer" (Mark 9:29).

Yet repeatedly Jesus emphasized the usefulness of collective, faithful, prayerful, informed, patient, loving action in resisting and removing evil from human beings and communities. This should give us both hope and direction. There is hope if women and men work together to re-imagine our spiritual context, reclaim our common divine roots, and require cultural and institutional changes that assert our equal authority and dignity in the face of evil principalities and powers.

Lou Schoen is a late-blooming lay professional in ecumenical ministry whose re-imagining has been aided importantly by his wife, three daughters, and two granddaughters. He is Director of Life and Work for the Minnesota Council of Churches, where he initiated the Minnesota Churches' Anti-Racism Initiative. He is also coordinator of cross-cultural and contextual studies at United Theological Seminary of the Twin Cities and coordinator of a study of multicultural-program collaboration for the Minnesota Consortium of Theological Schools. He earned a master of arts degree in religious leadership from United in 1992.

A Series of Miracles

NADEAN BISHOP

Perri Graham, lay staff member of Church World Service and a very pregnant lesbian, convened the first planning session for the inclusion of lesbian themes among the late-afternoon options at Re-Imagining. She was waiting for the miracle of her son's birth while the six of us who gathered for almost-weekly planning were about to experience several unanticipated miracles.

We chatted awhile and settled on an overarching title of "Listening with Our Hearts." The Friday session, which I agreed to chair, was subtitled "Prophetic Voices of Lesbians in the Church." The Friday group decided to deal with interpretation of biblical texts from a lesbian perspective, while the Saturday team chose to talk about lesbians in the contemporary church.

In keeping with the rest of the conference, we knew we wanted more than talking heads, so I invited Diane Christopherson, a doctoral candidate at United Theological Seminary of the Twin Cities, to play and sing some of her original songs for the gathering and meditation parts of the time together. Diane and I had met at the first national meeting of Christian Lesbians Out Together (CLOUT) in Minneapolis in late October 1991, the weekend I was a candidate to become pastor of University Baptist Church in Minneapolis and the weekend of the legendary twenty-eight-inch Halloween blizzard. We had weathered that storm together and therefore felt we could tackle anything that came our way.

Diane and I decided to invite three cofounders of CLOUT to join me in the panel discussion. Our first miracle happened: in one afternoon of phoning, I spoke directly to three of the busiest lesbians I know and received three enthusiastic acceptances. The Reverend Janie Spahr, who had been called to the Downtown Presbyterian Church of Rochester, New York, the weekend of the CLOUT snowstorm but was subsequently denied installation by the Permanent Judicial Commission of the Presbyterian Church (U.S.A.), is a lesbian evangelist. The Reverend CathyAnn Beatty is pastor of Spirit of the Lakes, a huge United Church of Christ congregation in Minneapolis. The Reverend Melanie Morrison is codirector of Leaven in Lansing, Michigan (an organization that provides resources and workshops in feminism, spiritual development, and sexual justice), and formerly pastored a gay/lesbian congregation in Kalamazoo, Michigan.

On that Friday afternoon, thirty copies of programs and bibliographies

23

on lesbian theology had been prepared for those we thought could comfortably fit in the assigned space. Our second miracle: more than a hundred gathered, sitting on every inch of floor and spilling out into the corridor. I was so thrilled my feet hardly touched the floor. A feeling of celebration filled the room as we sang, laughed, studied, answered questions, and shared stories.

I had a bright idea that Mary and Martha were lesbians. I used Rosemary Radford Ruether's article in *Sojourners*,[3] which suggested that Mary, Martha, and Lazarus were probably not blood kin but sisters and brother in an Essene community. I hedged my hypothesis with lots of qualifiers, but we reveled in joking about their typical lesbian squabbles over who would do the housework. I recounted the faith of Martha, expressed in a confession of the sovereignty of Jesus when Lazarus died—a confession parallel to that of Peter. I spoke of the love Jesus had for Mary and Martha and his attentiveness to their witness in their community. I exulted in the sensation I felt when I thought that perhaps Jesus had affirmed my chosen way of life. We left the session that evening, en route to hear Sweet Honey in the Rock, rejoicing in our sisterhood and planning future activities for CLOUT.

I wasn't prepared for the backlash. Several weeks after the event, we received an envelope addressed to the Governing Board at University Baptist Church. Enclosed was a photocopy of the two-page synopsis of accusations leveled by the *Presbyterian Layman,* with a highlighted paragraph about me as a leading lesbian heretic. The return address was Apostasy Task Force, First Baptist Church, Napa, California. Since (miracle of miracles) I was called to University Baptist Church as an out lesbian—the first out homosexual to be called to pastor an American Baptist Church—I posted the letter on the bulletin board with pride.

When Perri's son was born, our planning group enjoyed holding and caressing him. Maybe by the time Cameron grows up, we will welcome all people to be ministers of the gospel—a miracle devoutly to be wished.

The Reverend Dr. Nadean Bishop is a sixty-two-year-old lesbian grandmother who pastors the University Baptist Church in Minneapolis. She taught "The Bible as Literature" for twenty-five years at Eastern Michigan University, where she also served as chair of the women's studies program for three years. Her publications include several book chapters, articles on spirituality and sexuality in the poetry of American women, and a book of poetry. She received her master of divinity degree from Pacific School of Religion in 1985, and at age fifty-three she became American Baptist campus minister at the University of Michigan and pastor of the Northside Community Church in Ann Arbor.

Women at the Drum

KAREN ARTICHOKER

We arrived at the Re-Imagining Conference excited and ready to sing. We were nervous about singing because we did not have with us all of the women who usually sing, but we kept encouraging one another and telling ourselves that we could do it. We also felt reassured because to most nonnative peoples, all of our songs sound the same anyway. But to native singers, singing the appropriate song and singing it well are sources of pride.

The weather was cold and could affect the tone of our drum, but again we reassured ourselves that the audience was receptive and would share in our passion for our music—especially since it is unusual to see women at the drum and the conference was a woman event.

It was intimidating to walk into the huge conference room. We were surrounded by a sea of white faces, and no coffee was available for us. It's tough to sing for any length of time without a hot beverage. We were also disappointed that we wouldn't be able to do any teaching about our culture and our singing. However, being professionals, we worked to accept that we were there to entertain.

So we were somewhat out of sorts, tired, and wondering if we were going to have to sit through hours and hours of the program. One woman was already missing her baby. Another was certain she was going to have a panic attack from being in such a large crowd. (I had to poke her several times to get her to sing.)

My cousin Marlene Helgemo couldn't help but notice how grouchy I was and told me to behave. That helped, and I started working on being my usual, more cheerful self. Anyway, as the evening wore on, we began to enjoy ourselves more and more.

The singing was beautiful, and while we didn't always know or understand what was going on, we appreciated what we perceived to be the intent of the conference planners. Given our history with Christian missioning, a history that almost destroyed us, we appreciated the obvious: a forum to celebrate and respect the spiritual beliefs of other cultures, especially the woman culture.

We made the tremolo to let the other singers know we appreciated and respected their singing. We were moved by the famous woman who, after her presentation, came over to shake our hands, showing her respect and appreciation for us.

It was inspirational to see such a woman-focus and so many women coming together actively, trying to *do* and *be* different in a society that is so oppressive to members of any marginalized group. We understand because we've had our hard times, trying to sing at the drum when many in our culture have difficulty respecting our path and passion for the drum and singing.

We felt even more at home when we left to attend the reception and found that Marlene's car battery was dead. Even though we were tired and, by now, totally exhausted, we were in good humor and made a good time of it. (Besides, we all understand the trials and tribulations of car trouble.) While we waited for the tow truck, we listened to the tape we had made of ourselves and laughed at our mistakes.

In the natural world that we were meant to live in as indigenous people, we say that every process in the natural world begins with spiritual inspiration. The Creator gave us the mental capacity to think; and in the physical, we take action. Finally, we evaluate the outcome through the emotional.

When at last we arrived at Marlene's house, we felt energized and proud.

We are aware that there was some controversy following the conference. We know that it's not easy to help people understand the diversity of others' reality, but we're standing beside you. To the organizers we say: *Blihicyiye!* Take heart! Have fortitude! Be strong!

Karen Artichoker is a long-time activist in the area of violence against women. She is the executive director of the White Buffalo Calf Woman Society, a women's resource center located on the Rosebud Indian reservation in South Dakota. She loves her culture and travels to many pow-wows, singing and dancing. Karen is also the mother of Coya, age nineteen.

Home Security

DORIS PAGELKOPF

I look at my watch. It is 2:00 P.M., and soon I will leave my office to join the women I have come to know over the past few years as we gathered frequently to plan the Re-Imagining event. The day is finally here, and it is extremely difficult to keep my mind on work. Friends from all over the country will be there. They are friends I have worked with for many years on issues of sexism within the church and society.

The phone rings, and it is my husband, Don, saying with a very shaky voice that our house has been broken into and robbed. He had come home from work for lunch and interrupted burglars in the process of stripping our house of easily salable items. They left most of them piled at the back door. Don is not injured, just extremely shaken.

I drive home with trembling hands and a quivery stomach. Why today, of all days, should this happen? What if I'm late for Re-Imagining? When I arrive home, Don is beginning to calm down. As we quickly discover, this is not just an invasion of our home but an assault on our well-being and sense of security that will last for several months.

We spend some time cleaning up the broken glass, and I am able to break away to head downtown for Re-Imagining. As I walk into the convention center, it seems that every few feet I run into an old friend. These are friends of the heart and mind, who have shared so much on our journeys of life and faith. Here also are the steering committee friends who have given so much of themselves to make this event happen. A strong sense of security begins to enfold me. We all take our places and Re-Imagining happens. Herstory is made.

Just like the burglary, Re-Imagining had an impact on my life. However, this impact will endure much longer than the few months it took to heal my sense of insecurity. We installed a security system in our home to protect us and our possessions. Re-Imagining is the security system in my life that makes it okay to search and struggle with thousands of others in our faith journeys. Thanks be to God.

Doris Pagelkopf is a Lutheran laywoman who lives out her faith in the world as a nonprofit-organization executive. She has had a rich volunteer life within society and the Lutheran church. Recently, she has chaired the Commission on Women of the Evangelical Lutheran Church in

America (ELCA) and served on the national board of directors of the YWCA of the USA, chairing the national Racial Justice committee. She has also served on the national Vision for Mission Task Force of the ELCA and is president of the Lutheran Academy. Locally, she serves on the One to One board of directors and is president of Kaleidoscope, a children's nonprofit organization. Her career and volunteer life center on addressing racism, sexism, and children's issues.

Her Mother, Her Friend

RUTH CHRISTMAN MANDERNACH

Friendship is a rare and precious gift. Jean Cassat Christman, my mother, and May Jane Nesby (Jane) had such a gift.

Jean and Jane had decided in 1991 to go to Re-Imagining. This was simply one of the many plans they made together. Spending holidays in tandem, sharing theological discussions, going to visit archeological ruins in the Southwest, and generally supporting each other were natural outcomes of their compatibility.

In 1950 Jean Cassat had graduated from Princeton Seminary. Women could not be ordained, so she went into Christian education. She was hired as a faculty member and was the only female professor at that seminary. In 1980 she was ordained as a minister of the Word and Sacrament.

Jane was ordained a minister of the Christian Church (Disciples of Christ) on 10 December 1978. Jean and Jane met and became friends in 1983 while working for their respective denominations at the Interchurch Center in Phoenix, Arizona. Jane left for an interim executive church position in Washington State in 1992. She was to work one more year, then return to Phoenix. Both women would then be retired and have loads of time to travel, play, and study together.

In the winter of 1992 Jane was killed in a snowy, mountaintop accident. Her death devastated my mother. Often I would hear her speak of all their plans, which were not to be. Topping that list had been the Re-Imagining Conference.

I decided to go with my mother to the conference. Certainly she did not need my presence to attend, but I hoped that I could help her and that we would enjoy each other's company. We did. Between plenary sessions, Mom came to me with great sincerity and said that she felt Jane's presence. She realized that our time together was another gift to her from Jane.

My mother has always been light years ahead of me in the feminist movement. The conference was an uplifting event for her because she realized new levels of understanding are possible when one is exposed to new and different ideas and the people behind them.

I intend to join my mother on her journey—albeit several steps be-hind—confident in the effort, learning and leaping ahead at every opportunity throughout our lifetimes.

Ruth Christman Mandernach is a forty-year-old Presbyterian elder, living in southern Califor-nia. She is a licensed clinical social worker. She is inspired by her husband Bill; her children, Nathan, Josh, and Nick; and her friends and extended family. She embraces diversity.

Confessions of a Dance Monitor

MARGARET A. PFEFFER

Fall is a season that creeps in slowly, whispering change, not wanting to scare you. Fall is unpredictable. It's young maples going orange in a single day and old oaks refusing to show color until all the others are finished. Morning dawns warm and humid; and when you walk the dog at noon, you need a sweatshirt. Warm and cool temperatures are dancing the tango all the time.

But for me fall is a season of suddenly launching a new year of activities, negotiating schedules—who picks up, who drops off, who has an evening meeting—exciting and hectic. I don't want to change so fast. I want my hot and cold temperatures to take time to tango before I settle into any routine.

In the fall of 1993 I found my tango time by signing up for the Re-Imagining Conference. I could hardly wait to abandon my chauffeur's seat. I felt if I spent time re-imagining God, I might begin to also re-imagine myself and the communities around me. Like so many others, I had just reentered organized church life after a long hiatus. Both my husband and I had been raised as Catholics but left the church. We were sick of trying to dialogue with an institution so resistant to dialogue and change. It was like dealing with a two-year-old who only can say "no" and "mine." Still, we wanted to give our children some kind of tradition. I liked the rituals of Catholic worship. It became a matter of finding the right community.

The community we joined was a good match for us, providing nurture and guidance. One of the things I tried there was liturgical dance. This had not been part of my traditional Catholic upbringing. I loved it. I had loved dancing since I was a little girl, but my mother had thought it frivolous. She approved of things like dissecting frogs. "That," she said, "will get you somewhere." My children guided me to dance lessons—theirs. For a while I was happy to sit back and watch them. I felt my dance sun had set. Yet one day, in midlife madness, I signed up.

My teacher was one who was doing something a little different in church: dancing. At first I was too shy to do much, but soon I was dancing around the altar. My friends thought I was incredibly heroic to be dancing in church, since some parishioners didn't know what to make of all those women "up there," and they weren't shy about voicing their discomfort. My kids paid attention in church, hoping to catch mistakes but also happy and proud to see me there. I decided to let the awe of the children validate my dancing.

Through dancing I began to experience God differently. I visualized Alpha and Omega, the beginning and the end, as any point on a circle. I had a keen desire to tear down crosses and put up wreaths. This God of the circle was the movement of time in the seasons and the renewal of life through birth, death, and rebirth. I began to see a Movement as much as a Being in my prayers. My movement moved with all the Movement around me.

A week or so before the Re-Imagining Conference, a friend called and asked if I wanted to be one of the dancers in the rituals planned for the conference. At the rehearsal I realized I had never danced with so many women, all of different ages and backgrounds. The music and choreography made me feel for the first time that I was really doing sacred dance. It felt beautiful and powerful.

I looked at the dancers draped in brilliantly colored cloths of vivid purples, electrifying turquoises, intense reds laced with black and white. On one dancer the cloth became a shawl, on another a prayer cloth. They reminded me of our diversity—one of the Spirit's most precious gifts. With our colorful cloths, we danced in celebration and fun and joy, and I learned it's okay to laugh in church. We led participants in simple circle dances and chaotic conga lines that melted into a huge circle. The bonds of a community began to forge. I felt the power of community worship.

After the conference all of us were touched by the response of the larger community. The dancers were pictured as monitors, forcing people to participate. When people get caught up in the need to control others, they really have a hard time hearing the rhythm and beat so they can dance. Re-Imagining had more to do with choice than control. Choice left us with affirmation of ourselves and a chance to be equal, valued partners in a diverse community. Of course, if we all have value and power, there are no leaders and followers—only sharing circles for dancing, talking, or simply belonging.

We seem to be in a time that is like fall. The old oaks are holding out on change until everyone else has done it. In my heart I hope the strength of these old institutions doesn't succumb to internal rot before they decide to move on to the next season. I wonder if, as in nature, the slowness of the change isn't part of the plan; so I try to be patient and yet assertive at the same time, to feel my own movement and trust the Movement of the dance.

Margaret A. Pfeffer was born in Colorado but raised in various cities in the South. She has a bachelor of arts degree in anthropology from Washington University in Saint Louis. After two years living in Tokyo, going to Waseda University, studying Japanese, and teaching English in various corporations, she worked for six years in freight forwarding in San Francisco. She earned a master of arts degree in special education and taught for several years in California and Minnesota. She is married, with three children; she lives in Minneapolis, staying home full-time and writing—when not driving children around.

PART TWO

Finding God

In the gathered community, we listen to one another as the word of God is

proclaimed: the word written by the ancient ones and the word spoken by our

companions. As the stories are told, we look for God in the ordinary events of

daily lives and listen for God in lived experiences. We know that God has been

with us as we tell our stories

of re-membering . . .

and re-imagining. . .

In a Foreign Land

BARBARA PRICE-MARTIN

Dear Friends,

It's difficult to put my experiences of the Re-Imagining Conference into words. The overwhelming impression is of incredible challenge and nurture at the same time. I imagine that this conference must have been planned by women who have many children. Every detail was attended to, and much thought went into making welcome so that no one was left out. It's no accident that one of the gifts of the Spirit is hospitality. The event was steeped in this type of richness, captured for me by a number of symbols.

Now for some of you who read this, my description is going to sound like no conference you have ever attended. I think that was the case for most— if not all—of us. I liken it to going to a different country. Most of us do not immediately like foods from outside our culture, such as octopus or pickled pigs' feet. Yet to write something off as bad or offensive simply because it is foreign would be to miss a great chance to experience it. This conference was about stepping into a different culture, a foreign land. We thought new thoughts, felt new feelings, and reexamined our faith from new perspectives. If you live in another country for a long enough time, you stop seeing everything simply as different from your norm and begin to see its inherent beauty and meaning as an entity unto itself. So I hope you can be open to the reality that this conference was different. And, as I tell my three-year-old just about every day, different doesn't mean bad; it just means different.

For example, while driving to the convention center, my friends and I were discussing where we would meet if we were separated during the registration process. "How about at the front, maybe to the right of the podium?" I suggested. Then, realizing where we were going, I mused, "Surely there will be a podium up front?" We dismissed this with laughter. How else could it be done? It's always been done that way.

There wasn't a podium up front. It was in the center of the room, in the center of the participants, exactly where the prophets and ministers need to be. For where do women find themselves most often but in the midst of their friends and family and community? Not only were the speakers in our midst, but each one carefully turned the podium every few minutes so that she faced each quadrant of the room for some part of her address. We exchanged tables

37

each day so that all could have a turn at seeing and hearing equally well. While I was close to the center of the room one day, I was far away the next.

The music wasn't at the front either. It was in the four corners of the room, symbolizing both our diversity and our interconnectedness. Each musician had to express her own interpretation of the music and yet watch the others in order to make it beautiful.

The chairs were not lined up in orderly rows as they usually are at conferences, which allows chance or speed to determine who can grab the good seats fast enough, who can save seats for favored friends, and so on. We sat in assigned circles, gathered around tables with woven baskets filled with trinkets and remembrances from the earth. For those of us who think with our mouths, there was a gourd "microphone" to identify the speaker at discussion time. For those of us who think with our hands, there were crayons and markers to create while we listened. For those of us who think with our ears, there were little egg-shaped maracas so our applause would not disturb others. For those of us who think with our whole bodies, there were music and dance to celebrate and worship God. We were all welcome.

We were to bring remembrances from home—a piece of cloth and a vessel to share. And, of course, there were large tables with extra cloth and vessels in the outer hallway so no one was left out.

I know my description has not included the content of the conference. I imagine, however, that if you have been faithful enough to read what I have written, you are beginning to understand that some appreciation of, and perhaps more importantly, some respect for foreign culture is necessary to understand and receive this event. It is not my task to defend what was said or presented. Some things were said that were not especially helpful to me. But what I received far outweighs any distress caused by some "radical women."

Perhaps this is because I am not afraid of the new, even though I could not always have said that. You see, I think much of the controversy that followed the conference was about fear. I have no doubt that while our tradition has much to fear about that which challenges it, our God does not. Jesus Christ challenged a great number of religious traditions while remaining faithful to the Spirit of God. We can, too.

I do have one criticism of the conference. The table baskets should have contained tissues for those of us who think with our hearts and who cried tears for our own sense of longing and release.

I will count it a joy to continue to re-imagine how the grace of God can be experienced and received. I imagine, after all, that is the heart of the gospel I am called to preach.

Barbara Price-Martin is an ordained minister in the Presbyterian Church (U.S.A.) and a pastoral counselor in private practice in Wilmington, Delaware. She has been a hospital chaplain, specializing in neonatology and perinatal bereavement. A graduate of Westminster College in Pennsylvania and Princeton Seminary, she and her husband, Brad, are the parents of two children.

Womb of the Mountain

KATHERINE JUUL NEVINS

The real truth is I was nervous about this Re-Imagining thing. I signed up at the insistence of my friend Pam Joern who had teased my fancy over the last year or so with some of the planning committee's ideas and excitement. Then it was the night before the first night, and I started reading the material I'd been sent in preparation. I was supposed to bring a gift to give to a perfect stranger who would be at my conference table. I was also supposed to bring a vessel to maybe give away or keep as part of some ritual, and I was to bring a piece of cloth that held meaning for me. What? A group experience—with strangers—and I'm supposed to share important parts of my spiritual self, precious and deeply personal symbolic objects, with women I don't know, may not like, and won't see again? I hit the buttons on my touch-tone phone, tracking down Pam at a downtown hotel, already in the thick of running a convention.

"It's okay, Kathy. You don't have to share anything you don't want to. You'll be fine. It might even be fun." . . . Right.

At least I knew where I was going, if not to what. I parked where Pam suggested, maneuvered the maze of elevators and escalators, muscled my way to the registration table, got my packet, and focused on finding my seat for the opening ceremony.

I'd read the table layout map, but when I entered the plenary room, anxiety began to have a tinge of awe. Round tables. Everywhere. Forced personalization? Will it work?

I wasn't the first to arrive at the table, nor was I the only one who strategized a seat facing the speaker's platform in the center of the room. I played a bit of musical chairs with myself, eyeing the others at the table surreptitiously, trying to sense any gushiness so I could sit as far away as possible.

As the others sifted through the room to our table, we made small talk: Hello, how are you? Where are you from? Where are you staying? Where did you park? Nice banners. What's this stuff on the table?

I parallel-processed during this time, one ear tuned to my neighbor, the other to the similar conversations going on around the table. My analytical mind drew the following conclusions:

1. *We were a fairly subdued and reserved bunch.*
2. *There were some pretty high-powered I-know-who-I-am-and-where-I'm-going women.*
3. *I was definitely in the minority as an evangelical (whatever that means these days) and as a never-been-to-seminary person, and as an I'm-not-sure-who-I-am-or-where-I'm-going person.*

Action plan: zip the lip, keep shields up, watch, and listen.

I spent that first session mostly with my head buried in my ritual book, guessing when we were supposed to chat with each other and about what. It was a night of tentativeness. When encouraged to draw on the paper table-cloth, we fought internal battles with our critical voices; and when it came time to explain our doodles, many of us could not/would not.

Yet with the music and the dancing and the breaking of bread, I saw spirit behind the formal reserve of these women at my table. Together we packed up our basket and table drawings but left singly after that first night. I felt I had a table I belonged to, but not yet a circle of friends.

Friday: different seat, different location in the room, the faces at the table were the same. Or were they? Maybe lack of sleep loosened us up; maybe Nancy Chinn's encouragement and modeling freed us to draw while someone was speaking. Whatever. We doodled, and we drew, and we colored. I started a braid of green and yellow and red and blue across my coloring space, stopping when I felt myself intruding on Beth, the Brethren pastor's, canvas. I put my pastels down for a minute, letting my eyes wander around the room as I listened. I happened to glance over at Beth's work and was captivated. She was stretching her doodles out from her drawing to meet mine! She looked at me with asking eyes; I want to do this—is it okay? I picked up my crayons and started redirecting my braid toward her streamers of green and blue and gray.

Soon, others at the table joined their doodles with their neighbors' until each drawing was connected with the one on either side. Then the Spirit moved. Catherine, I think, was the first to stretch out of her chair and begin connecting her drawing with those across the table. No line was a straight shot through, and the outline of a circle made up of many lines began to take shape in the center of the paper. As its presence became more noticeable, table members began accenting its shape and creating beams of color that bridged the space between the center circle and the personal symbols of themselves spread around the table's edge.

One drawing was by Suzanne, whose destiny as an ordained priest of the Church of England was being decided by Parliament the very weekend of the conference. Suzanne, who used her middle name, Chris, on her business card to avoid discrimination and whose last name, Challenger, spoke of her courage.

Another belonged to June, a seminary graduate from Canada who had refused ordination in her church, believing she could serve more effectively and be less burdened by cumbersome issues if she remained a layperson. Now in midlife she ponders changing her name to Grace.

The pasture scene was Ida's, a woman from Kentucky who once massaged hands for a living. She was now a woman of dignity, wearing a look of wisdom gained only from learning what life can teach us over seventy plus years.

Beth drew a green whirling dervish with a red tear in its center. She shared a ministry with her husband, pastoring a Church of the Brethren congregation. We cheered for her when she joined other Brethren attendees to affirm a name change for her church that would recognize her as a believer.

Catherine shared a post with her husband in a Lutheran church. She had taught preaching in a seminary for a while, but she and her husband were facing a painful transition out of the pulpit ministry for the sake of their personal health and their family. The spirit of ministry was being sucked out of them by unforgiving politics and intraparish conflicts.

Other pain was present, too. A minister recently divorced to escape an abusive husband faced a new job in a new town. She was still deeply wounded and fearful of how her ability to serve God might now be compromised.

A church council secretary, so burned out and defeated by pettiness and politics, could not worship with meaning. She was isolated, no longer hearing her name when the pastor talked of the brotherhood of believers and absolution of the sins of man.

All of these, along with Connie from Missouri, Ginny from Iowa, and me. We connected our drawings through the circle in the center, connected our lives through shared experience.

The conference planners wanted us to have a new paper tablecloth the next day and later to tear it into individual pieces to carry away from the conference. Not this table. Not our talking circle. The tablecloth had become a sacred symbol of our connection to God and our connection to each other. We carried it with us to the last assigned seating place and unveiled it for ourselves one more time. It was whole as it was.

The spiritual high of the conference is a sustaining memory. I have the tablecloth we made hanging in my stairwell. I look at it to remind me of those nine women who brought me home to God through our connections. I pray for them as our lives extend beyond the conference.

Suzanne was ordained in May 1994 in grand style in the largest cathedral in England. Many of us were with her in spirit.

Beth and her husband have survived one more budgetary crisis at their church and continue in their work in spite of her "rash" behavior in joining the movement to petition a name change for her denomination.

Claudia is no longer a church secretary and has begun an inner exile, reading and journalizing and creating, in an effort to reawaken her soul. We talk once in a while and have shared a few meals together, even though she lives fifteen hundred miles away.

Ginny is still semisecurely in place in the Presbyterian hierarchy of Iowa. During her review last summer, her attendance at the conference was never made an issue, and she was granted another five-year term just in time to help her daughter prepare a wedding.

Catherine has left the parish ministry and writes curricula for Augsburg Fortress, as well as wonderful poetry. She leads weekend workshops, but the part of her that was meant to lead a congregation in the sacrament is sadly neglected. I know, because I saw and felt the Holy Spirit during one of her last times preaching.

Connie wept at the end of the conference because she said we were close to each other in Minnesota and she was having to go home to Missouri alone.

What was the precipitating factor? What was the catalyst that transformed a table of strangers into friends of the spirit? What was it that calmed my anxieties, melted my shields, and opened my heart? I can only imagine.

Katherine Juul Nevins, Ph.D., is professor and department chair of psychology and on the counseling staff at Bethel College in Minnesota. She is a mediator, trainer, and facilitator for the Mediation Center in Saint Paul, helping to resolve divorce and child custody, civil, organizational, and special-education disputes. In her spare time, she loves doing other people's home-improvement projects, reading, travel, sports, music, jigsaw puzzles, writing, theater, and learning new things.

A Place at the Table

MARVIN A. MARSH

The program booklet began, "Welcome to Re-Imagining, a conference by women for women and men. We anticipate our time together will challenge and expand our horizons in undreamed of ways, will enrich and nurture us spiritually, and will provide the opportunity to dialogue with women and men from around the world." [1] Those words set the tone for me, and they continue to be a good description of what happened there—even though the proceedings have been labeled unbiblical, heretical, and shocking by some and have prompted an interesting array of defense, apology, back-pedaling, support, explanation, and even some genuine dialogue.

Make no mistake about it: I feel for those who are embroiled in the controversy—whether being attacked or attacking. The pain, frustration, and aggravation are very real for those on all sides of the issues. My greatest feeling, however, is one of gratitude for having been included as a man in the conference. I didn't agree with everything said, everything done, or even everything hoped for. Neither did there seem to be an expectation that anyone or everyone would. The conference was not offered as a time of teaching or instituting, but rather as a time of exploring, trusting, and believing that God is secure enough to endure the uncensored expression of the questions, dreams, and prayers usually reserved for the silence of our own souls—especially women's souls.

Throughout the conference, I sensed a general permission to participate or not to participate according to one's taste and/or conscience. I saw individual men and women sit through respective times of silence (perhaps even separation) and, at other times, be enthusiastically involved. The truth is that I felt less manipulation here than I have in many other, more traditional religious gatherings. There seemed to be a determined expectation for all of us to be present on our own terms, not for the benefit of someone else. We were an assembly of honest seekers, trusting God to be God while we rearranged the trappings for a clearer view of God, Creation, and our own place within it all.

What happened for me? What did I gain? I had quite an experience. What excites me is what happened for and within me as I attended the conference. The rest of what I have to say is a bit like my own diary; I offer it as confession, prayer, and celebration.

First, I discovered a difference between affirming my own interests and standing in solidarity with someone else. For years, my wife has been nudging me along, helping me get out of my own way as a man in the midst of a sexist society. Her work began years after a conservative Illinois farmer challenged me for using sexist language in the pulpit, failing to include fully his daughters and wife in the explicit grace of the gospel. Throughout those years of learning, I became clearer about issues of inclusion and the prevailing politics of exclusion. Along the way, it also became clear that freedom for women meant freedom for men, too. Stereotypes are a pain for us all, and I've never enjoyed the expectations laid on me simply because I happen to be male. All things considered, I eagerly became an advocate for women's rights.

However, at this conference, a new reality sunk in. At some point it dawned on me that freedom for women was not primarily about my liberation—as good a thing as that might be. I cannot allow the foundation for my solidarity with these sisters to be equated with the conviction that what is good for them is also good for me. As true as it is, the latter remains a male-centered conviction, still confirming myself as the entitled one. To be an advocate for women's rights and freedom is to believe in the call for women to live the abundant life of grace, spirit, and giftedness as each discerns in and for her own life. It is to believe this for them, for their salvation, healing, and ministries—not primarily for my own.

Secondly, I discovered a more balanced view of political correctness. Politically correct language gets mixed reviews these days. Some complain bitterly about it as another form of tyranny. Others demand conscientious obedience to its ever-evolving wisdom. When preparing to go off to Minneapolis, I confess this was a source of some apprehension for me. I really did expect to be schooled more intensely in some version or another of political correctness.

The surprise came as the sessions unfolded. Instead of a common glossary, I found real diversity. I was becoming less concerned with using the right words and more with hearing and being heard, whether the words were quite right or not. Trust, not correctness, was the primary issue.

I still value a measure of political correctness. After all, we can do violence to one another with words, and some words deserve to be marked for the violence they inflict and perpetuate. However, among this diverse gathering, I felt freed to pursue discussions and concerns more germane to the sort of trust, understanding, and communication that require more persistence and grace than a prescribed glossary can manage. It was the difference between relying upon a tourist vocabulary, trying to make one's way through a territory to which one doesn't really expect or even hope to belong, versus a willingness to immerse oneself in a culture, ready to cope with the frustrations of miscommunication in order to build on common experience and honest interchange.

My third discovery was my need for a place at the table. During the final session, we were invited to share expectations with one another around our table. The first statement we were asked to complete was: "To be in solidarity with me in my struggle, I need you to. . . . " The question was implicitly geared to solidarity with women. However, by this time, the same eight women and two men had been sharing with one another around a common table for each session. We had formed a measure of community that allowed me to say "my struggle is to learn how to be in solidarity with women while setting aside my sense of entitlement, increasing my ability to listen, coping with the expectation of others that as a male I'm going to dominate, and growing in my sense of freedom while not getting in the way of others. What I need from you is the trust that you'll hold me accountable for those things. I don't want *the* place at the table, just *a* place at the table. So most of all, I ask that you continue to allow me a place at the table."

Was it the right thing to say? I have no idea. But it was an authentic thing; and after we had all shared, it was apparent we each had new strength and new insight. There was hope that it was possible to re-imagine life together as partners, female and male, equal and free. How appropriate that the sermon to follow was titled, *"Es Posible . . . It Is Possible!"*

We sang a final song as we marched. Or was it a dance? The words sang of marching in the light of God, and the march was one of smiles, tears, laughter, joyful movement, and grace. What might happen if we prayed for God to re-imagine us in new patterns of peace and equality, not leaving us to those social realities which seem so certain and so stifling?

I'm glad I was there. Perhaps one had to be to understand.

The Reverend Dr. Marvin A. Marsh is white, male, Terryl's husband, ordained, American Baptist, and pretty sure that there's enough life to go around for all. He lives in King of Prussia, Pennsylvania. He has served as a local director of neighborhood ministries in Rhode Island, as a pastor in Scranton, Pennsylvania, and as a denominational staff person. He has a bachelor of arts degree from Culver-Stockton College, Canton, Missouri; a master of divinity degree from Andover Newton Theological School, Newton Centre, Massachusetts; and a doctor of ministry degree from Drew University, Madison, New Jersey.

An Unexpected Gift

JEANINE DORFMAN

My friends Pam and Chris and I left the conference a little early Thursday night. Not, you understand, because the closing ritual wasn't wonderful, but because we were thoroughly exhausted from driving all the way from Nashville to Minneapolis. As we walked out into the main hallway, we spotted Bernice Johnson Reagon sitting by a table of Sweet Honey in the Rock merchandise. Did you hear me? I said Bernice Johnson Reagon! Not only did I hold enormous admiration and respect for her because of her role in forming, guiding, and participating in Sweet Honey in the Rock, but that very night I had listened to her with my whole being while she talked about being in the storm rather than trying to find shelter from the storm. She seemed to reach deep inside me and stir up my soul, my pain, my anger, my strength, my faith, and my determination.

So there she was. I nudged Pam and Chris, who are big fans, too. "Hey, do you guys think we should try to talk to her?" Someone was doing just that, so we slowly kept on walking, whispering frantically about whether we should turn around. Chris and I were in an a cappella women's group at divinity school, and we liked to perform some of Sweet Honey in the Rock's songs.

We finally got up the courage to approach her. Even though I knew it was silly, I was really nervous at first; I think as I introduced myself, I must have sounded star-struck. But after telling her what big fans we were and how wonderful her talk had been, I explained about our singing group's desire to learn "Beatitude." I think I expected her to say something like: No, there isn't any sheet music for that one, but I wish you luck trying to figure it out. Instead, she asked some questions about our group and then proceeded to tell us there was a trick to performing that song; the part we had been thinking of as a solo really needed to be understood and felt more as an interplay with the other parts. After explaining how they fit together, Bernice said, "Here, let me show you. You sing this part." And she sang a few words. I repeated what she had sung, and she came in with the other part. She motioned for me to keep going with my part, which I did, all the while thinking, I can't believe this! I'm singing with Bernice Johnson Reagon!

When we finished, she assured us that figuring out the rest of the song would be easy; we just needed to fill in the harmonies above and below the part I was singing. She then wished our group luck and told us to send her a tape sometime. As we walked away from her, I know I must have been glowing.

Jeanine Dorfman is currently searching for a practical application for her master of divinity degree and making a home in a new city—Rochester, New York. She is trying to find/create her place in the church as an openly lesbian woman. Some of her spirit foods include singing, creating, walking in the woods, enjoying her relationship with her mom, and making a family with her partner, Teri, and their cat.

Behind the Scenes

JO RINGGENBERG

Label me a Re-Imagining nonattending attendee. I paid my registration early; I worked diligently to have all the details in place and enough volunteers so that we planners who wished to attend could. Re-Imagining flowed by, and things kept happening.

When the conference ended, I realized I had not attended any of the daytime presentations in its entirety. I had spent only a few minutes in a few of them. I didn't get to the reception for presenters and planners or to my denominational gathering. As one of the persons in charge of local arrangements, I experienced a different conference.

My Talking Circle Became the People I Saw and Served at the Information Table

One of the volunteer interpreters said, "It was hard to do a good job, so I'm going to buy the tapes, translate them, and send them." (Re-Imagining then bought the tapes for all four of the interpreters.)

I gave a desperate-to-attend, uptight woman a chance to crash the conference by being a needed doorkeeper inside the ballroom. She arrived with an anxious frown and left on Sunday with a smile on her face and a spring in her step.

I listened to a young woman's account of being ousted as one of four roommates. That was sad and disturbing. We found her a different room; coincidentally, that solved the problem of another woman, whose roommate did not show up.

I participated as all two thousand of us put our dishes on the floor and later watched as ninety percent of us walked out, leaving the dishes under the table for someone else to clean up.

I Was Aware of Miracles Happening

Two thousand people left the ballroom each day to stand in the lobby for a few minutes, then pick up their meals, and return to the ballroom with no grumbling. Those same two thousand people found their tables in a different

49

place each day, picked out afternoon options on a first-come/first-served basis, and survived without verbal housekeeping announcements or reminders.

Money came in so that all who asked for scholarship help received some, and we covered expenses that came up after our first naive budget.

In spite of needed changes in individuals' and groups' plans, which continued to happen until the closing hour, everyone seemed to be accommodated at a reasonable level of comfort.

I watched the tentativeness and anxiety of expectation on Thursday evening become the happy chorus and dance of solidarity on Sunday morning.

I Learned a Lot besides Theology

Some costs, if evaluated on a per-person bottom line, would have been ruled out as too expensive. Those same costs, evaluated on people's needs and gains, were worthwhile and necessary. For example, we were able to extend financial assistance to internationals and persons with a limited income. Their being there improved the total experience for everyone.

One must walk the walk before one talks the talk. The map seemed to say it was there, but I misdirected scores of people to a phantom skyway. (Sorry.)

Providing accessibility assistance is often complicated and expensive. It took over an hour of phone calls, another twenty minutes of leg work, and forty dollars to arrange an eight-block, round-trip ride for a woman and her wheelchair.

Specialists abound at many levels in many fields. This is wonderful for the professionalism and perfection it brings, but it is frustrating when you need to cross boundaries or accomplish a multipurpose task. In many instances, this came into play. The grand-piano saga is a good example. After locating the music companies that rent grand pianos, I still needed to talk to the grand-piano renter at those companies. Only certain haulers handle grand pianos. It took twenty-one phone calls to seven different people on fifteen different days to get the pianos rented, delivered, and returned. To complicate it further, it seemed as though all the Twin Cities grand-piano haulers were deer hunters and were gone for the opening of deer-hunting season the weekend of the conference.

We are a group who either stretch or ignore deadlines and who push boundaries. We question the process and change our minds. That's okay, but frustrating for those charged with carrying out the plans.

Simple multiplication adds up, or simple addition multiplies, when inspired amateurs set out to develop their dream conference. Preparing for two thousand is ten times the preparation as for two hundred, the number with which many of us had dealt previously. Offering services for seventy-two hours is twelve times the services for six hours—another familiar number. And ten times twelve (people and services) is 120 times the details and complications. Factor in thirty-five presenters, forty-five group leaders, special friends, and international participants, along with human error and plan changes. It could have been a nightmare—instead it was a hectic dream.

The conference couldn't have happened without giving of time, talent, and effort. Many said, "You can count on me, I'll be there to help." Some should have added: unless I forget or change my mind or get so engrossed in the goings-on I can't break away. Some volunteers were there all four days; some helped who weren't scheduled to help. Most did much more than was their responsibility. (Thank you!)

The whole four-year adventure was a genuine pleasure, a once-in-a-lifetime opportunity, a valuable experience, an awakening. I'd try it again.

I worked near artists in words, music, color, liturgy, drama, and diplomacy. I worked with professionals who were learned, experienced, caring, creative dreamers. We re-imagined conference arrangements so that context, content, and presentation could work together to let re-imagining happen.

I also worked near professionals who were knowledgeable, experienced, accommodating pragmatists who seldom set up a room with the stage in the middle of two hundred tables and three grand pianos. These professionals pride themselves in delivering services, such as orderly presentation of meals to neatly accessorized tables.

These two worlds needed to fit together. It was like letting a loaf of bread dough take its own shape, knitting a sweater for a pubescent teenager the summer of the growth spurt, or piecing a quilt without a pattern—scary, risky, stretching—but worth doing.

Jo Ringgenberg is a Presbyterian laywoman and elder living in Plymouth, Minnesota. She was a member of the ecumenical gathering that began the discussions and dreaming leading to the Re-Imagining Conference; she served as a member of the conference steering committee; and she continues as treasurer of the coordinating council of the Re-Imagining Community. Jo enjoys the freedom of retirement from nursing and townhouse living in Plymouth, Minnesota, while continuing to carry out the responsibilities and privileges of being wife, mother, grandmother, and volunteer in Presbyterian and ecumenical roles.

Here's to You, Mr. Robertson

MELANIE MORRISON

In mid-May 1994, seven months after the Re-Imagining Conference, two friends in different locations called to say that they had heard my voice on Pat Robertson's television program, *The 700 Club*. The callers explained that they had been flipping through their cable channels when they heard a familiar voice on a most unexpected network. Apparently Robertson was playing a segment of the Re-Imagining tapes in which I addressed participants.

I don't know the exact nature of Robertson's commentary. Based on other segments of *The 700 Club* that I've seen, I can venture a guess. The clip of tape he played was from the Saturday morning plenary session at Re-Imagining. I was not a scheduled speaker. My name was not in the program for Saturday morning. How I came to stand on the speaker's platform that day is a story I want to share.

The racial and ethnic diversity of the presenters at Re-Imagining was breathtaking. Leadership for the workshops was also impressively diverse in terms of race, religious background, and sexual orientation. Nevertheless, some of us who are lesbian began to grow uneasy because when all two thousand participants gathered for presentations, no one was speaking in a lesbian voice.

Afternoon presentations and workshops definitely had an out-lesbian presence, but afternoon events were optional. We learned that one of the plenary presenters planned to make a strong and personal coming-out statement at the closing worship service. But we felt there should be lesbian voice and visibility before the closing worship. After all, here was an ecumenical gathering with representatives from many denominations, most of which have repressive policies and statements regarding lesbian women. We felt that no one should leave a conference highlighting the Ecumenical Decade: Churches in Solidarity with Women without having to wrestle directly with the question of what it means to be in solidarity with lesbian women.

Fearing that this question otherwise might not get raised when all of us were gathered, we decided to approach the conference steering committee and ask for time during Saturday morning's plenary session to make a brief statement to the participants. After much negotiation, the conference planners agreed to give us a few minutes to make an unofficial statement. As co-chair of the Coordinating Council of CLOUT (Christian Lesbians Out Together), I was selected as the spokesperson to issue an invitation from the center stage inviting all lesbian, bisexual, and transsexual women to circle the platform and sing, celebrating our courage.

Only a handful of us knew what was going to happen that Saturday morning. We hoped enough women would come forward to complete a circle around the stage, but we could not be certain. We knew that for many women—clergy and lay—it could be very risky to come out in front of members of their denominations, who could then go home and tell their bishops or others with power over them.

I introduced myself and explained that I work with CLOUT, an ecumenical movement celebrating the miracle of being lesbian, out, and Christian. Then I said, "We are keenly, painfully aware that the world is not safe for lesbian women and that often the *least* safe place is the church. We call upon all of you—whatever your sexual orientation—not to leave this holy place without wrestling with these questions: What does it mean for us to be in solidarity with lesbian, bisexual, and transsexual women in this decade, and how can we together re-imagine our churches so that *every* woman may claim her voice, her gifts, her loves, and her wholeness? Acknowledging that my white skin may put me in a place where there is less at stake in coming out, I invite every lesbian, bisexual, and transsexual woman who is willing and able, to come forward and join hands, encircling this platform, facing out."

As soon as I issued the invitation, women in every part of that great hall left their tables and started moving toward the center of the room. At least 150 women circled the stage three rows deep and spilled up onto the platform. I intended to ask the people remaining at their tables to stand in solidarity with us. But when women began to stream to the center, a roar went up from the crowd as people rose spontaneously to their feet and gave the women a long and thunderous ovation.

It was glorious pandemonium. From where I stood on the platform, I could see tears running down the faces of many who stood at their tables. People were cheering and waving their arms. The women who circled the stage faced the cheering people, clasping each other's hands and raising their arms in a triumphant gesture of pride and strength. I reminded all of us that there were women standing at their tables who wanted to be in this circle, but who did not yet feel safe enough to join us. We sang a song together, and then the room erupted in more applause, hugs, and tears.

During the remainder of the conference, woman after woman told us how she experienced what happened Saturday morning. Some said that this was the first time they had ever dared to come out in such a public way. Others said they did not feel safe enough to join us, but they felt supported and affirmed by the action and the applause.

Many straight women sought us out to say that they were deeply appreciative that this challenge had been issued and tangibly enacted in such a compelling way. One woman said, "What you all did was the most powerful moment in a very empowering conference." We also heard many testimonies about how our act of vulnerable courage broke open conversation at the tables in a new way.

I suspect that none of us who planned this event on Saturday morning dared dream that the support would be so dramatic and demonstrable. But it seems that the time was right to name this wound in the body of Christ. The cathartic power of what erupted that Saturday morning signifies how much the Body has suffered from enforced closets and threats of expulsion. The eruption also testifies to the tenacious, indefatigable spirit of healing that returns when individuals refuse to collude with fear any longer.

As I stood on the stage, I knew that nothing could ever kill the memory of that grace-filled moment. And that memory has carried me through some frightening times, when I've been face to face with people who insist that lesbians and gay men—not heterosexism and homophobia—are purveyors of division and disease within the church. In the aftermath of Re-Imagining, when campaigns to discredit the conference were calculated to divide participants from one another by fanning the flames of homophobia, I have been sustained by the memory of that moment when courage and solidarity were so palpable.

The attacks on the Re-Imagining Conference include a variety of charges and caricatures, but blatant homophobia runs through them all. The front of a fund-raising envelope included in the January/February 1994 *Presbyterian Layman* was just one of many examples. It read,

> *Did you want*
> * *your Presbyterian church money spent on a conference to worship the female goddess "Sophia"?*
> * *your Presbyterian National staff planning a conference where leaders rejected the atonement of Jesus Christ, celebrated lesbianism, and called for adding books to the Bible that could then be used to justify radical feminist and homosexual activism?*
> * *your Presbyterian National Staff participating in a pagan worship ritual?*

Rumor has it that some conservative groups are scanning photographs of this Saturday morning event, hoping to identify particular women. I was moved to tears when I heard the response of one Lutheran heterosexual sister who said, "If that happens, then those of us who are heterosexual will have to step forward and say, 'I was there! I was in that circle! Didn't you see me? Maybe you can't see me in that photo, but I was there!'"

When I first heard that tape of my voice on *The 700 Club,* I felt a mixture of fear and rage. I could hardly bear the thought of this attempt to profane such a holy moment. Then a friend told me that he had been giving thanks for the fact that God was using even *The 700 Club* to get the message out to lesbian women. When I realized he wasn't joking, my fear and rage were transformed into delight and gratitude. For surely, some lesbian women who have been taught to despise themselves watch *The 700 Club.* And some of them might have been warmed and encouraged by hearing the thunderous applause that surrounded the lesbian women at the Re-Imagining Conference. Perhaps they heard, via *The 700 Club,* that they have a community of sisters and brothers waiting to receive them as they come out and come home. And wouldn't that give new meaning to the old expression that God moves in mysterious ways Her wonders to perform?

Melanie Morrison is an ordained United Church of Christ minister. She is codirector of Leaven, a nonprofit organization in Lansing, Michigan, providing resources and education in the areas of feminism, spiritual development, and sexual justice. The author of three books, including The Grace of Coming Home: Spirituality, Sexuality, and the Struggle for Justice *(Pilgrim Press, 1995), she is completing a doctor of philosophy degree in practical theology at the University of Groningen in the Netherlands.*

Escape from Patriarchy

PEG A. B. CHEMBERLIN

I walked into the room, the big room, already full of people, mostly women. None of us outside the planning committee knew what to expect, and even the planning committee members were having anxious thoughts about this event. Which direction is front? I wondered to myself. The stage was cluttered with stuff that looked like four large blank canvases and painting paraphernalia.

Finally I found my table. Like the others, it was covered with paper. Art supplies were in the center of it. Oh no, I thought. They're gonna ask us to do something crafty to share ourselves with each other. Soon we were into the welcome and introductions, and the crafts were explained: we would have no assignment; the art materials were here for self-expression or even doodling. Okay, I thought.

Seated at a round table, my back was to the speaker's podium. I could have turned around, but I like having a table to rest my elbows on (when Mom's not around of course). And I liked those Cray-Pas. Nice colors. Blend well. I could scribble and blend and just enjoy the colors. I discovered that my place at the table also offered me an excellent view of the stage.

It had been explained that the stage was for the artists-in-residence. They were going to paint the event, or their impressions of the event, or some reflection of the concepts and ideas being brought forward, or some abstract response to the event, or something. I wasn't clear, but I was clear that this was not going to be a project that had any relation to anything else I had ever watched. I mean, what is art after all? You pick a subject and then copy it, right? But they seemed to be painting, simply adding paint, and images would show up on the canvas. Then they would switch and each work on a different canvas.

So I color-blended and the speakers spoke. I liked the rhythm of engaging the coloring part of me while listening to the speakers, interrupting myself for a moment here and there to applaud a particularly well-spoken phrase or inspiration or to look around at the crowd. Getting a little bored with making colors, I asked myself: What would you really like to draw? The response came back: The red hills of northern New Mexico. But since I'd been into blue, I decided to do something with blue instead.

As it turned out, my table was always near the stage, even though the tables moved every day. I watched with awe as image after image emerged, and then to my shock the artists would paint right over some marvelous image. No, don't! I liked that one, the curve of it or the color appealed to something in me. But the image was gone, replaced by a new image, a new icon, which opened up some new inspiration in me. I wasn't aware of the direct connections with what was being said. There was a jungle: thick greens of many variations, vines, and big leaves like the leaves of the dinosaur era. Now a sky, a dark red sky, as if the planet were still new and hot and heating the sky. Now a cooler sky and stars emerging. She's setting it on its side. Oh no, don't take away the sky! Oh, I see, it's a landscape—yes, a lovely landscape.

What courage, I thought. To let go of some piece of beauty to make room for another. They must have great confidence in their abilities to pull this off. But soon I began to wonder if perhaps their confidence was not so much in themselves but in the process or maybe in the cocreative nature of this whole thing. Whoa! If that's true, maybe all these years I have been thinking wrongly about this art stuff.

I had always wanted to create with color, but all my stuff was laughable, almost cartoonish. Nobody—I mean *nobody*—had ever encouraged my efforts. And it was understandable. If I set out to draw a horse, it looked more like a dog, a dead dog. But what would happen if I abandoned the old way for this new thing like they were doing? I had to stop and think about the old way. Well, it was a linear way. You start at Place A, the blank piece of paper, and decide that you want to get to Place B, the horse. Then you try to figure out the shortest distance between those two points and proceed with the task.

Okay, so I was going to intentionally lay aside that procedure, but what was this new one? Just start, pick a color, make a line, fill a space—even a tiny space—and be in that space for a while, then step back to see what has emerged. Okay, here goes. It was, after all, paper just for doodling. No assignment here.

A rust color, a line that twisted and turned like viewing an ancient river from the air. Then a red line alongside it, thickening in spots. The feel of putting lines down, of giving them space, giving them voice in a sense, was a feeling so satisfying and so different from most of my work. Now, a gray shadow and a dot of black, blend here and blend there. Almost as if the paper asked for what it needed. It became a process that was less conscious at one level and reached deeper consciousness at another—less rational, more mystical.

So the presentations went on, and I was hearing them. They related to what I was doing: giving voice to something inside me not previously heard (at least not out loud); experimenting with a new part of myself in a place that was safe; learning to trust a process of cocreation that was clearly more than my actions alone; connecting with a new muse, a new spirit—perhaps the creative aspect of God?

Later I would speak to Nancy Chinn, the artist-in-residence, and tell her about my experience, and she would say, "Congratulations. You have just escaped patriarchy." Emerging, not straight-lined, not sufficient unto myself, but finding myself through relationship to what is going on around me, discovering the prompting of the Spirit in ways that I could never have seen without risking, stepping off into the place.

Then it was time to move into the workshops. So I put away the Cray-Pas, wiped my hands, sat up straight, turned my paper on its side, and there they were: the red hills of northern New Mexico.

Peg A. B. Chemberlin is executive director of the Minnesota Council of Churches. She received her master of divinity degree at United Theological Seminary of the Twin Cities and is ordained in the Moravian church, with dual-standing in the United Church of Christ. She is an avowed and practicing ecumenist and feminist, both for herself and for the sake of her daughter.

Chung Hyun Kyung Gets Her Apple

MANLEY OLSON

One of the hopes of the conference planners was that the table groups would coalesce and the participants would form a community that would provide a home during the conference. This certainly happened at the table where I sat. We were a diverse group: ordained, lay, religious, and seminarian; young and not so young; female and male; mobile on feet and mobile on wheels; Catholic, Lutheran, Reformed, and Independent; from all parts of the country and with a variety of experiences and viewpoints. Yet it did not take long before it was clear that we had developed a sense of caring for each other.

We found ways to circle dance so that our friend in a wheelchair could be included. We became especially sensitive to our youngest member, who was from an independent conservative church. She came as a guest of her future mother-in-law and admitted to knowing very little about the beliefs and practices of other churches. As the only man in the group, I was fully accepted; and, in fact, others often asked if I felt comfortable and able to contribute.

Several members of the group brought small gifts to share. I had not, and I began to think about what I could do. What I finally selected became not just a gift for my group, but one that found its way into the larger gathering and became for me, and perhaps others, a lasting symbol of the conference.

When Chung Hyun Kyung was introduced at the opening session, mention was made of her words in *Inheriting Our Mothers' Gardens*[2], in which she wrote of sitting with all her mothers under Eve's tree, eating an apple. One of my tablemates suggested we should be eating apples at our table. That gave me the idea I was looking for. The next day, I brought apples for each of us, and we began to eat them as the program started. However, there was an empty chair at our table and thus an extra apple. When I asked if anyone wanted a second apple, someone suggested giving it to Dr. Chung. We agreed, but no one wanted take it to her. So I did. I gave her the apple just before she was scheduled to speak. I think she was somewhat surprised, but she graciously accepted it.

Before beginning her talk, Dr. Chung announced that she had been given an apple by a white, Anglo-Saxon, middle-class-looking brother. She noted that this was a small sign of the redemption of patriarchal Christianity and that it had deeply touched her. Then she took several bites from it. From

59

the applause of the group, it was clear that those gathered appreciated the symbolism of the gift. Here we were, all sitting under Eve's tree and sharing her apple.

I did not speak to Dr. Chung again until the end of the conference, as the wild, joyous dance was coming to an end. As we shared a hug, she again thanked me for the gift. This time it was my turn to thank her for her words that the apple was a sign of redemption. We parted with the fond hope that one day we might meet again and share an apple.

Though I heard a few comments about the apple incident during the conference, I was not fully aware of its symbolic impact until later. At the beginning of the first meeting of the steering committee after the conference, the co-chairs of the group presented each committee member with a pin in the shape of an apple. As we received our pins, I was surprised by the extent to which the apple had come to be a symbol of the sharing and the hope of Re-Imagining.

Manley Olson is a Presbyterian elder and a seeker after and worker for inclusiveness, justice, and peace in the church. He served on the Re-Imagining Conference steering committee. Currently he serves the Presbyterian Church (U.S.A.) as co-moderator of Presbyterians for Disabilities Concerns and as co-chair of the Ecumenical Decade committee. In addition to serving on the coordinating council of the Re-Imagining Community, he is part of the planning group for a regional interfaith conference on religion and disability. He is a poet and hymn writer, a birder, and a historian, and he has been a college dean for twenty-five years.

Chosen by God

KATHI AUSTIN MAHLE

Saturday lunchtime. Finally I found a time to sit down, catch my breath, and relax a bit. It had been a hectic and stress-filled morning behind the scenes at Re-Imagining, so eating lunch and laughing were a joy. Then someone brought the note.

My husband had called security at the convention center. Ardith Force, a member of the church I serve, had been taken to Fairview Riverside Hospital. She was in a coma. The family needed to reach Virginia Anderson, her daughter, who was attending the Re-Imagining Conference. She and her mother shared a registration for the conference.

I found Virginia and told her about her mother; we left for the hospital together. When we got there, we learned Ardith had had a heart attack while in the hospital, on top of what was presumed to be a stroke. It was serious. Her other daughter, Laurel, and son Roger were already at the hospital. Over the course of the next couple of hours, the doctors ruled out a stroke. It was possibly meningitis. Her condition was grave.

Ardith Force was a very special woman. I had known her for many years prior to my serving at Hamline United Methodist Church. She was involved with Annual Conference leadership and United Methodist Women. She had been on the original Ecumenical Decade committee, representing Church Women United. She was one of the many volunteers at registration for Re-Imagining on Thursday and had attended the conference that evening. Ardith was a woman of deep faith and supported other women on their faith journeys.

Late Saturday afternoon, I prayed with the family around her still body, knowing that I would probably not see her again. When I checked in later in the evening, Laurel reported that as soon as Allen, their older brother, arrived from Texas they would make the decision to turn off the respirator. It was meningitis. I grieved. Many others who knew Ardith would grieve the next day at her death.

In the midst of celebrating new life and a new way to be community, we dealt with death. In order to have new life, there must be a dying. We experienced that with Ardith and grieved with her family.

A week later, we celebrated her life in a wonderful service of resurrection and remembering. Women and men from all over Minnesota gathered to remember and rejoice in all the gifts she had given us. The worship folder from her service reflected Ardith's life: her faith, her love of music, her commitment to family, and her work with church women. At the end, her family wrote these words: "From all our sharing and remembrances since her death, we see the Re-Imagining Conference and its vision of re-imagining what the world can be, as a culmination of our mother's life."

Reflecting on the events of that weekend, I realized that what was important to me was ministry with people—being with people in the times of their deepest pain and times of celebration of new life. We experienced both during the conference. My pastoral role extended on Sunday to those who knew Ardith and were her friends. Even in the midst of worrying about conference details and organization, the very real human needs of grieving women became paramount. Tears flowed, arms reached out, and the care and love of Sophia hovered around.

We are all chosen by God for ministry. Compassion becomes the bedrock of all we do: in our singing, in our teaching, in our administering, in our preaching and pastoring, in our daily living. A re-imagined world based on compassion and love and peace with justice was Ardith's dream, and it is the dream we all share in the never-ending love of God.

The Reverend Kathi Austin Mahle serves as the lead pastor at Hamline United Methodist Church in Saint Paul, Minnesota. She served as co-chair of the Re-Imagining Conference steering committee and continues to serve as co-chair of the coordinating council of the Re-Imagining Community. She is a past president of the board of directors of the Greater Minneapolis Council of Churches. She is active in the life of the United Methodist Church at the Annual Conference and general church levels.

A Simple Gift

JENNIFER BLAGEN

When the director Julia Carey first asked me to participate in a reading of the play *Simple Gifts,* I must admit my interest lay more in working with Julia than in performing a play about Shakers. I come from a decidedly secular background, and though many of my formative experiences with organized religion have been pleasant, I've always had the feeling that I was sitting in on something that didn't have anything to do with me personally. Church seemed to belong to the other people in the pews.

Once we'd actually read through the play, my attitude changed. The play itself was very good, but the attraction was strongest to the lives of these amazing people called the Shakers. Their lives were constantly in a state of appreciation of sacredness. They felt that everything one does in life should exude what is sacred about us as humans. They had an uncanny ability to create beauty; but at the same time, the beauty of human sexuality was completely taboo. What a strange combination, and what delight as an actress to be able to explore the role of a young Shaker grappling with the contradictions of the faith in which she'd been raised.

In researching the material for the play, we read diaries, poured through photographs, read histories, and saw as much film footage as possible. We tried to become as familiar with the everydayness of Shaker life as we could. One thing was overwhelming to me: despite all of the unusual aspects of their beliefs, like shaking and celibacy, they were *so normal.* Their diaries were filled with entries like "Oh boy, I have to go work in that darn dye house again; I really hate that job sometimes." And they were so practical. They were the first people to bottle medicine; they invented the flat broom and the round barn, among a bejillion other things. They traded happily and without prejudice with the outside world. These fascinating people were (are) so complex and so real. I felt myself becoming involved somehow with these ideas, and it made me happy.

Yet another unusual element in working on this piece was performing in a church. Have you ever done anything as selfish as rehearsing (for something that has nothing to do with next Sunday) in a church? What a weird feeling. I sensed a satisfaction, almost defiance, in some of the members of the cast and crew. I put that down to the fact that, despite the secular society we all live in, it's really difficult to be neutral about working in a church.

So here we are, spending a mere (very mere by theater standards) three hours a day rehearsing *Simple Gifts* by Pamela Carter Joern. We go through our own personal journeys and receive our own personal rewards. But then comes opening night—it is now time to share our exploration and work with an audience that we worry may have more concrete experience with the subject matter than we do. Well, let's be honest, we know they have a better understanding of the whole religion thing than we do, but we also know we have poured our hearts and souls into this work and that we have something truly beautiful, heartfelt, and personal to share with the strangers attending the Re-Imagining Conference. It has been a process of self and communal discovery, and now we are to give it away for the first time.

I keep getting stuck when I try to explain the unusual and enormous impact of that first performance. Have you ever *really* wanted to tell someone something *really* special and *really* important, and to your surprise and delight they *really* wanted to hear it? If you can magnify that joy and satisfaction a million times over, you might come close to the privilege of communion that we experienced that night—and every night of the conference. I have never felt the force of an audience like that in my life. It was a spiritual event, and I count it among those things with which I am blessed.

Jennifer Blagen is currently a full-time student at the University of Minnesota, studying Russian language and literature. She lives with Peter, her boyfriend, and Hecate, her cat. She hopes to be training at the Moscow Art Theatre in Russia during the fall of 1995.

a meeting of roots

KAROL E. HENDRICKS-MCCRACKEN

seon joy and kyu moon, korean born, now citizens of minnesota
a six-year-old daughter, a four-year-old son
chung hyun kyung, korean born, korean citizen
professor of theology, keynote speaker

seon joy longs to meet her birth mother
chung hyun kyung has recently met her birth mother
much in common
they must meet
dear god go before me and speak to her heart
ask
yes

seon joy and kyu moon
chung hyun kyung
a meeting
a pleasant exchange
a blessing
a recognition of life-blood flowing among the three
culture acknowledged and shared

momma a lady from korea touched me
she said i had an ancient spirit
she said i had a strong spirit
momma do you think our birth mothers look like her?

Karol E. Hendricks-McCracken is currently on sabbatical from professional life so she can experience a stable family environment with her three young children and husband. She is a Stephen Ministry leader and member of the Feminine Face of God study group at Calvary Lutheran Church. When employed, Karol taught public speaking and interpersonal communication skills at the university level and coordinated volunteers at the regional hospital. Often asked to speak on her faith journey within her community of Bemidji, Minnesota, she has been quoted as saying, "I would rather give a sermon than work in the church kitchen any day."

Emerging from the Tomb

DONALD R. KEYWORTH

The Re-Imagining Conference was exciting for me from start to finish. Being one of the eighty or so men in a group of nearly two thousand women was particularly moving during the singing. Though I (and I am sure the other men) sang along during the general assembly sessions, all that could be heard were treble voices. I frequently stopped singing just to listen. How beautiful it was! Not only in quality of sound, but also in what the celebration symbolized.

And then I remember the laughter. It was transforming for me. Events and comments that did not seem funny to me often brought roars of glee from the crowd. Usually a moment or two later I would catch on and see the humor flowing from the context of all these people who had striven so long to break through the walls of an oppressive theological and ecclesiastical system. During the play *Simple Gifts,* one of these humorous epiphanies was overwhelming. Since I know Pam Joern, the playwright, I had heard about some of the actors struggling to grasp the humor of lines that were written to be funny. The rehearsals had been successful, the actors were all professionals, but they did not share the same religious context or history. Then during the opening moments of the performance, the actor portraying the Playwright said, "I have been plagued by religion all of my life."[3] The audience of eight hundred erupted! And before our eyes, we could see a person transformed. What had been someone else's story was now hers: her voice, her actions, even her eyes became animated as she and the other actors merged with the audience in a common struggle. It was a moment that is as vivid for me now as it was those many months ago.

Another treasured memory is the session on Jesus. I owe a great debt of gratitude to the three speakers, Delores Williams, Kwok Pui-Lan, and Barbara Lundblad. Their presentations have provided much needed nourishment to my impoverished soul and revived my spirituality.

Oh, Jesus, who are you?[4] (asked over and over)

I had been taught we are supposed to know who Jesus is, not to ask. I had stopped asking. The answers I had heard so often were no longer palatable to me. The old notions still held immense nostalgic appeal for me, but the spooky magic of atonement had become so morally offensive that the central

66

symbol of my faith had become little more than a rosy blur. When the speakers asked us to re-imagine Jesus, I immediately thought of how this could be done in our hymns and spiritual songs. So many of them portray Jesus' suffering as only external. "Let this cup pass from me" (Matt. 26:39) and "My God, my God, why have you forsaken me" (Matt. 27:46) seem relegated to the subtext at best. Surely this is a denial of the incarnation. If, as the Scriptures maintain, "Jesus was tempted in all things as we are" (Heb. 4:15), then we need to think and picture and sing about his inwardness rather than settling for our usual misinterpretation of his seemingly flippant resistance to the devil in the wilderness.

The incarnation of the Spirit came through Mary's body. . . . Jesus is God and Mary. [5]

One insight that was very productive for me was the feminist/womanist emphasis on starting with the Spirit as discovered in my own religious experience and moving from there to a sense of who Jesus and God are, rather than the traditional path from God to Jesus to the Spirit. Though I am a philosopher by trade and make my living by manipulating abstractions, I find in my own journey little substance to the concept of God as a starting point. Instead, personal religious meaning for me must begin, as one speaker said, with listening to my own inner gasps, groans, songs, and celebrations and deriving from them, in community with other seekers, concepts and pictures that are essential to identifying the place of God and Jesus in the stream of my life.

In the early morning hours, I have often gone with my sister Mary Magdalene to the tomb with spices in my hand: all my anger, all my questions, everything I just can no longer say. I have gone to the tomb to bury Jesus, to be done with him once and for all. And then when I get there in all my emptiness, trying to throw everything away, I hear a voice that says, "Barbara." And then Jesus says, "Do not hold me! Do not hold me in the old categories that no longer touch you. Do not put back the stone that has been telling you that this is a story of death and not life. Do not hang on to the right answers that come from somebody else." And I could not then bury Jesus, for he had said my name. [6]

Talk about a resurrection experience! This was certainly one for me. I heard him say my name, and I began to emerge from the tomb of abracadabra (ending every prayer with "in Jesus' name") and of tribal gore ("washed in the blood"). I could feel the binding grave cloths begin to fall away, rags of my frustrated rebellion against all the caricatures that the power-hungry media Christians have drawn and labeled "Jesus." In spite of all the injustice and wrong that have been committed under the authority of Jesus' name, I cannot bury Jesus. And I cannot remain silent about this. To paraphrase Martin Buber: We cannot cleanse this image and we cannot make it whole; but defiled and mutilated as it is, we can raise it from the ground and set it over an hour of great care.[7]

Donald R. Keyworth is professor emeritus of philosophy at Drake University in Des Moines, Iowa. He taught philosophy at Drake University for thirty-seven years and served as choir director at Westover Baptist Church in Des Moines, Iowa, for twenty-six years. His paramount spiritual choice has always been to be a reflective Christian or not to be a Christian at all.

Early Morning

MARILYN HUGH

The choir director asked me for suggestions for replacing a male pronoun in a song. "The word *God* fits," I responded. I guess I was getting a reputation for asking speakers to remove their pronouns and for singing different words from everyone else. Take Sophia.

A priest I met used the name *Sophia* to talk about the Holy Spirit, explaining it was the biblical word for *wisdom*. I liked that idea. So when I went to the Re-Imagining Conference, I was thrilled to sing "bless Sophia, dream the vision, share the wisdom dwelling deep within"[8] as each speaker was blessed before speaking to us. It was a way of asking God to share through this person the wisdom implanted within her.

I stayed with my brother during the conference, and he took me to the convention center early each morning on his way to work. I looked forward to spending that time reading the daily newsletter to see the latest installment of information about the history of using *Sophia* to refer to God. I did not perceive at any time that we were worshiping a goddess or making God into a different image. I was comfortable with new words and enjoying new insights.

Another early morning highlight for me was spending time with Nancy Chinn's sculptures, *Even the Stones Cry Out,* depicting ten stories from the Bible that support abusive attitudes toward women. Each sculpture has a reflection sentence. As I stood there looking at the yellow painting of an apple cut in half with an egg emerging, I remembered all those times I had heard Eve referred to as the source of evil in the world. I thought about my own ability to risk and to grow and to not accept the judgment upon Eve.

As I looked at the blue rose in the Mary painting, I thought about a line in the song "The Rose" which speaks of one who is afraid of dying never learning to live. Nancy's words said, "Our sexuality and our lives are holy."[9] I felt like shouting: Yes, Lord, we are sexual beings reflecting your love just as Mary gave birth to Jesus in the usual way, receiving the usual shunning from her culture.

The most meaningful sculpture of all was Lot's wife, with its skyscraper and falling stones and the reflection "Survival is not worth destroying who we are."[10] I think that was the essence of the whole conference for me. I survived.

I wasn't destroyed. I didn't feel forced to change. I felt affirmed. I enjoyed the people at my table. We drew. We connected. We shared. We accepted each other exactly as we were.

Marilyn Hugh is a fifty-seven-year-old professional volunteer and lifetime Lutheran. She is an avid reader and supporter of many kinds of diversities. Her volunteer work includes hospice, learning ministries, hunger walks, and homeless shelters. Marilyn lives with her husband in suburban Chicago; they have one adult daughter.

Two Thousand and One

KARLA MCGRAY

As two thousand women gathered at the Minneapolis Convention Center re-imagining the church, I sat at home re-imagining a childhood. As two thousand women danced in beautifully designed rituals, I danced between the medicine chest and my sick child's bed. As two thousand women sang sacred hymns and deeply moving chants, I sang quiet lullabies to help ease my daughter into a feverish sleep. As two thousand women took their long-held yearnings and created a safe place together, I created a safe place for my sick child, the child I had long yearned for.

When people ask, "Did you attend the Re-Imagining Conference?" I need to respond, "Yes, but. . . . " I need to add that I could only attend the first evening. I was there long enough to sample the banquet that was going to be served. I was there long enough to sit at the table, look into the faces of nine other women, and taste their stories. I was there long enough to sit in a circle of women filled with anticipation of what was about to happen. I sat in a circle of sisters for one evening, and then the circle was broken. My chair sat empty as my daughter's fever rose over the next three days.

Even though I wasn't able to return to the conference, I continued my contact with the women in the only way possible. Each day I handed my ticket through my front door to a grateful woman who had heard of my situation and was most eager not to let a ticket go to waste. One of these women was from El Salvador. She was a woman who had taken great risks with her life to be one face of God to a desperate people. She happened to be visiting Minneapolis, unaware that Re-Imagining was taking place. She was thrilled to go, and I was very pleased to share. It made my absence take on new meaning. And it proved how the communication network of women works so effectively.

Another visitor at my door was one sweet soul from my Friday evening table. She brought me a bag of clay. The clay had been shared at our table by each woman, then used as a creative medium for expression. The experience was very meaningful to her. She wanted me to have this experience, too. I was touched by her thoughtfulness, and it felt good to be remembered.

But I have a confession. While it felt good to be remembered and to create an opportunity for others to attend, I felt a sense of loss with each meeting at the door. In the midst of it all, I had this deep knowing that something revolutionary was taking place, and I wasn't part of it. It reminded me of when I was a new mother, and my daughter had just arrived from Korea. I remember sitting in a rocking chair with Kate in my arms, watching a protest demonstration at the Honeywell Corporation on television. I remember thinking how important and necessary the protest was at that point in time and how glad I was that others had the energy and freedom to be there when I couldn't.

Two thousand women were called to gather, question, challenge, and celebrate their faith. At the same time I was called to mother, pay attention, heal, and quietly celebrate my most fundamental ministry in life. Two thousand women gathered to re-imagine all the possibilities within our Christian faith and to create an experience the church had not been able to give them. I gathered my daughter in my arms to re-imagine for her all the possibilities of her childhood that my own working single mother was unable to give me.

It seems to me there was an abundance of God's presence in all that we women were struggling to do that weekend. Yet God's presence is not without complication and complexity. It often can create a tension between two points. It is a tension that I, as a clergywoman and mother, live with every day. It is a tension that I hear other women share. It is a tension that can be difficult at times, but it is one for which I am grateful. Each of the two points fuels the other, makes the passion stronger. Out of this is born a re-imagining power that is unlimited. It is a blessing to the church and a childhood.

The Reverend Karla McGray entered seminary when her children were one and two years old, after twenty years in management in business and nonprofit organizations. She attended United Theological Seminary of the Twin Cities and graduated in 1991. Upon graduation, she received a wooden desk plate from her family reading "Reverend Mommy," a sign of future struggles she did not yet understand. She was associate pastor at Judson Memorial Baptist Church in Minneapolis for three years, but now her ministry continues outside the church through denominational work and consulting in an effort to balance what God has called her to do and what God has called her to create, her family.

Lingering Impressions

MARY HAGUE GATES, AS TOLD TO PAMELA CARTER JOERN

Over gyros and Kalamata olives, Mary Gates talked about Re-Imagining. Mary, along with Jo Ringgenberg, co-chaired local arrangements for the conference. Mary was in charge of exhibit space, child care, and the sale of commemorative items, along with myriad other details. She is also president of United Methodist Women in Minnesota, a voluntary organization of nearly twenty thousand women, whose mission focus is women, children, and youth. These women raise an annual budget of $545,000 from individual contributions, chicken suppers, and bazaars.

The conversation had barely begun when Mary said, "I need to write you a note." Puzzled, I handed over my notebook. Seated at the next table, she wrote, is a clergy couple who were ringleaders of the opposition against Re-Imagining. It turns out that the husband had written an article criticizing Re-Imagining for Good News *and had led the negative attack at the United Methodist Church Annual Conference in June 1994. We chuckled at yet another of life's ironies and got on with our business. In fact, getting on with business is a Mary Gates trait. She talked about her lingering impressions of Re-Imagining in snippets of insight.*

The conference reinforced what I already knew about working with women. It's exciting . . . things could fall apart at any given moment, but they never do. Sometimes you feel you are holding things together by the sheer force of personality.

I was very touched that all the presenters agreed to come for a common honorarium. I'm sure it was less money than many of them usually receive, and I wouldn't expect them to set aside their fees for every occasion. But it was very gratifying to me as a woman that they were willing to come together in this way for this event.

It was a holy moment or maybe the essence of awe to be working with so many well-known, gifted, and knowledgeable people.

I came away with tremendous respect for Jo Ringgenberg. And we are still friends.

Coordinating the exhibits and displays was a tremendous task. People tended to relax once it was up and running. But beforehand, the exhibitors were anxious (understandably) about recouping their investments. At first, I said "never again!" No more exhibits. That lasted a year. Now I'm saying that people want these resources, and maybe we should do it at our regional conferences—on a small scale. It's a little like childbirth: if you wait long enough, you're ready to go through it again.

I spent a lot of time and energy trying to get ethnic minority women to attend. I also coordinated a reception on Friday night for United Methodists which was funded by five separate groups. That took a lot of calling, begging, and cajoling. So, I had responsibilities related to the steering committee and other responsibilities that I took on as a United Methodist woman. Sometimes when it got a bit much, members of my support group would say, "Don't you want to chuck it all?" But I would never have given up this experience.

I was zealous in insisting that every contributor should be recognized in the program booklet: denominations, organizations, and individuals. Later the organized conservative religious groups used that information as a way to pressure people to withhold their denominational support and to raise funds for their own efforts to uphold what they believe to be the true faith. Still, listing contributors was the right thing to do.

United Methodist Women have a history of progressive thought and action on social issues. I have regretted that our national Women's Unit responded defensively at first to what might have been an educating moment. Now we have moved into the educating mode.

I still have visions sometimes of schlepping all those boxes and asking myself: Is this what this is really about? I learned after a while that walking the length of the convention center was easier on the carpeted second floor.

I didn't anticipate not being able to attend the conference. I knew there would be last-minute things, but it seemed like some of us were called out constantly to deal with questions no one else could answer. The office was on the second floor, which turned out to be a long way away.

People tend to think we did this conference with a full staff of professionals working around the clock. The truth is we did it with volunteers who recruited other volunteers. As volunteers go, some were priceless, and some didn't show up.

I remember a moment when I was trying to track down the name of the librarian at Luther Seminary to get a list of books by our presenters. I said, "I don't want to worry about the theology of it all. I'll just get it done." Randy Nelson, a member of the steering committee and a faculty member at Luther Seminary, laughed because he said that captures the fundamental difference between Lutherans and United Methodists. Lutherans worry over the theology, and United Methodists roll up their sleeves.

I comfort myself with two thoughts. First, most people were not aware of the problems behind the scenes. They experienced a smooth event that was more sensitive to their needs than many other public events. Second, the things we worried about most never happened. I think I'll just keep those worries to myself.

I was upset by the negative response at first. The nature of the attacks was so vicious. The issues weren't new, but somehow we were blamed for bringing them up. I went to speak to a group of concerned United Methodist churches in Minnesota. When I was asked questions about theological issues, I responded by saying "I am not a theologian." A woman in the back of the room stood and asked how I dared to present myself as president of United Methodist Women in Minnesota if I am not qualified as a theologian. That hurt. However, the churches that were represented that day have decided not to withhold their giving, so maybe it did some good for us to try to talk together.

It was exhilarating to take on something bigger than life. We shouldn't have been able to pull it off, but we did.

Mary Hague Gates is an active member of Simpson United Methodist Church and currently serves as president of the Minnesota Conference of United Methodist Women. She was observer/representative at the United Nations Conference on Women in Nairobi and at the World Methodist Council and the World Federation of Methodist Women in Singapore. A life member of the Girl Scouts, her many volunteer positions include president of the board of directors of the Girl Scout Council of Greater Minneapolis and national volunteer for Girl Scouts of the USA. A graduate of the University of Minnesota and employed for nineteen years as an admissions counselor at Metropolitan State University, she and her husband, Clyde, have four grown children and five grandchildren.

God Is Like That

ROBERT E. LUCAS

In all of the reporting about the Re-Imagining Conference, little has been said about the wonderful and powerful images of God which would have found broad acceptance among the conference's critics. The presenter who made a deep impact on me was Rita Nakashima Brock. She recounted her own personal story and described how her mother and father had become separated when she was an infant. Eventually, there was a divorce and a remarriage. Rita grew up believing her stepfather was her birth father.

After her Japanese mother died, Rita learned of her adoption. Eventually, she found the name of her birth father and an old address in Puerto Rico. She went to find him and, in the process, discovered an entire family that she had not even known existed. She met her grandfather, who had prayed every day of his life for the little granddaughter he had never seen. And she found a grandmother who had kept Rita's baby pictures tucked into the frame of the mirror on her dresser and who had continually looked at those pictures, sure that she would not die before seeing that child in the flesh. These grandparents had waited and hoped and prayed for a day they so earnestly wanted to come.

Then Rita said to us, "My grandmother's commitment to loving me did not rest on my knowing her, but on her memory of me. *Abuela* Maria loved me although she was unknown to me."[11] I heard Rita saying she thinks God is like that.

Well, so do I, and I am grateful to Rita Nakashima Brock for providing me with a new image of God.

Robert E. Lucas is a Presbyterian Church (U.S.A.) minister, serving as the executive presbyter of the Presbytery of the Twin Cities Area in Minneapolis.

Standing Up Straight

CHERYL DUDLEY

I looked forward with great expectation to Re-Imagining. I had heard about it while serving in my former post in the Midwest prior to moving to a new ministry position, and I had mused about the possibilities of such a gathering. I took time to talk to friends, cohorts, associates, and acquaintances about the coming together of women to reflect on our experiences and hopes for the church. I even recruited conferees by sharing information I had received. Being a community organizer by inclination, I wanted to be sure that this gathering had faces, forms, and spirits familiar and recognizable to me. Generally speaking, an environment needs to be personally comfortable in order for me to ingest content meant for my intellectual and spiritual edification. Nevertheless, it sounded to me as if Re-Imagining had the makings of being a historic, phenomenal event, and I wanted to be there.

Those whose presence I anticipated were womanist and feminist theologians and other women of faith—those firmly grounded and theologically sound, as well as the seekers, the faithful, the pushers, the promoters, the courageous, and those who felt that in the midst of it all they had lost their way and needed to be reconnected. Another expectation was that I would see many women that I have known in other life experiences related to our faith. I was right. These persons were present, but I was surprised that other persons I would have expected to be there were not: the persons who have been in the forefront of conferences for women and/or women in ministry planned or sponsored by the American Baptist churches. I wondered if they thought Re-Imagining was an unsafe place for them or if they chose not to attend for other reasons.

Of the two thousand persons who were there, I had met only a very small number before. It was said that hundreds more wanted to attend but could not because the conference space could not accommodate them. I know of women who tarried on waiting lists hoping that those who had secured a place early would be unable to attend. Imagine: all these women and a few men from various places had sojourned to this cold location in November in search of intellectual and spiritual stimulation, *koinonia* or sisterhood, respite, even healing.

Walking into the ballroom, site of the plenary sessions, that first evening was almost overwhelming. The organizers' hard work was evident right

77

away. All participants were assigned to tables and sections of the ballroom coded by number and color. Such organization! My table assignment was fifty-four. At first glance, it appeared to be nowhere in sight; I thought there must be hundreds of tables. But I found it, and as those of us assigned to table fifty-four gathered around, I began to hear the stories of these few women. It was clear that they had come to Re-Imagining to receive something: healing, affirmation, empowerment, vision, connection to the family of God from which they may have been estranged where they presently do ministry, and simple bonding with sisters and allies.

We began with ritual: singing and praying, liturgical dance, and provocative words from wise women. (The next several days brought more of the same—perhaps much more than any one person could comfortably ingest. I was relieved to discover that tapes were being made; I could purchase them and digest later at an easier pace.) The evening was meticulously orchestrated, each segment patently timed to the point of irritation. Some acoustical failures occurred, as well as a few glitches in choreography—however, a tone of expectation burst forth.

The women's stories were varied: a woman serving as pastor of a Mennonite congregation with her husband in a midwestern town; another woman pastor trying to discern a sister's place in the Church of the Brethren (language is a powerful tool); a United Methodist laywoman, a college professor, identifying herself as a seeker struggling with a call to ministry; a seminarian hungering for an environment that encourages nontraditional theological reflection. Then there were the women who sat quietly together, seemingly not fully engaged, pensively listening and talking about their Christian rearing in a Southeast Asian country. There was a woman who appeared as if she could have been a pillar of her community or church, or a Junior Leaguer, or a Mary Kay consultant; she was meticulously groomed every day. She had a distinctive style of speaking and seemed to choose her words carefully. I also shared from my own experience, although somewhat guardedly. We gained a superficial knowledge of one another in the several days we were together. Although I could not accept or understand all the words of my sisters on the platform or in the seats next to me, I could listen and rejoice with them when crippling spirits disappeared or diminished at the end of our days together. I joined with the crowd on the last day in dancing and rejoicing for the good things Christ had done in our midst.

During Re-Imagining, a personal celebration occurred within me. It was a felt recognition of the possibilities for a spiritual merger of my head and heart with respect to my womanist Christian faith. I think too often we function in a compartmentalized fashion. A specific example is the emotional separation of my womanness from my faith journey. I enjoy being a woman; and as a womanist, I look for ways to affirm my womanist thinking both inside and outside the church. As a woman of faith, I've presented myself as un-apologetically Christian to my sisters who may be Jewish, Muslim, Buddhist, formerly Roman Catholic, straddlers, or agnostics. In my experience, the presence of the reconciling Christ in the midst of these different women often has been both apparent and powerful.

At times I've felt a twinge of loneliness at gatherings of women who do not share my faith, but I contend that this sense of spiritual isolation is nothing in comparison to isolation felt in my own company of believers who have disregarded my experience as an African American woman in society and in the church.

I wanted to unpack my experience at Re-Imagining with acquaintances or colleagues. I longed for the company of the ones with whom I had cove-nanted to do this experience: coworkers and a close friend from seminary days. What were they thinking? How were they feeling? What were the points of resonance for them? At what points did they feel dissonance? I wanted to talk to persons I knew who would disagree without necessarily becoming disagree-able or overly polite, persons in whom I could recognize a nod of agreement or a furrow of questioning. I had a strong desire for ongoing life: an internaliza-tion, utilization, and implementation of the tidbits (at times) and the tidal waves (at other times) of revelation and understanding about myself and others. I wondered who the women around my talking table were to those who saw or knew them in their communities. Were these women affirmed, scorned, or simply a part of the scenery? Were these women my sisters? And if they were, would they continue to be so after we departed from the conference?

A text from Luke has come to mind in the months of reflection since the conference:

> *Now he was teaching in one of the synagogues on the Sabbath. And just then there appeared a woman with a spirit that had crippled her for eighteen years. She was bent over and was quite unable to stand up straight. When Jesus saw her he called her over and said, "Woman, you are set free from your ailment." When he laid his hands on her, immediately she stood up straight and began praising God (Luke 13:10–13).*

There is no doubt that many women at the conference experienced the living and healing Christ. It seemed as if many of my sisters were stooped or stumped in their faith, in their experience in the church, or in their ministries. I heard expressions of healing while in Minneapolis and in days since the benediction of the conference. Let me name two examples.

Women from the Church of the Brethren went before the assembly to affirm their rightful place in their communion. I believe these women felt empowered through the spirit of Christ to stand erect in the church (which is theirs) and to serve with dignity, recognition of merit, and equity. The Re-Imagining assembly rejoiced with them as they received their corporate healing.

My friend from seminary has served as an associate pastor in two churches. She is presently a doctoral student in religion and women's studies. My evangelical, spiritually disciplined friend, with charismatic leanings, was harassed at her last pastoral post for introducing Jesus as a feminist and suggesting feminine aspects of God in her women's Bible study. That experience had a lasting effect which caused cloudiness and uncertainty; however, it may have served as a springboard for her matriculation into the doctoral program. I recently talked to her about Re-Imagining, and I was inspired by the fervor in her words, declaring that she now knows what she is supposed to be doing. She has clarity of vision and purpose of step. "Woman you are set free from your ailment. . . . She stood up straight and began praising God." I rejoice with her and others who, because of Re-imagining and other experiences, can now stand up straight, praise God, and serve.

Cheryl Dudley is a Christian womanist thinker and minister living in Pennsylvania. She is an ordained Baptist minister. She is also a product of and participant in the Baptist missionary traditions. She has served in ministry in New Jersey, Illinois, North Carolina, and Pennsylvania. She was reared in the free-thinking, Christian mystic, community-action traditions and remains in that vein.

Frances

CAROLINE CONKLIN

That last morning at Re-Imagining, I clung so hard and so long to a kind table-neighbor's hand that her fingers must have been numb for hours. Why? Because I was trying not to sob aloud. My tears were mostly from relief: from finally understood heart-knowledge, some suppressed for decades. Yes. That's how it is. How it has always been. Yes! For instance, Frances.

Frances is a gently contoured, thirteen-inch, Effanbee girl-doll. She stands on my bookcase now, with her cap of waved, honey hair only a little mussed and her graceful fingers only slightly chipped. She wears a yellow cotton, puffed-sleeved dress with tiny pearl buttons up the back.

When I first saw Frances half a century ago, I was six. She, misty in pink tulle, floated from my grandfather's Christmas tree. I was awe-struck.

"Is she mine?" Gentle laughter rippled, even from Grandfather, normally a gray, distant, scolding man.

"Yes, dear. Thank Grandfather."

"Thank you, Grandfather!"

"You're welcome, Caroline. Play nicely now."

Frances came with the dress she floated in and a couple of others that were cheaply made and soon to disintegrate. Plus a red cardboard suitcase. The suitcase was filled with clothes my mother sewed with tiny stitches and miniature trim:

the dress she wears today,
a blue pinafore with pink roses and an elastic waist,
a red plaid school jumper,
a white dotted Swiss blouse,
a cream-colored nightgown trimmed in red,
a pair of green slacks with a yellow polka-dot top,
a rose taffeta, lace-trimmed party dress,
and, over the next few years that I played with Frances daily, any other
garment I felt we needed.

Frances herself was deadpan and poky-hard, impossible to sleep with (though I tried). In her clothes, though, she was me. Not as I was, but as I meant to be, could be: a wise inventor of replies to injuring remarks; a brave marcher-forth to scary times just ahead; a confident, hopeful beckoner to the shadowy future.

Adults who came across me as I played with Frances, my lips moving in dialogue, would say, "Wasn't it nice of your grandfather to give you such a beautiful doll?" Head down, I would nod. And so it was. Nice of him. It may even have been his idea, though it's hard to believe he would have concerned himself for an instant with a matter so minor.

But one kind of heart-knowledge that came to me at Re-Imagining was this: My little Christmas doll, Frances, possessed more life and more value than anyone knew (except for me, and I soon learned to unknow); and every bit of the life and value Frances possessed came to her through my mother's boundless care and skill. For Frances and for her millions of sisters, those lost except to memory and those still in sight, thank you, Mother.

Caroline Conklin received her bachelor of arts degree from Radcliffe College and her master of arts degree from the University of Montana. She has worked as a public school speech and language pathologist for twenty-four years. In June 1991, she was ordained a permanent deacon in the Episcopal church. She and her husband, Bill, have three living children, two adopted and one natural-born; their fourth child is with God.

An Experience of the Sacred

JANET KALVEN

I'm a Jewish Catholic crone, born to a middle-class reformed Jewish family, converted to Catholicism in my twenties, attaining cronehood at seventy (a crone, according to Mary Daly, is a woman who is untamed and has survived[12]). In my eighty years, I've attended hundreds of conferences and have organized scores myself. I was deeply impressed by Re-Imagining. I don't think I've ever been at a gathering that was so well prepared and that succeeded so magnificently in integrating the arts, social-justice issues, ethnic diversities, rituals, and theologizing—and all this in a highly participative format. It was energizing, inspiriting, hope-filled. I left the Minneapolis Convention Center refreshed and renewed.

I felt the presence of the Spirit throughout the four days, but the high point for me—the moment that moved me most deeply and brought tears to my eyes—was on Saturday morning. At the end of the opening worship, a young woman stood on the central dais and invited the lesbian, gay, and bisexual persons among us to come forward, if they wished to do so, and make their presence visible. There was a moment of silence, of weighing the risks and making the decision. Then from all parts of the room, I saw women rising and converging on the center platform. There was another moment of suspense as I waited to see how we would respond to this intervention. Suddenly, the whole assembly rose to its feet, applauding and cheering. For me, both of these suspense-filled moments were experiences of the Holy, the Spirit moving in the minds and hearts of the gathering, enabling us to transcend our private fears and prejudices and to respond to each other in loving affirmation.

After the session, I ran into a close friend, a woman with whom I have worked for many years and know intimately. She is a hard-headed political organizer, brusque and unsentimental. With tears in her eyes, she said to me, "I've never come out in public like that before. A lot of these women were taking a big risk. It was an incredible experience."

Two footnotes to my story. First, I am and always have been heterosexual. Second, I met Melanie Morrison, the woman who issued the invitation from the dais, a few months later. "When I invited people to come forward," Melanie told me, "I was not sure that anyone would respond."

The Spirit blows where She wills (John 3:8) and was surely present at Re-Imagining.

Janet Kalven is a Jewish Catholic crone, born in 1913, a member of the Grail since 1942, and one of the group that founded Grailville in 1944 as a center of empowering education for women. Retired from the University of Dayton in 1986, she lives and works at Grailville in Loveland, Ohio, organizing programs in feminist theology and spirituality and writing a book on the history of the Grail in the United States, tentatively titled Fast Women in a Slow Church.

A Midwife's Renewal

JEAN FITCH JUSTICE

For many people, the Re-Imagining Conference was an experience of spiritual rebirth and renewal. I am one who would make that claim. However, unlike most attendees, my spiritual renewal did not come during the days the conference was held. It came before and after the actual event.

When I agreed to serve as coregistrar for the conference, my greatest fear was that I would spend most of the conference sitting behind a registration desk rather than participating in the sessions. That fear was well grounded. I was only able to attend parts of two general sessions. Though I had wanted to be one of those giving birth to new spiritual insights and dimensions in my life and the lives of the women around me, I found myself instead in the role of midwife, enabling others to participate fully. After dealing with my disappointment and grief at my loss of opportunity to be within the gathered community, I found a sense of acceptance and even gratitude for the privilege of being a midwife to such an energizing experience for others.

Later I had my own spiritual renewal as I listened to the tapes of the conference presentations. Because I was hearing these speakers for the first time at the same time that I was reading volumes of backlash material generated by those who opposed what had been said and thought-provoking commentary by those whose minds were open to re-imagining, I had a different perspective than I would have had in the audience during the conference. What I heard were the voices of prophecy.

Mary Farrell Bednarowski: "The work of re-imagining theology needs to be work that sets us free rather than ties us up." . . . "We are not at the mercy of our theologies; we are responsible for them."[13]

Bernice Johnson Reagon: "I only know God in a personal way because of the storm." . . . "If there is a storm, you should be in the roughest part of the storm—probably in a ship without a sail—so that you cannot anchor until the storm is over."[14]

Heard in the storm of the aftermath, these words seemed even stronger, even more compelling, even more hope-filled and inspiring than they may have been when they were presented. As I listened to the tapes, I felt the storm and I felt the strength of a new kind of sheltering: women brought together out of a hunger of their spirits and fed by the work of the Holy Spirit among them. I heard answers to questions I had not dared to ask as well as answers to questions I had been asking for years.

The most meaningful presentation for me was one that received some of the most vitriolic attention: Delores Williams's presentation on "Re-Imagining Jesus." I am a Christian laywoman with no seminary training. I have not been exposed to much formal theological instruction other than materials I have read or discussions I have had with other Christian and Jewish lay people and clergy—all of which most assuredly is important theological discourse.

When I heard Delores Williams say that our emphasis must be on "not what Jesus died for but what Jesus lived for,"[15] I felt an immense sense of relief. I have long been uncomfortable with substitution theology, with the idea that our redemption comes from the event of Jesus' death on the cross to remove our sins, but I always figured I must be aberrant in my thinking. Hearing Delores Williams speak so confidently about questions I had been afraid to ask was an affirmation I have long needed. I am no longer hesitant to say that I do not find comfort in a theology that says an innocent person was tortured and killed to remove my sins, nor can I put my faith and trust in a God who would choose that way to assure redemption for the world. Instead I can confidently state what I have long believed and what Delores Williams so eloquently proclaimed: that the most important thing about Jesus was how he lived, not how he died; that Jesus lived for justice and healing and peace; that the value of this death for me was his willingness to risk on behalf of others and to stand up for what he believed no matter what the cost. Her words were full of faith and sharing and light and renewal for me.

Another time of spiritual renewal came to me slowly but steadily in the months, then weeks, then days leading up to 3 November 1993, when I had the privilege of being part of the steering committee for Re-Imagining. Within that group, I enjoyed the new experience of working closely with a multidenominational group of Christian women and men who were committed to establishing a time and place where people could join together to blend their unique spiritual voices into a common song—a song of wisdom and strength, of beauty and justice, of hope and rebirth. I am hopeful.

Jean Fitch Justice is a United Methodist laywoman, active at local, district, and conference levels as both a professional and volunteer. She is an adult Christian educator, speaker, writer, quilter, family historian, wife, and mother. She is secretary of the Re-Imagining Community and lives in Eden Prairie, Minnesota.

Distant Friends

ALIAS M. CHACKO

Dear Rev. Sally. L. Hill, Conference Coordinator,

With pleasure I should say about the conference that it was a great experience for me. I never had an occasion to attend such a big and planned conference abroad. The conference made me to re-imagine; and as I am from the Orthodox church, I will share my experiences with people of my country, especially with women. During next month, I may attend conferences where I will pass the message that I got from Minneapolis. My heartiest congratulations to you, as the program was well organized and a grand success. You do deserve all admiration, and I do pray for you all. Also my sincere felicitations.

I am also very much anxious to know the follow-up action you are taking as a continuation of the conference. Do you have any plan to conduct a conference anywhere else? Please let me know, as I can extend all my help for such functions, in case you need it. In my opinion, you should chalk out a plan of activities to pass the information to others who could not attend the conference. You can organize regional symposia or small meetings. You can also entrust others for these programs, but your group is the right source for all those activities, as you have the initiative and spirit and resource persons. You can focus it on Third World countries by giving more importance to their needs and considering their issues. You should also involve men in these works for better awareness. Since Re-Imagining was a seminar organized by women, men didn't have participation to express their views and opinions. God's grace and blessings are with you. Please do continue your ministry.

Once again, I thank you for all the help you have extended to me in my effort to attend the conference. My wife Mini, my son Gregory, and my daughter Hannah join with me to convey our love and regard to you all. Please pray for us, too. I take this opportunity to invite you and your family to our country and especially to my state, Kerala.

I hope by the Grace of God Almighty your family and yourself are keeping fine. Kindly convey my family's regards to everyone at home.

With prayers,

Yours in Christ,
Alias M. Chacko

Alias M. Chacko is from Kerala, India, and is business manager of a Christian journal. He is associated with Christian Workers Fellowship and is also an executive of an industrial organization. He is from the Orthodox church and involved in ecumenical activities.

Why I Painted a Naked Lady

NANCY CHINN

Why did we paint a naked woman on one corner of the four panels that we painted during the Re-Imagining Conference?

Some background to the painting would be helpful. I wanted to paint during the conference as a demonstration to the people drawing at their tables that the process of layering, discarding, and imagining that they were being asked to do was straightforward. I wanted to paint as encouragement, as a model of the process the people were invited into.

When it came to me that it was too easy to paint the four canvases by myself, I wanted to ask someone else whose work and ideology I did not know. I wanted to bump against someone whose ideas would be fresh to me in this context. I wanted to dialogue visually with her, just as the people at the tables were potentially doing.

Winn Rea and I had met two years before at a gathering in Ames, Iowa, and we had occasionally corresponded about our art and our mutual interest in the church. A letter arrived from her at the time that I was making this decision, and it seemed right to ask her: a woman who I knew made art and thought deeply about her faith, a woman much younger than I and from a different part of the country, a woman who seemed willing to expose the intimate process of painting to a crowd.

Neither one of us had any idea about what to paint. We were completely open to reflect what we heard, saw, and felt. We talked briefly about how to begin and how comfortable we each were about our own space being painted on. While I instructed the people at the tables to make gesture lines, Winn made similar lines across the four panels. That evening, we decided to each paint on two panels, and the shape of the woman began to come from one of the gesture lines that Winn had made. I recall it came something like the sequence shown in Figure 1.

This was never intended to be a goddess. It was intended, as organically developed, to reflect the generative power of femaleness. If it were possible to paint something more basic to my interior as a woman, I would have. This painting, for me, is about rejoicing in my experience as woman and about beginning from my experience as a woman to re-imagine a world where femaleness is valued. Rediscovering that I too, as a woman, have been made in God's image is a radical reshaping of what, for me, has been oppression.

Figure 1

This is not to say that I am advocating some sort of matriarchal power structure. Replacing patriarchy as a system with women in the same structure will not be the solution. I believe that what is needed is for women to value ourselves enough to see ourselves as partners to men—just as Winn and I saw ourselves as partners. Then we might cocreate a way of seeing the world that reflects our dialogue, our relationship, and our mutuality.

I am interested that some of the response has been to take offense at the nakedness of a woman. Nudity here seems to be taken literally as an interpreted goddess by the same folks who tell me that we should reflect God and God's creation of human beings as male and who ask me to understand that *He/Him* is an inclusive term. They seem to suggest that we can expand meaning of the male metaphors, but we cannot expand the meaning of an image of a woman. It has been good for me to see the link between the nude woman and male metaphors—that is, literalism of any metaphor limits and hurts all of us.

Upon further reflection, I wish I had painted her belly more completely. What is she pregnant with? The world? The Spirit? Her spirit? She seems clothed in the sun to me. Should she have feet on the crescent moon? A crown of stars? Is there a dragon (Rev. 12) that is trying to destroy what she is carrying?

We did not attempt to create her as ideal, as beautiful, as any particular race or age. That is why her features are coarse and undefined and she has no hair. Her hands are as important to me as her nudity. She does hold an apple, representing to me the choices we all have to risk to bring change. Personally, I celebrate and cultivate that freedom. During the conference, she shifted many times in her gestures and in her limbs. On her head appeared a sign introduced to us at the conference as a marking of God's presence within each of us. She has energy inside her and Winn's personal mark over her heart.

The painting was purchased by United Theological Seminary of the Twin Cities. It is valued as an archival work of the conference, and it is not complete.

I am pleased that an image has such power to help people wrestle with the proclaimed word. As a liturgical artist, I have dedicated my life to the work of bringing a visual language to the theological discourse. This has been an affirmation and an encouragement to keep working. There is much to do ahead, much to re-imagine, much to create. I am glad that we artists are a serious part of the conversation.

No one can do this discourse alone. I believe it must be done through dialogue, through many of us clearly stating our truths and listening well to each other. I am concerned that such dialogue is a lost value in the church. In our passion for and conviction to what we believe is truth, we have been disrespectful of the truth of the other. In this time following Re-Imagining, I have felt attacked, persecuted, censored, and misunderstood. Assumptions about details have replaced any attempt to hear my truth. How can we have a conversation if no one will listen?

Yet reformation is in the air. As artists, we play a significant role in re-imagining. Let us loose, and the church will never be able to stay content with its memories of what it once was. We will show you visions and encourage you to dream dreams, and each dream you make will demand that you change.

I believe Christ is always calling us to change our hearts. At no time do we completely understand what God would have us know. But wait: Jesus tells us more than that change is in the air. Jesus tells us the name; like Moses before the burning bush, we hear the name of the revolution. It is love:

> *your love of my passion as a human being,*
> *your love of my brokenness as an artist, of my imperfections, of my*
> *glimpses yet through a mirror darkly,*
> *my love for you who resist and my compassion for the cost of change,*
> *my love for you with your loyalties and set assumptions.*

It is in the name of that love that I offer you the truth as it is revealed to me. It is in the name of love that I will try to listen carefully and respectfully to what you are saying to me. It is my hope that others can offer the same for me. In the place between, I hope we will glimpse God.

Nancy Chinn is an artist who works with feminist images and creates banners and installations for festivals, conferences, and liturgical seasons. A frequent lecturer and instructor in the area of connecting art and worship, she has won numerous awards.

PART THREE

Lamenting

The community must pray. All come to it with brokenness, anger, resentment. We come having hurt and been hurt. We come craving justice; we come needing mercy. As the gathered community shares its laments, we know that behind each prayer is a story

of re-membering . . .

and re-imagining . . .

Try

CAROLYN STAHL BOHLER

Imagine two thousand people of Christian faith packing their bags, getting their families and work in order so they might leave for a long weekend to explore, in community, their faith.

Imagine two hundred circular tables in a giant room filled with huge note paper, crayons (to be donated to children after their use here), musical egg shakers, and flowers.

Imagine being at a table with nine people of diverse ages, backgrounds, and geographic locals—to talk, pray, reflect.

Imagine solidarity with churches as the theme.

Imagine singing, listening, hearing dialogue, entering into dialogue, praying, yearning, crying, and laughing.

Imagine each speaker being blessed by the mostly gray-haired, generous crowd, before the speaking.

Imagine logistics, caring for these people with local arrangements, in the midst of northern November cold.

Imagine leaving the gathering with notes, experiences, questions, learnings, longings, joys, dissatisfactions—and deeper faith.

Imagine several months later being treated as a witch—hunted down.

If Christians decide not to trust women to think, worship, pray, disagree, and dialogue;

If Christians decide to oust women, emotionally, spiritually, and economically;

How many other cheeks do they expect women to have?

Imagine a church

> *without questioning,*
> *without dialogue.*

Imagine the church

> *bowing to Jesus, who rose;*
> *searching for women, who are off searching for Jesus;*
> *content with the status quo, when Jesus turned that over.*

Try.

Re-imagining the church without women who re-imagine.

Carolyn Stahl Bohler, Ph.D., is a mother of two, a United Methodist clergywoman, and professor of pastoral theology and counseling at United Theological Seminary in Dayton, Ohio. She is the author of Prayer on Wings: A Search for Authentic Prayer, When You Need to Take a Stand, *and* Opening to God: Guided Imagery Meditations on Scripture.

One Fell Thud

CAROLYN BULLARD-ZERWECK

Back to reality—with one fell thud. After four days of affirmation and support from the gathering of over two thousand women (and a few good men) in Minneapolis for the Re-Imagining Conference, my reentry into the world of patriarchy and male dominance was going fairly smoothly until I read an article in my morning newspaper. Then I was painfully aware why I went to this conference and why it was so important. Facts from the United Nations' 1985 women's conference ending the United Nations Decade for Women say it well.

Women are one-half of the world's population, constitute one-third of the world's labor force, work two-thirds of the world's working hours, receive one-tenth of the world's income, and own one one-hundredth of the world's property. Domestic work represents an invisible contribution of $4 trillion by the women of the world. And because women have the primary responsibility for domestic work—which includes caring for and nurturing children—women have fewer opportunities to pursue an education, follow a career, or enter a political activity.

There's more. Women constitute 34 percent of the paid labor force worldwide. However, in no country have women reached wage parity with men. In the United States, a woman working full time earns an average of sixty-nine cents for every dollar earned by a man.

Worldwide, the illiteracy rate for women is 10 percent higher than for men, the lives of 125 million women are endangered by health-care discrimination, and 90 percent of all refugees are women and children.[1]

Here at home, in "the land of the free and the home of the brave," every fifteen seconds a woman is beaten by her husband or by a male partner, and every three to six minutes a woman is raped. What fuels this violence? Could it be the patriarchal systems of male dominance and abuse of power that have been justified in the name of a religious faith that believes that "if God is male, then the male is God," as Mary Daly suggests?[2]

The VISN Women's Television Project has reported, "Violence against women and children is as old as recorded history. The authority of men over women and adults over children has been approved and upheld for centuries by civil and religious authorities. . . . Every four seconds a woman is violently assaulted somewhere in the United States."[3]

A woman who has grown up knowing father as her mother's batterer and/or her own sexual molester finds little comfort and healing from the image of God the Father. The Reverend Marie Fortune, executive director of the Seattle-based Center for the Prevention of Sexual and Domestic Violence, notes that "one in every four members of a church or synagogue is a victim/survivor of sexual or domestic violence."[4] What does the faith community offer to these people? Unfortunately, the faith community is often the last place they turn for help.

The writer in my newspaper labeled those of us who attended (and enjoyed) the Re-Imagining Conference as pagans and feminists. A pagan I am not. The gathering was the most spiritual experience of my life, and I refuse to allow anyone else to define my religion for me. The charge of being a feminist is true, although the term is greatly misunderstood in my area of the country. A friend of mine defines a feminist as one who believes that God created female and male equally human. Pretty radical theology—right out of Genesis 1!

What we did in Minneapolis was to re-imagine God as the One who is big enough to include the entire range of human diversity. We re-imagined names for God that would be healing, nurturing, and empowering. We re-imagined a church where women as well as men could be affirmed and supported. We re-imagined a world where women could be safe and nurtured and free to be who they were created to be. We re-imagined community for all people, community in solidarity with those who struggle for justice, community that works for the rights of the world's poor and disenfranchised.

The writer claimed that feminism is destroying our society and our world. I challenge that. Male domination and oppression resulting in ever-increasing violence and chaos are the sins we must face and name and for which we must ask forgiveness. Men, as well as women, are wounded by the abuse of power and authority. As Letty Russell has said, echoing Martin Luther King Jr. from the Birmingham City Jail, "no one is free until all are free."[5]

Carolyn Bullard-Zerweck is an ordained minister in the Christian Church (Disciples of Christ) and has served as associate pastor and campus minister. Currently she is a program associate for child advocacy for the Greater Dallas Community of Churches in Dallas, Texas. She is married to a minister and is the mother of two daughters and a son.

Where Were the Latina Voices?

ADA MARÍA ISASI-DÍAZ

To my sisters who coordinated the conference,

I want to thank you so very much for all the work you did for the Re-Imagining Conference. Since I have had the privilege of organizing and staffing similar conferences, believe me I know the amount of work that went into gathering us. I salute your dedication and sisterly care. I also want to thank you for inviting me to be a presenter and to serve on the advisory committee for the conference. May we all reap abundant fruit from your commitment and dedication.

As the conference unfolded, I waited in vain for the voices of Latinas—for the voices of women from Latin America to dream the vision, to share the wisdom that is ours with the gathered sisters at the conference. I talked with a number of women during the conference, and we all kept wondering why we were passed over. Why was our reality and wisdom not lifted? Why were we not given an opportunity to share our struggle with those called to re-imagine the church? Of course, I realize that there were several of us who were presenters in the afternoon sessions. So I am referring to our absence at the plenary sessions.

I realize that it is impossible to include every single perspective in a conference, and I know from experience that no matter how hard the organizers try, someone is always left out. But here I am speaking about a group, Latinas in the United States, who at the end of this century will be the largest racial/ethnic group in this country; I am talking about Latin America, which is the exploited and oppressed area of the world closest to the United States. I am not even arguing that you should have given us an opportunity to make a presentation at the plenary, though it would have been wonderful. But our absence was almost total. Not even when the wisdom of sisters from different eras and cultures was read during one of the rituals was the wisdom of Latinas and women from Latin America included. The one short song in Spanish and the one line in Spanish in another song certainly felt like tokenism to me.

You also need to know that by asking me to be on the advisory committee and then not using me to try to figure out how Latinas could be present in the plenary sessions and in the rituals, well, in reality I feel tokenized. My community has the right to hold me accountable, to ask why I did not protest our exclusion. And I did signal to you that I was willing and able to take seriously my advisory duties when, though I was not asked, I sent in my comments about using Spanish in the conference.

You may think that I need to take responsibility for not taking the initiative. And I do, partially. But from the materials I received before the conference, there was no way I could know anything about our absence from the rituals, from the great variety of things that happened at center stage. Maybe I should have been more aggressive, but then it is hard to be so when I don't know any of you personally. Besides, echoing Chris Smith's statement before she preached, I am not the only one responsible for the inclusion of voices of the Latinas; we all are. We all have to take seriously the struggles of the poor and oppressed among us, and with African American women and American Indian women, Latinas are certainly the most marginalized in this society.

I heard during the conference that Elsa Tamez had been invited, and she could not come. But Elsa is not the only woman from Latin America of the stature of the women who did speak during the plenaries. Among all Latinas in the United States, many could have served as a plenary speaker; many of us could have participated in the rituals so our rich religious heritage would have been part of the wisdom of the women we celebrated during the conference.

I opened my presentation in the afternoon with a few words in Spanish. At the end of the presentation, many of the Latinas who were there came to thank me for what I had said and for saying a few words in Spanish. I noticed an older woman waiting on the side until the end. I finally turned to her and greeted her in Spanish. Shyly, she approached me and thanked me for my presentation. Then turning to go, she stopped and turned once again to me. Choking with tears, she said, "You made me feel so proud of being a Latina." Her words are the reason I write this letter. Latinas seldom find ourselves reflected in society; our values, rituals, and customs are so very often ignored. We need to commit ourselves to change this, for if we are not part of the solution, we certainly are part of the problem.

Thank you for reading through this letter. Again, I am most appreciative of all you have done for many of us women by giving of yourselves so abundantly in organizing the Re-Imagining Conference. I pray that what I point out to you in this letter becomes part of the wisdom we receive from Sophia, and that such wisdom will become an intrinsic part of who we are and all that we do.

Sincerely, *en la lucha*—in the struggle,

Ada María Isasi-Díaz

Ada María Isasi-Díaz is a mujerista *theologian and a professor of ethics and theology. She was born and raised in La Habana, Cuba. She is a* mujerista, *a Latina committed to the struggle for liberation of Hispanic women living in the United States.*

Reclaiming Visual Language

WINNIFRED C. S. REA

Some weeks after Re-Imagining, when fallout began to cloud the sky like dust from Mount Saint Helens, I was invited to create an illustration for the cover of *Church & Society,* a journal of the Presbyterian Church (U.S.A.). A May/June 1994 issue was being prepared to detail the content of the Re-Imagining Conference. Little did I know that my work as a visual artist would soon suffer the suffocating dust of editorial caution. My encounter has affirmed the power of visual language while causing me to struggle with what constitutes artistic integrity and how to respond when my language is threatened with censure.

Nancy Chinn invited me to collaborate with her at Re-Imagining on a four-panel painting to be created in response to conference plenary sessions. Our collaboration magnified many smaller collaborations between participants who used art materials on papered tabletops to dream a new way of seeing themselves and the church. Early in our collaboration, the image of a nude, seated female figure came to Nancy. As the painting evolved, Nancy and I both modeled her features, revealed her gestures, and felt her presence. Her strong, nude body spoke of new birth and nurturance of a reunited spirituality and sexuality. Over four days, the tables and our painting became tapestries of new vision.

But after the creative environment in Minneapolis, our reclaimed visual language was subjected to crueler forces, who twisted our images to their own ends. The *Presbyterian Layman* detailed the nude figure of Woman without our permission on the cover of their January/February 1994 issue. The headline touted "Return of the Goddess." Around the image of the nude woman, the *Presbyterian Layman* excerpted words from a litany spoken during the conference that celebrated women's sexuality as a gift from God. The recontextualized image tapped into repressed fears of women's sexuality and the holistic understanding of God which arises from reuniting our spirituality and sexuality. The image of Woman on the cover of the *Presbyterian Layman* became a lightning rod for conservative fury across the country.

Meanwhile, *Church & Society* was in the works. The special-issue editor asked me to create the cover illustration and smaller images for the article headers. I created a circle filled with smaller thumbnail images representing different aspects of the conference (**see fig. 2**). Among other images, I included a dancer to recall Carla De Sola's inspiring movement, a serpent wrapped

Figure 2
"Re-Imagining": First version of illustration created by Winnifred Rea for the
cover of *Church and Society,* May/June 1994.

around a stained glass window to remind us of the temptation of relying on old
forms, a drum to recall the native beat that unified our hearts, and international breads on a plate to remind us of breaking bread together. I also included the nude, seated figure who had become a symbol of Woman for Nancy
and me as we painted. She had come as an inspiration, almost like an angel. In
her international appearance, she represented all women without exclusion.

    In my cover illustration, with its variety of images reflecting the wide
scope of the Re-Imagining Conference, it was the thumbnail image of Woman
that was found objectionable. I was asked by the special-issue editor to make
her look more like a woman, to give her hair or some other "feminine"

features, and to change her posture to make her look less like a goddess or Buddha.

As a creative artist, I had followed inspiration in the painting of the woman during the conference. Now, as a commissioned artist, I struggled with how much my voice should be subjected to the editor's voice. Was there any way to remain true to the artistic vision and satisfy the editor's objections?

In a letter to the editor, I stated my concern that "the image is threatening mainly due to the *Layman*'s use and abuse of it. I can't help but think this is the ongoing story of Woman—scorned as temptress Eve, denied power as passive Virgin Mary, and now condemned as a god-supplanter." In the second draft of the cover, I dissociated the figure of Woman from the serpent image, I changed the apple in her hand to a dove, and I placed a globe in her belly to more fully indicate the spirit in which she was created; we are women pregnant with possibility (see fig. 3). I wanted to use the figure of Woman in a positive manner to counteract the abuse of the figure by the *Presbyterian Layman*. To leave the figure of Woman out was to make woman invisible again. To leave the figure of Woman out was to have visual language taken away.

The editors said they respected my decision, but they would not be able to publish the cover illustration if it included the nude figure of Woman. She had been the lightning rod for too much pain. The senior editor of *Church & Society* felt that presenting the image on the cover of a Presbyterian Church (U.S.A.) magazine would incite more controversy. The logo for Re-Imagining was used on the cover instead. Proposal drawings for the Re-Imagining logo appeared inside the magazine. The special-issue editor told me that she had anticipated editorial battles over verbal language in conference lecture transcripts, but she never suspected she would run into editorial problems with visual images for the magazine.

I was deeply hurt and left with many painful questions. Why was my visual language silenced? How could the actions of an antagonistic press rob me of an image that had been empowering for so many women? Why was I prohibited from reclaiming that image in a positive light? Why were the national leaders of my church trying to keep the peace? Why were they acquiescing to coercive tactics and silencing themselves through self-censorship? Why were they selling out the creative soul of the church to preserve its hollow shell?

The passionate questions above undergird more rational questions:

> *How do we reclaim vocabulary of spiritual and bodily wholeness when opposition groups persist in taking that language and distorting it to incite fear in their audience?*

Figure 3
"Re-Imagining": Second version of illustration created by Winnifred Rea for
the cover of *Church and Society,* May/June 1994.

How much do we censor ourselves in order to be heard?
How can the Protestant church reclaim visual language that it deemed
    too sensual and threatening during the Reformation?
In a church that clings to tradition, how can I as an artist move
    beyond illustrating *old forms to* embodying *new forms of faith?*

The power of reclaimed visual language has been confirmed by the
negative editorial actions of both the *Presbyterian Layman* and *Church & Society.*
Re-Imagining provided a glimpse of what creative vision might be. It was a

moment of breath moving freely, of the spirit moving freely over fertile waters. Outside of Re-Imagining, the air is much closer and clouded with the dust of fearful caution. Is there enough breath to reclaim what is good in our faith and breathe a new vision?

Winnifred C. S. Rea is an installation artist stirring the waters from Brooklyn, Iowa. She earned her master of fine art degree from the University of Iowa, where she served as an adjunct art instructor. She combines painting, sculpture, and multimedia in installations that address spiritual concerns. She has offered workshops in Wisconsin, Iowa, and Illinois in which participants explore issues of faith through art.

Song of Lament

M. SUE SEID-MARTIN

A glorious and wonderful event was finally unfolding at the stroke of 5:30 on that Thursday evening in November 1993. At the last moment, I had scurried into a black dress after a day of preparation and rehearsal that began at 6:30 in the morning. Almost twelve hours later, I was so tired I could barely talk. At the same time, it was exhilarating to see the room prepared and nearly two thousand people gathered in anticipation. There was high energy, and we were about to begin.

"The process is more important than the product," we had said all along. And what a process it was! So many people gave so much care to each moment: its sounds, its look, its people. Almost all of the ritual was handcrafted, not lifted from anybody's prepared ritual books but inspired and guided by those books and all the praying we had done for years. With that richness as backdrop and guide, we came together over two years' time to prepare material specifically for this event—this time and place—born out of women's experience, which we collectively knew in our bones, but for which no time and place for expression had yet been found.

As the event unfolded, there was much rejoicing. People seemed genuinely touched by the abundance in the baskets on the tables. The singing was full-bodied, the dancers were beautiful, the ritual breads were fresh and enjoyed by all, the complicated sound system was working, and the meal was splendid. We laughed when clearing the tables took so long that Nancy Chinn simply asked us to stuff all the debris under the tables. The clock was running, and we needed to get started.

That was when my song of lament began in earnest. I realized that the time schedule we had struggled over for so long had begun to unravel. All three of the presenters were fabulous, but all spoke longer than anticipated. The slow, easy movement of the podium that allowed Mary Farrell Bednarowski, Chung Hyun Kyung, and Bernice Johnson Reagon to be engaged with all corners of the gathered assembly was like a counterpoint to the speed with which the clock was running. Bernice was so profound in her message through word, music, and passion about "keeping on keeping on" that when she was finished, the participants' bodies and spirits signaled that the evening was over. And the clock certainly suggested that as well.

But what we ritual people knew—some 150 of us in all—was that the music and movement designed to go into those places where words cannot reach was only *now* supposed to begin. We had poured our hearts into an anticipated forty minutes of celebrating the many voices of women's experience in other languages, in music and dance, in lament over dreams unrealized and voices unheard in almost two thousand years of Christianity. But the decision was being made for us by the participants; they were leaving. We had no decision-making process for dealing with this crisis moment, and the ritual was simply aborted. We fast-forwarded to a closing song, and the evening was over.

The weeping, however, had only just begun. The ritual team cried with each other, asking how this could have happened. In some ways, we were undone by our own abundance in the whole of the evening. But we also felt abandoned; dropping one of the speakers was never considered an option, but the artistic work was allowed to die a horrible death. Others sympathetically suggested that we could perhaps salvage the aborted ritual for another time in the coming days. But the work that was so carefully planned and developed as a continuum made that impossible. In addition, some people who were contributing specifically to this Thursday evening ritual could not rearrange their schedules at the last minute.

The hour of anguish that followed everyone's departure was torture. The image that kept coming to me was that of so much of the work of women over centuries, simply poured into the ground and lost. We are in a new age and a new time, and yet it was happening again. A central message of our faith, which we call *paschal,* was lived again that Thursday night with the death of Holy Play. The conference continued and built toward a ritual resurrection on Sunday morning. So we continue to believe beyond believing that life can spring from death, even in conference plans and dreams gone unfulfilled.

M. Sue Seid-Martin is a retired liturgical musician living in Saint Paul, Minnesota. She has held teaching positions at the University of Saint Thomas School of Divinity in Saint Paul, Minnesota, and the University of Notre Dame in Notre Dame, Indiana. She served as ritual coordinator for the 1993 Re- Imagining Conference.

Welcome to Washington

PHIL LENOX

We like to plan ahead. Several years ago, we bought a house in the state of Washington, thinking we would like to retire to the Pacific Northwest. Early in 1994 while still in our planning-ahead mode, we decided to practice retirement by taking an extended vacation in this second house. Though it would be several months before we would sell our house in Minnesota and make the final move, my wife and I thought this would be a wonderful preview of the next stage in our lives. It would also be a chance to get to know some folks and to find a new Presbyterian church home to which we could transfer our membership after retiring.

We first tried a church about twenty miles from our house. Unlike our Minnesota church which resembled a gymnasium with a cement floor, this church had dark woodwork, carpeting, and a balcony that wrapped around the sanctuary. The choir sat in the balcony at the front of the church, looking down at the crowded pews. It seems it was not only Boy Scout Sunday, but many people had turned out to say goodbye to some navy friends who had received new orders, apparently a common occurrence in this military-base community.

The worship service started with various announcements, one of which began, "Have you seen the *Presbyterian Layman*[6] with the picture of the goddess Sophia on the front?" The minister went on to tell us that an ecumenical group of women had met in Minneapolis and had, among other forms of worship, actually prayed to this goddess who was the font of all human life. The group that published the *Layman* reported that this awakening conference was possibly heretical in nature since it proposed supplanting Jesus Christ with Sophia as our Lord and Master. A woman named Mary Ann Lundy, who held a high Presbyterian office, was a leader of this conference, and she had perhaps overstepped her powers. Some $400,000 of Presbyterian money had been spent on this three-day meeting.

A short time after the service started, those attending for the first time were asked to stand and identify themselves. Since we qualified, I gave my name and my wife's name, stated that we came from Minnesota, and said that, coincidentally, Mary Ann Lundy was a member of our congregation. This caused quite a stir.

After the excellent two-hour service concluded, my wife was approached by several women wanting to know our feelings about Mary Ann, the conference, and the *Layman* article. We had not read the article, but we both vouched for Mary Ann. Soon after, we met the minister, who took us to his office and gave us a copy of the article to read. We told him of our plans to move to the area and where our house was. He suggested that we might be more comfortable with a United Methodist church nearer to our home since they were concerned with problems such as the AIDS epidemic.

We didn't tell anyone that we are conservative Republicans.

Phil Lenox made the best decision of his life forty-five years ago when he married his current lover. He tries to value diversity and enjoy extremes, savor what time is left, enjoy the uniqueness of all people and animals, and give thanks for all of it.

Silenced Voices Speak

MELODY MARTIN AND PAMELA ARMSTRONG

After much avoidance and soul-searching, we make this attempt to capture in words part of our experience of the Re-Imagining Conference. We do not write this dialogue to point fingers at individuals, for we have already spoken with some of those who were involved. Rather, we write to tell a part of the Re-Imagining story, hoping it will prevent similar experiences in the future.

Melody: I am a woman with a disability. I have cerebral palsy, which affects my muscle coordination and speech. My speech is slow but can be understood if people take the time to listen. In addition, I have a hearing loss. I am also a theologian whose passion is kindled when engaged in dialogue about those basic questions we ask throughout our lives: Who is God? Who am I? Why am I here? Where does Christ fit into all this? My answers to these questions, like most of my life experiences, are shaped in part by the fact that I am a woman with a disability. My experiences around the Re-Imagining Conference were no exception.

My contact with Re-Imagining began when I called a member of the steering committee to ask what was being done to include women with disabilities at all levels of the conference. As a result of this question and some last-minute shuffling, I was invited to do a workshop, talk with organizers about accessibility issues, have a part in the Sunday morning ritual, and introduce one of the main speakers. It was within the latter events that I experienced the pain of oppression and the gifts of solidarity and empowerment. Here's what happened.

I arrived at the convention center on Thursday afternoon for the rehearsal of the Sunday morning ritual. We had a short time to run through it before the conference got under way. After a few starts and stops, we were told that this would have to be a run-through without further stops because of the constraints of time. I found myself standing on a stage in one corner of the room. Similarly, the other three voices were in their respective corners of the room. I could not see or hear the other three speakers well. A piano was in front of me, and directly behind me a choir was singing. I was told that I would have to speak directly into the microphone or else my voice would not be heard; I would have to do this while holding and reading the script. Other people were starting to come into the room already. (This was certainly different from the first rehearsal, where the four readers sat around the table in a small conference room, going through the script.)

I realized quickly that, due to the logistics of the ritual, it would be difficult for me to perform in a way that could be understood and heard. This realization became public when it was my turn to speak. The words were slow to come out; I could not hold my head up to the microphone and read the script; and I could not keep my mouth close enough to the microphone for the words I spoke to be heard. The tension around me and within me was thick.

After I read a few more lines, the person who offered me the role was standing in front of me, beckoning me to follow her. She told me that the rehearsal would go along without the two of us and that we needed to talk. She sensed that I was frustrated and close to tears, and she acknowledged those feelings. She asked me what could be done. Given the logistics, time constraints, and my feelings, I just shrugged my shoulders. By this time we were both crying. She asked me who we could get to do the part; I told her I would ask my business partner, Pam. She told me where I could use a phone, and she went back to the rehearsal.

I called Pam, told her what had happened, and asked her, through my tears, if she would do the part. She said, "No!" She said the only way she could agree to do the part would be if I were allowed to do it with her. I was surprised and deeply moved. I gave Pam's proposal to the woman, and she agreed—on the condition that we meet for another rehearsal to see if it would work with two voices.

Pam: Re-Imagining began for me with Mel's pain-filled phone call on Thursday afternoon, explaining the problems with the Sunday morning ritual. It was unthinkable to do the worship experience without her, my sister/friend who had been my intimate partner in the struggle to name, grieve, and transform the oppression that threatens the community of people with disabilities. Reading it together seemed an appropriate embodiment of the interdependency on which our relationship is based.

Melody: During the course of the next two days, I observed the ritual around the introduction and blessing of a main speaker. The person making the introduction had to stand and hold the microphone for the singer and herself while holding any notes she had about the speaker. Given what had happened at the rehearsal, I knew I needed some things to be different.

I brought my concerns to Chris Smith, a friend, colleague, and the speaker I was to introduce. I told her that it would be better if we could be sitting while I introduced her. I also said it would be easier if someone else held the microphone for both the singer and myself. Chris responded that we would do both. We asked the coordinator who had spoken with me on Thursday, and she agreed. Finally, I told Chris that there was a possibility we would get on stage and I would have difficulty getting the words out. Chris said that would be fine—we would just be in silent solidarity with one another. Chris's presence and responses empowered me to state my accessibility needs and to be myself on stage without apology.

Pam: The Re-Imagining experience was paradoxical for me. During the conference, I was moved by the stories of liberation and solidarity that were unfolding. We embraced so many sister communities and celebrated their value, realizing that our re-imagining depended on their presence in our midst. With the power of our solidarity, we blessed their journey.

Melody: Later, I was told that we must stand during the blessing because the woman performing it believed it was inappropriate to do a blessing sitting down. My reaction to this was mixed. Physically it was not a problem for me to stand during the blessing; my request to be seated was only for the introduction. However, the implications of her statement touched my core. What was this woman saying? Was she saying that it was inappropriate for my sisters who use wheelchairs to give blessings and to receive blessings? The woman's statement brought to the surface the oppression of people with disabilities and the need for re-imagining perceptions of us within our religious communities and our theologies.

Sunday morning came.

Pam: I woke up on Sunday morning feeling anxious. I was not worried about the service—we would do fine. It was the disturbing realization that no one knew our story. We had not been named, nor had we named ourselves. Most participants would have little choice but to receive us, especially Mel, with the stereotypical emotions they had been taught to have for people with disabilities: sympathetic tolerance and patronizing pride. This is not an insult to those participating in the conference. Five years ago, I believed that those emotions were good, not realizing how oppressive they are to me and my community. The disability community is finally gaining the strength to name the oppression and to educate our society, and our society is just beginning to recognize the need to be educated. Given all of this, I knew that I had to say something.

As I was getting dressed, the words I needed to say came to me. Although they have become more polished with time, the words went something like this:

In seminary, when I was unable to put what I knew in my heart into academic language, Melody gave me words, gave me voice, refusing to do theology without me. When the technical logistics of this morning's worship service made it impossible for Melody to be understood, it was my turn to give her words, to give her voice, refusing to do it without her. When you leave here to re-imagine theology in our world, pay attention to our words, seek out our voices. Refuse to do theology without us.

I felt that these few sentences may have introduced Mel as the theologian that she is. They may have introduced the idea that women with disabilities have a distinctive story to add to the creative energy of re-imagining. They may have offered a new emotional paradigm of respect and mutuality, replacing the negative energy of sympathetic tolerance and patronizing pride. They may have.

They were never said. They should have been said at the very beginning of the day, so that people would know why the two of us were reading the part of one voice. I approached a committee member and explained what I wanted to say and why. I was told that too many changes to the program had been made already and that nothing could be added, for fear of running out of time. I was stunned, understanding of her dilemma, and compliant.

A few minutes later, the main speaker asked this same woman if she could begin her talk with an additional page-long statement. She was told that it wouldn't be a problem. The statement was about the persons who had not been represented enough in the conference, and she listed women with disabilities among them.

Melody: Once again, someone else was speaking for women with disabilities rather than women with disabilities speaking for themselves.

Pam: I angrily said to another reader that I was going to make my statement anyway, but I didn't. I held back—too scared and too conditioned to cooperate. Thus, I utterly failed my community. I do not excuse the actions of the organizer. If she had said yes, I would not have hesitated to speak. She does not excuse herself. She later told me that when she examined her denial of my request, it was the ableism in her that made it easy to tell me no. Yet, ultimately, it was my story to tell, and no one could have stopped me if I had chosen to speak.

The moment to speak passed; the ritual began. We read with blended voices. Later, Melody introduced the speaker with the intensity and flair she puts into most of her work. There were spontaneous announcements from other groups. The ritual ended with a snake dance, which excluded anyone who could not navigate the narrow aisles. When it was over, I looked at my watch. We had twenty-five minutes to spare. That was when the rage and grief that I had been suppressing began to rise to the surface. The conference was over. Our chance to share our story, to enter the discussion of re-imagining, and to celebrate our existence with the affirmation of our global community was gone.

I have forgiven my silence. And now I truly understand repentance, because I will not be silenced again. Yet forgiveness does not erase the painful consequences of my silence. I regret the wasted opportunity to introduce to the re-imagining community new perspectives about people with disabilities. I regret the lost opportunity to name ourselves and have that naming be validated and celebrated in community. I regret that I denied myself and my community the chance of experiencing solidarity rather than isolation.

Most of all, I regret the pain that Melody, my sister/friend, experienced because I was silent. She was the one who was the focus of that oppressive negative energy. She was the one who received the pats on her shoulder from strangers who, in high unnatural voices, told her how proud they were of her. She was the one seen as the token disabled person. She was the one unnamed. She was the one described in a newspaper article as "the woman with cerebral palsy who hesitantly introduced the speaker."[7] She is the one who forgave me into forgiving myself. She is my mentor, teaching me never to be silent again.

Melody and Pam, together: When doing the work of re-imagining, refuse to do it without the voices of people with disabilities as part of the dialogue. Empower all to live the question, "Is it possible?" into the proclamation "It is possible!"

Melody Martin is a radical theologian/activist, currently disguised as a mild-mannered accountant. With Pam Armstrong, she is in a business partnership/ministry called Made in the Image, located in Minneapolis, Minnesota. They provide disability and/or theological consultation.

Pamela Armstrong is a mild-mannered church secretary/minister's wife who is working hard to redefine both of these roles. With Melody Martin, she is in a business partnership/ministry called Made in the Image, which provides disability and/or theological consultation. She lives and works in Minneapolis, Minnesota.

Down at the OK Corral

VIRGINIA WEST DAVIDSON

(Fade In. Outdoors. Rugged. Church against skyline in background. Camera closes in. Pans up. Boots. Blue jeans. Bibles in holsters. Three men leaning on a fence. Action.)

Hey, fellas! Guess what? We left the gate at the corral unlocked and the gals got out—went to Minneapolis and come back with some reel crazy idees. Don't that beat all? Now what're we gonna do with 'em?

Fer gosh sakes, who's this Sofie anyway? Prayin' to some new goddess we ain't ever heerd of, these wimmin wuz. Nobody tole us 'bout a Sofie in seminary—or in church. What're these gals up to, anyhow? Prayin' to some goddess instead'a Jeezus. That's pagan stuff, shore 'nuff.

Geez, I wish some of us hadda bin there with 'em. Now we only got tapes to figger out what happened. Fer the life o' me, I cain't understan' how come they didn't know that was no meetin' to go to—after all we've larned 'em these years. Shucks, I always read the slick promos reel careful 'fore I sign up fer any sech thing. I ain't gonna be corrupted intenshionally. No sirree! Not me! An' they won't even criteek what they heerd, dang it. Cain't even get 'em to say what they larned.

What's worse, they went ahead and spent money we give 'em. That's the last time we oughta give 'em anything to spend, 'cept mebbe a little bit for the heatin' bill at church in the winter—cain't trust 'em any further than you can twirl 'em. They 'jes don' know how to handle money, least ways. Remember Thelma and Louise? Ha!

Strikes me they'se sorta like them Currinthian wimmin Paul wrote about—took their head scarves off and let their hair fall right down in church. That was shameful in those days. An' even spoke up in reel loud voices while the men wuz worshippin'. Uppity wimmin, too, they musta been. No wonder Paul had t'write what he did—to keep 'em in line.

Mebbe the answer is no more money, no more plane tickets, no more wimmin preachers or teachers even, no more high-falutin' larnin' in seminary for these gals, too. Jes' get 'em back in the OK Corral, that's what I say. We'll keep 'em busy there, y'all can be darn shore. Matter of fact, we oughta thank the Layboys fer alertin' us t'what happened. Otherwise, we might notta knowed, least not for a long time. Now the cat's outta the bag an' they're gonna have t'pay for what they went and did—the gals an' the few good men they say wuz there too. Say, ain't that what they call the marines: a few good men? Hey, fellas, do you know who any of them men wuz? Mebbe we oughta find out summa their names too. We gotta do sumthin' reel soon 'fore they blow the whole dang church outta the water!

(Camera closes on faces. Angry. Camera pans down. Boots. Fade out.)

Virginia West Davidson is a lifelong Presbyterian, with children and grandchildren, who is currently co-moderator of advocacy for the More Light Churches Network, a movement working for full inclusion of lesbigay people within the Presbyterian Church (U.S.A.). She is a member of the Downtown United Presbyterian Church in Rochester, New York, and an ordained Presbyterian elder. In the 1970s, she served as vice-moderator of the General Assembly of the United Presbyterian Church in the U.S.A. (UPCUSA), chair of the UPCUSA Task Force to Study Homosexuality, and then enrolled as a student at Colgate Rochester Divinity School. She was awarded a master of arts degree in church history and theology three weeks before her fiftieth class reunion at Wellesley College.

The Conference I Did(n't) Attend

HEATHER MURRAY ELKINS

From the moment I heard Re-Imagining Steering Committee member Sue Seid-Martin lay out the rhythms of this women's gathering in the feminist liturgy group of the North American Academy of Liturgy, I intended to be present. I ordered tickets for plane, hotel, conference, and even concert. I pinned to my clipboard marked *Urgent!* the precious postcard admitting me to all events, and I began "Feasting in an Age of Fasts," the first chapter of my book *Worshiping Women.*

Shortly before the conference, the first of the firestorms over Sophia blew in. Susan Cady, one of the authors of *Wisdom's Feast,* had been the Nelle Morton lecturer and preacher at Drew Theological School in the spring. As professor of worship and chair of the chapel committee, I arranged the printed liturgy. I presided with Reverend Cady at the table. The service was composed of scripture, the historic words of institution, and prayers from *The United Methodist Hymnal* and *The United Methodist Book of Worship.* It met our tradition's sacramental standards, yet a colleague who left the chapel after the sermon wrote an essay denouncing Reverend Cady's sermon and the service as heretical.

There was little reaction from the outside community when Dr. Thomas Oden's essay "Encountering the Goddess at Church" appeared in *Christianity Today* in August 1993. That changed radically when the essay was mailed anonymously, without the author's permission, to the offices of our general boards, agencies, and bishops in several jurisdictions. Calls to my office began—the callers assuming that I was either the unnamed "highly visible feminist leader," with "her uncommon fixation of the worship of the goddess Sophia," or responsible for inviting a preacher who bragged about driving away members. I explained over and over that the following sentence was simply not true: "It was a 'victory' story in which a pious United Methodist lay leader and other members were driven out of her church and forced to join another after they challenged her authority to offer the Lord's Supper in the name of the goddess Sophia."[8]

The factual errors were triple: the story was not about Susan Cady or her congregation; communion was not mentioned at all, let alone in the name of a goddess; no one was driven out, unless the affirmation of United Methodist diversity from a pulpit constitutes excommunication. Reverend Cady's sermon and her lecture the evening before were examples of Christology interpreted through the scriptural tradition of wisdom/sophia. She stated in the lecture that she did not use the term *sophia* as goddess. The sermon and sacrament had been offered according to our tradition of word and table in honor of Christ. Dr. Oden had not attended the lecture and had departed prior to communion. Each caller to my office, however, had read his account that a heretical communion service to a goddess had been offered in our chapel.

The calls ranged from cautious warnings to threats of charges. A *Newscope* brief, a weekly news digest from the United Methodist publishing house, headlined the essay on 22 October 1993. The calls escalated, and I began to be questioned about the service as I traveled and made presentations in church gatherings. I provided to several agencies and bishops a written account of the service and the service itself. A supporting letter from the dean was mailed to the United Methodist bishops, yet the controversy, which eventually led to a jurisdictional joint review committee, continued to build. The liturgical scholars and bishops who had seen the text of the service found it orthodox, but there was no platform for sharing that news.

The Re-Imagining Conference was now four days away. My editor alerted me that Dr. Oden's essay was part of a book that would be published in the fall. He suggested including my account of the service at Drew as a footnote in my book. If I could finish the chapter on communion and mail it by Monday, my text would be published first. I stared at my tickets, then at my chapter, "Feasting in an Age of Fasts." I was in the middle of an explanation of the ancient eucharistic text of Hippolytus. Surely, I thought, the ecumenical Christian world will be strengthened when this early church's cup of milk and honey is returned to "the children of God for the healing of the bitterness of the human heart with the sweetness of His word."[9]

A conference of worshiping women or a footnote to defend worshiping women? I sent my tickets to a Presbyterian friend who was taking a group of women to Minneapolis. I sat at the computer screen for the next three days wondering if I would ever recover what I was missing.

As they returned, electricity poured out of those in our community who attended. "This was *the* women's event of a lifetime," said my colleague David Graybeal. His affirmation made me feel like the foolish virgin who ran out of oil for her lamp. My chapter was in the mail, but I had missed the real presence of the Spirit. He then delivered the paradoxical news: I *did* attend Re-Imagining. The organizers were so overwhelmed by the crowds that they insisted no changes could be made in the nametags. I had registered, so I was there. At least my name was there—worn by a Presbyterian sister I've never met.

Not only was I there in name, apparently I was also there in spirit. The woman who wore the nametag was elegant and reserved in speech, careful in gesture. As the energy at her table began to build and the imaginative force of the gathering grew, her style began to loosen. The change was so obvious that tablemates began to comment. "Oh," she would say, waving off their questions, "this isn't me; this is Heather." Presence. Real presence through the body and heart of an unmet kindred spirit.

The gift of the Spirit's whimsical presence sustained me as the controversy over worshiping women at Drew and Minneapolis magnified. It was public, intense, yet curiously lonely. I alternated between strength and shame as I struggled and seemingly failed to protect the hospitality and integrity of the Christ table placed in my institution's keeping. Other faculty members added their assistance, but the flawed essay took on the destructive force of a whirlwind. A grievance was filed against Bishop Susan Morrison and was fueled by the controversy over Drew's communion service. All charges would be dismissed unanimously by the jurisdictional joint review committee, but that relief was ten long months in the future.

Unexpectedly, I received an invitation to join a small group of women in New York for strategic response to the criticism of Re-Imagining. I was heartened yet puzzled, having not attended the conference. I called the number given, and someone answered. I promised to be there, but why was I invited? Did they know that I hadn't actually attended the conference?

"Oh, yes," she answered, "but you seem to be in as much hot water as the women who did. We want you to come." It was a time of hope. It was a time of threat. It was definitely a matter of wisdom. I headed for the Big Apple, where I joined eight other women in defense of a conference I did(n't) attend.

Heather Murray Elkins is associate professor of worship and liturgical studies at Drew University, Madison, New Jersey, and an ordained United Methodist in the West Virginia Annual Conference. Her recent publications include Worshiping Women: Re-forming God's People for Praise *and* The Storyteller's Companion to the Bible: The Prophets.

A Different Dance

KATHIE BOMSTA

13 November 1993

Dear Committee:

Thank you for your invitation to the thank-you party. However, I will not be there. As I wrote to Pat Schuckert and explained my feelings to her, I will try to explain to you.

I did not really know what the conference was about. When I first heard of the conference, what caught my eye was the name Carla De Sola. Then Pat called and asked if I would like to dance with the dancers. I was honored and said yes. I have always enjoyed dancing with Pat. She is gifted with a wonderful ministry and is a powerful and graceful dancer.

But that has nothing to do with this. I loved the procession dance and the dance with the bread. But when the speakers began, and I really began to listen and think, something in me was really stirring.

The more I listened, the more I realized I was in the wrong place. Although some good was said, most of it was against my beliefs. I wanted to voice some of my opinions in the talking circle, but our talking circle never happened. At first, I thought that maybe on Sunday I would be able to say what was in my heart. But by then I knew that I would not return.

I scanned the booklet we were given when we received our official nametags, but I didn't really look at it. On Sunday afternoon, I opened it and began to read it. Then I was sure that I was at the wrong place—for me. I love the Catholic church, the entire church, and all that it stands for: the pope, the sacraments, everything. I may not agree 100 percent with everything, but I would not change anything. I couldn't agree with or accept anything in that book. I believe it is wrong to pray to our Maker, Sophia. Our Maker is God, and our Mother is Mary, Jesus' mother.

I just felt I needed to explain, and I thank you again for the invitation.

Kathi Bomsta

Kathie Bomsta is a liturgical dance minister at the Catholic Church of Saint Paul in Ham Lake, Minnesota.

Departure under Fire

MARY ANN W. LUNDY

On 19 May 1994, the following statement was issued from the executive offices of the Presbyterian Church (U.S.A.): "James D. Brown, Executive Director and Mary Ann Lundy, Associate Director, of the General Assembly Council, today announced that Ms. Lundy will leave her position as of July 1, 1994. Circumstances have made her goal of effective service to the church unattainable."

Behind that brief statement lay seven months of turmoil and strife within the 2.9 million-member denomination. Strong feelings were reflected in the rapid, vociferous responses to the announcement, ranging from those who rejoiced that the denomination had rid itself of a "heretical" leader to those who were appalled and outraged that a political attack by the right wing had succeeded by outrageous tactics in removing a feminist church leader: me.

Most observers closely linked my departure with my role in the Re-Imagining Conference. The conference has been described as an earth-shaking (some have said a "gender-quaking") event for the emergence of feminist theology as a vital force within the American church, if not the world. For those of us responsible for it, Re-Imagining surpassed our original dreams and hopes in its process, its attention to detail, and the leadership of the theologians in its inspiring plenary sessions.

During the conference, many of us were uneasy about the presence of a large number of right-wing reporters from journals historically critical of mainline denominational staff. One reporter had been assigned to me for the previous four years, taking down every word at meetings and speeches. This was nothing new for me. But as these reporters hovered over tables with their cameras flashing, some women expressed their fear that "this may not be a safe place for Christian feminists." Little did we know how correct we were and how betrayed we all would feel by the accusations of heresy, goddess worship, and paganism.

Soon after the conference, hundreds of Presbyterians received news alerts with these accusations along with calls for the withholding of funds for denominational programs and for the resignation of all staff present— particularly me. Angry letters poured in from churches demanding my resignation, an apology, or an explanation. Letters of support came in more slowly as more liberal Presbyterians were not aware of the controversy perpetrated by the conservative factions. The executive director began to press for my resignation, even though there were, I felt, no compelling reasons.

The General Assembly Council, the church's elected executive body, met in February 1994 and devoted more than half the agenda of the four-day meeting to investigating my involvement in the conference. In a two-hour inquiry, a fact-finding group questioned me about such things as the procedures that had been used, my role in the planning, my judgment in staying in the process, and my knowledge of the potentially controversial aspects of the conference. My contention that the terrible aftermath was being created by the right-wing reporting of the conference, and not the conference itself, fell on deaf ears. Underlying the debate about the conference were years of frustration among conservatives with the denomination's leadership, which did not necessarily have anything to do with me. However, I had become an easy target, fed by the fears of feminist and "radical" thinking created by the religious right.

I began to realize that the General Assembly Council felt it had to do something to appease the right wing. In a personnel report distributed to everyone present—including the press (clearly against the denomination's personnel policies, which call for confidentiality in an executive session of the council)—the only charges were vague statements about a lack of judgment in foreseeing problems. I was never permitted to speak to a plenary session of the body. In a final step to do something about me, a motion was made to do a special evaluation of my work. It failed by a vote of thirty-two to thirty-one. I was seemingly cleared, but the executive director was given the power to evaluate my work in an ongoing process to determine my ability to be effective in my position.

By now it was clear that the strategy of the church leadership was to separate itself from me. The executive director failed to defend me in public statements while privately supporting my work. I believe he was clearly distressed and unsure of what to do in the face of terrible pressures from the conservative members of the General Assembly Council as well as the far right.

The following months were difficult ones for everyone, but especially for me, as the right wing, smelling blood, intensified its campaign against me. My leadership of the Women's Unit and its programs, actions, and feminist theological base came under scrutiny, and staff members were maligned by innuendo and nuance. Personal attacks raising questions about my personal life, my sexual orientation, and my family appeared on PresbyNet, and phone calls from males—particularly from two geographical areas—became rude, threatening, and violent so that I no longer answered my phone directly. "Do you know what I would do with you, Little Girl?" "Resignation wouldn't be good enough for you; I'd lock you in the basement." Pressure mounted for my resignation, but I would not resign. I believed that I had done nothing wrong and that my leaving would not only fail to satisfy the critics, but would appear to give in to the accusations and pave the way for attacks on other staff.

At the same time, I received strong support from a large number of colleagues at the denominational headquarters and in regional offices. The sixteen male synod executives called a special meeting with the executive director to assert their strong support for me and request that he make a public statement of support. He issued a statement the last week of April, stating his confidence in my leadership and my competency and citing the strong support of my colleagues across the church. I breathed a sigh of relief. But it was to be short lived.

Only three weeks later, on 19 May, the executive director called a meeting with me to discuss developments in the crisis—especially in light of the impending General Assembly, the denomination's annual gathering, held in June. Immediately after this meeting, the statement announcing my departure was issued. Church personnel policies require confidentiality about the details of staff departures.

Talk of schism began to be whispered as overtures about Re-Imagining poured in for General Assembly consideration. Nearly fifty of them criticized the conference and called for negative actions against the denomination and punishment of Presbyterian participants in the conference. The committee named to investigate the conference brought a report that was conciliatory: it supported participation in ecumenical gatherings, asserted that the conference may have gone beyond the boundaries of the Reformed tradition, acknowledged the denomination's failings on behalf of women while pledging support for women's theological quests, affirmed theology as central to the life and witness of the church, and recommended study of the implications raised by the conference. It called for an end to the polarization and harmful criticism so that healing could occur and trust could be rebuilt.

After the nearly unanimous adoption of the committee's report, with tears, spontaneous singing, praying, and thanksgiving, five commissioners rose to microphones to ask the assembly to express its appreciation for my eight years of work as a staff person of the General Assembly and to ask for prayers for me as I left my work in the Presbyterian church. One at a time, they were declared out of order. Silence was again the order of the day for those who dare to re-imagine faith.

Mary Ann W. Lundy, although no longer an employee, is still a member of the Presbyterian Church (U.S.A.).

No One

JO ANN LUCAS

I am deserted . . . cut off . . . isolated . . . as one with plague.
Called witch, whore, lesbian, destroyer, perverse, evil
   And called that, not to my face, but to all the folks I go with to worship
   And called that through the mail, in newspaper form
Has great power that I know not how to combat.

Some call it a point of view, some call it slander, I call it a lie.
Who has asked? No one.

Jo Ann Lucas is a married grandmother businessperson.

Under Siege

JUDITH A. STRAUSZ-CLEMENT

Little did I realize the implications when I accepted the invitation. The Twin Cities Area presbytery executive asked me to be the representative of the presbytery at a mid-1988 gathering of the ecumenical community of Minneapolis and Saint Paul. The conversation was to center on the Ecumenical Decade: Churches in Solidarity with Women and how we might promote it. This conversation would eventually result in the Re-Imagining Conference, and the subsequent dialogue would shake up my denomination.

Having been a part of the planning of Re-Imagining from its inception, it was hard to leave the Twin Cities six months prior to the conference and move to Pittsburgh, but I looked forward to new beginnings following my marriage to John.

John and I returned to Minneapolis for Re-Imagining. I can remember standing in the lobby of the auditorium before the opening worship service, feeling overwhelmed by the number of people, mostly women, who were eager for a conference that would examine the church and its relationship to women. I felt the excitement of something that was about to take place that would probably change us all forever. I did not realize then how true that would be.

About mid-December we were alerted to a forthcoming article in the *Presbyterian Layman,* a newspaper published by Presbyterians, though not officially associated with the Presbyterian Church (U.S.A.). The paper planned to report that Re-Imagining involved goddess worship and was pagan and heretical.

After the report appeared, daily attacks came from various sources about that "awful" conference in Minneapolis. Many individuals knew I was from Minneapolis. Should I tell them that I had attended the conference, that I had been part of the steering committee that planned it? As the firestorm enveloped the denomination, my fear began. I did not speak about Re-Imagining to others, yet it was seemingly in everyone's conversation. I felt I was cowering in a corner. I struggled about making my involvement known. I was terrified. How would I survive in this area of the country where the reaction was so strong?

I was being hired to serve as a full-time interim pastor in a rural, small-town church north of Pittsburgh. I had to join the presbytery and be questioned at its monthly meeting about my statement of faith and my prior

ministry. I was fearful they would ask me about having lived in Minnesota and
about "that conference." My anxiety increased when at the presbytery meeting, just before I was introduced to the gathering, the outgoing president of
Presbyterian Women gave a report and closed with "like it or not, what the
Layman is saying about Re-Imagining in Minneapolis is true." My heart sank,
and I was filled with dread and despair. What would happen to my career and
my whole being as one who is called to proclaim the love of God as a minister
of the Word and Sacrament in the Presbyterian Church (U.S.A.)? But somehow, no one in the Presbytery meeting chose to question me about Re-
Imagining, and I was received as a member.

The attacks on the conference intensified, and the conversation at home
between John and me constantly centered on Re-Imagining and who was
saying and writing what. Both of us felt under siege. He was being attacked
publicly for having attended the conference, but he kept saying that because
of all the publicity being generated, Re-Imagining was now a well-known
history-making event, a watershed, and Christianity would never be the same.

One midwinter Saturday evening, John and I attended a small dinner
party to which the Reverend John Buchanan was also invited. Eventually "that
conference" became the topic of conversation. I acknowledged my attendance
and my involvement with it. I told what a tremendous experience and safe
place it had been for me and for most who attended.

Still, I had not yet spoken publicly about my attendance or involvement.
At another presbytery meeting (where the harangue against Re-Imagining
went on for over an hour and ended with a resolution that called for an
investigation of the conference), several clergywomen spoke against the conference, even though they had not attended. I sat in silence during the entire
proceeding and came home sobbing. I was afraid for my own personhood and
my career. I felt attacked for who I was—not because of what I'd done, but
because I was female. I was dying inside. Several times I was asked to do
speaking engagements, but I declined for fear of being found out.

Finally, I made the decision to speak out about what I had experienced at
Re-Imagining—that extraordinary safe space and life-giving conference. I had
preached about justice issues during my entire ministry, and I could no longer
be silent. I made plans to tell the session (the governing body) of the church
where I was serving. I made up a packet of information about the conference,
both pro and con, and gave it to session members with a statement of my
involvement. I was afraid that they would ask me to leave. But they did not
ask for my resignation, and for that particular congregation it has been a non-
issue, at least publicly.

I also made plans to tell the clergywomen of my presbytery about my involvement at a luncheon in early May. Their reaction was mostly disbelief. Statements ranged from "Oh goody, now we'll find out what really happened," to "Did Christian women really plan that conference?" There was some curiosity but little dialogue. At a later gathering of clergy from my presbytery, only one woman came to hear about it; the other twenty or so members of the clergy were men. The result has been a shunning of me by the women of my presbytery. I believe they fear that being connected to me might label them and endanger their careers.

At the denomination's General Assembly in June, the review committee, chaired by the Reverend John Buchanan (whom John and I had met at dinner six months earlier), convened to respond to the controversy surrounding Re-Imagining. The compromise document from the review committee was adopted with no amendments by all but four of the six hundred voting delegates. It stated that "theology matters" and affirmed women doing theology. At the close of the assembly, the Reverend John Buchanan gave me a hug and recalled the dinner back in January where it all began for him. With new appreciation and a sense of God's involvement in all of this, I realized the serendipity of that January dinner party.

During General Assembly, I earnestly prayed that I could let go of the emotional attachment I had to the conference. Re-Imagining had begun a life of its own and was reshaping the church. We in the Twin Cities birthed this conference, and it was a welcome, refreshing, visionary, and safe place for many. Yet the resulting controversy had cut up, trampled, and battered Re-Imagining so much that it was often seen as a completely different event from what it was. I prayed that the church would begin to dialogue with the issues brought forth by Re-Imagining.

At a meeting of my presbytery following the General Assembly, a man who served as one of the commissioners made a report about Re-Imagining. He announced that Mary Ann Lundy, Associate Director for Churchwide Planning, had been "forced to resign" and then said, "We have not seen the last of Mary Ann Lundy; she is out to destroy the church." The Reverend Kenneth Hall rose to speak. With a quavering voice, red face, and clenched jaw, this well-respected former moderator of our denomination said that even though he disagreed theologically with Mary Ann Lundy, he valued her commitment and dedication to her church. He further commented that the personal attack was absolutely uncalled-for and inappropriate for our denomination. Incredible relief flooded my senses. Maybe, in fact, we could hope to disagree in love about theology and engage in dialogue about the issues that came out of Re-Imagining.

I continue to be elated about the Re-Imagining Conference and the ensuing dialogue that is beginning in our church. This conference was a history-making event, and I am proud to have taken part in making it all happen.

Judith Strausz-Clement, a Presbyterian pastor, graduated from United Theological Seminary of the Twin Cities. She was part of the original steering committee to plan the Re-Imagining Conference. She is a codeveloper of the Urban Waters Parish of Minneapolis and is now living and serving a church full-time in Pennsylvania.

Heresy

JEANETTE STOKES

I have been rushing around inside my feminist theological brain for the last few months, trying to keep up with the onslaught against women disguised as critique of the Re-Imagining Conference. It is open season on feminist theology and on women. In a widely circulated article about Re-Imagining, Elizabeth Dodson Gray names the issues as power and naming.[10] The men can't stand it that a whole bunch of women got together to talk about the Holy and did not ask for their response. Move over, buddy. We are here now, and even though you treat us badly, we are going to keep saying what we have to say.

And what is it that we have to say? That Christianity to date has been self-serving for men. That males created God in their own image. That Mary was not a virgin. That there were not twelve disciples, and they were not all men. That Mary Magdalene was not a prostitute but a leader in the early church who lost power and then was marginalized.

The Re-Imagining Conference, and feminists along with it, are accused of heresy, blasphemy, and paganism. Heresy is defined as opinion contrary to accepted religious opinions. If that is so, then what we are saying is heresy. So was the Protestant Reformation. Blasphemy is taking on the characteristics of God for yourself. No, feminist theology is not blasphemy. Blasphemy is what we have been living with for centuries: males taking on the characteristics of God for themselves. What we are trying to do now is to correct blasphemy. As for paganism, people should know that a legitimate, respectable pagan movement exists in this country that would probably be insulted to have the worship at the Re-Imagining Conference called paganism.

The criticism of the conference has been so wide-ranging that I finally stopped and said out loud to myself, "Okay, which issue do people really want to talk about?" So far, I have read or heard comment on: imago Dei, atonement, suffering, Sophia, biblical authority, milk and honey ritual, inclusive language, violence against women, lesbianism, and giving thanks for women's sexuality. Someone is liable to throw in abortion soon. This conflict could be a sign of health. If the church is so split open by this debate, then these may be issues of real disagreement.

The part of me that has the personality of a lawyer sort of enjoys this fight. I stayed up until two o'clock in the morning recently, reading theories of atonement and suffering. It was good for my brain. Atonement theories can seem a little ridiculous. God sent God's only child to earth and then sacrificed him on a cross so that God could love us? What? Jesus saved us? From what? The wrath of God who created us? I believe that Jesus was a Jewish reformer who was politically dangerous and was killed by the Romans through their puppet Jewish government. Jesus' followers were devastated by his death. The story of the resurrection may have been spin control. The church is the body of Christ, the resurrected body of Christ.

Then there's Sophia. Some have said that the problem with the use of Sophia was that it did not conform to the reformed trinitarian formulation for God. Neither does "Rock of my Salvation," but we use that language all the time and people don't start screaming about rock worship. I am not personally devoted to the trinitarian ascription for God. One of the things we have been pushing for is expanding our images of God. When I ask other women how they imagine God, I hear lots of formulations outside of God the Father, Son, and Holy Spirit, and outside Creator, Redeemer, and Sustainer. The use of Sophia was an attempt to try something new but something biblical. It always surprises me that so many people get so upset when we replace male language for God with female language. It reminds me that they must believe that God is male.

Some have criticized the milk and honey ritual for being a substitute for Holy Communion. Every invitation to a feast sounds like the words of institution, like being called in for supper. Can we have no other rituals at all? What about the Moravian love feast? Is that also blasphemous? The problem is how to make safe spaces for exploring new rituals without being reprimanded.

Why do some people keep trying to stop the debate with an appeal to the peace and unity of the church? It sounds like power and control to me. Do they think we are going to blow ourselves to pieces? Conversely, why would conservative publications want to keep talking about these issues? Such debate may have a liberalizing influence in the long run. Some day we may thank the *Presbyterian Layman* and the *Good News* folks for the publicity and for raising feminist theology to the level of national debate.

Most days I don't really care what church commentators say. They can vote their votes and issue their papers. The church is changing. While some may try to stop it and others may try to push it faster, change is all around us. Women are leaders and preachers. Many churches use inclusive language for people, if not for God. The new United Methodist worship book includes a liturgy for healing from miscarriage. It may be slow, but I do believe that in the last twenty years we have changed the landscape of religion in America.

Jeanette Stokes is a Presbyterian minister. She founded the Resource Center for Women and Ministry in the South in 1977 and served as its executive director for almost eighteen years. She lives in Durham, North Carolina. She is married and a graduate of Smith College and Duke Divinity School.

A Contemporary Morality Play

A CLERGY FAMILY

Time: January 1995.
Place: A kitchen table. Tape recorder in the middle of the table.
Characters: Dad, a middle-aged Presbyterian pastor. Mom, active with presbytery women and the Fellowship of Christian Athletes. Three daughters: ages seventeen, sixteen, and eight.
Background: Mom and two other women from the congregation attended the Re-Imagining Conference. The two congregational members were upset about lesbian participation in the conference. After months of attempted dialogue, a vote was taken by the session of the church to dissolve the relationship with the pastor. He was given three months severance pay, housing for four months, and insurance benefits. The family is currently relocated and serving a different congregation.

Dad: I had conversations with both women following the conference. They were not able to evaluate other parts of the conference because they were focusing on the homosexual dimension, particularly the moment when CLOUT (Christian Lesbians Out Together) took the platform. By February, conservative literature from the *Presbyterian Layman* and the *American Family Association Journal* was coming out. James Brown, Executive Director of the General Assembly of the Presbyterian Church (U.S.A.), sent a letter to the churches. I duplicated the letter and passed it through our congregation. One of the women who attended the conference was a sponsor for a confirmand in our church who made a reference to Brown's letter. The woman responded by stating that Brown's letter was about some other conference, not the one she had attended. Later, when she realized it was the same conference, she became very angry and demanded a meeting with the session. She expressed that she felt she had been duped into a betrayal of her faith and a denial of her commitment to Jesus Christ; that she had been in a place where her denomination advocated a homosexual lifestyle; that she had unwittingly participated in pagan worship; and, to add more trauma to her spiritual life, she had now lied to a young person whom she was sponsoring in the faith. She blamed me for not taking care of her as she believed a pastor should by protecting her from this experience. The session shared her anger and shock. Taking their cues from the *Presbyterian Layman,* they were upset that $66,000 of Presbyterian Bicentennial Fund money was used in support of the conference. We tried to interpret the wider use of the bicentennial money, including four significant projects in our own area, but none of those interpretations mattered much.

The session asked where I stood on the issue of homosexuality. I told them I had problems accepting the book of Leviticus as the sole rule of faith and practice. I affirmed our church's constitution, which states that the only basis for membership is belief in Jesus Christ. One's particular orientation or any particular sin are questions neither for membership nor for continued participation in our fellowship. I accept and support our denomination's position that homosexuals are not to be ordained; I understand it to be a political compromise that is intended to hold our church together. I also knew there were members of our congregation who are homosexuals, and I felt a responsibility to them as pastor.

I preached a series of sermons about forgiveness, understanding, and compassion and said we must not allow ourselves to be enslaved to a restrictive law. The sermons didn't make much difference. The session decided that my leadership had been compromised and asked for a resignation. I did not resign. There was a dissolution process according to our constitution. Meanwhile, rumors circulated that we had raised the money for the conference, that we had planned the conference, that we had housed homosexuals in the manse, and so on. People came with their minds already made up to the meeting to vote on dissolving my relationship with the church. The proposal was that we dissolve our relationship without cause and that there would be a severance package. If they agreed to the severance package, I would not contest the dissolution-ment. I did not speak in my defense, because I had not been charged with anything. There was simply a vote, and the vote was twenty-nine to eight that I should not continue to be pastor.

Daughter (eight years old): Kids downstairs kept saying he had to go. I didn't think they were being respectful. The kids at the church were being very mean. I don't know what came over them, but they wouldn't let me do anything with them. *(She cries and cannot continue.)*

Daughter (seventeen years old): I think what bothered me most was that the woman who brought up the whole thing was our youth director. And her whole point was that she didn't feel she could be a leader and help us with our faith after attending this conference. But to me, I cannot see how she could not even respect someone . . . when you're a Christian you're supposed to love everyone . . . I can't love everyone, but to take a whole group and hate them because, in her mind, they sinned . . . everyone's a sinner. You can't say "I hate all homosexuals"; that's like saying "I hate all African Americans" or "I hate all American Indians." I don't think she even knew any homosexuals. She

can't know how they feel. When someone cheats on his wife, no one gets riled
up about it. I know there are people who do that; and she knew about those
people, and she didn't hate them at all. It seemed to me that she was being
very prejudiced, and I lost a lot of respect for her.

Mom: This happened back in April, but we're still grieving. My grief is
that I lost a community that I didn't feel ready to leave. But at the same time,
I've told my husband those were some of his greatest sermons, because he said
we would continue to walk in love. Our entire family would not take on a
vindictive spirit. We would continue to walk in love, and by the grace of God
we did that.

One of the marvelous things for me to see was how these teenagers were
running around asking their dad, "Are you okay, Dad? How you feeling today,
Dad?" I thought: Are these our teenagers here?

Dad: I was moved by people who came to visit us in our home to express
their concern for us. I think of one in particular who left three hundred dollars
in cash on our kitchen table.

Mom: This brother left his father's funeral to come and be a comfort to
us. And there were others who came to talk with us and continued to pray for
us. That's what got us through.

Daughter (sixteen years old): I found it difficult that the people in our
congregation who went to this conference could not find anything good about
it. Out of a conference with about five hundred workshops, they could only
notice everything that was negative.

I took it very personally to see my family being torn apart day by day. I
didn't understand why the congregation went straight to the pastor and tried
to throw him out because of this conference, which he had absolutely nothing
to do with: he wasn't a leader there; he didn't speak; he didn't take part in it.

(She has difficulty speaking.) It was hard for me as a youth in school at the
time. After I knew he would lose his job, I didn't know whether I would be
able to finish the school year, and I didn't know where I would attend the next
fall or whether I would have a place to go.

I sometimes had a hard time answering people's questions: "Is your dad
being fired because so and so said . . . ?" That was probably the only thing
that really got me was having to straight-up answer questions like that.

One thing that was also real hard for me to deal with was that one of the
other youth members in our church . . . his confirmation sponsor was the
woman who went to the conference . . . it came down to every day in school

we would talk about the Re-Imagining Conference, and it would just turn into a big argument. And he was a friend of mine. We tried to tell each other we weren't going to let this come between our friendship, but it never worked.

Another hard thing for me to deal with was that the woman who instigated the fight was a very good friend of the family, and it seemed to me like she just turned on us. I felt abused and hurt. She was also our youth leader. She said she couldn't come back to our youth group and share her faith with us because she felt she had done something wrong by going to this conference. But during our youth meetings, we did not have any discussions on the Bible; it was more of a fund-raising group. It was hard for me to understand why she couldn't be a leader to us, because she wasn't a biblical faith leader for me anyway. I didn't think less of her for attending the conference. But after she had begun the fight to dismiss my father from his position, I lost a lot of respect for her.

Above all, I think the hardest thing for me was not to be angry with the people of the congregation but to continue to try to love them through the whole thing. I gained a lot of respect for my father, seeing how he handled the situation, knowing that all the pain he was going through was worse than what I had to deal with. But he still told us to love them and to keep peace and not have any hatred or revenge toward them.

Mom: One of the things that I was asked was how I could go to a conference like this and speak positively about it. I would still speak positively about it. If such a conference were held again, I would attend. Before I went, my prayer was that I wanted to be able to express God's love to people; and somehow I wound up in a conference that dealt with respect and compassion. The conference had so much to say about issues related to the persecution of women, and it was eloquently designed so that every voice could be heard. Yet because of one thirty-minute segment in which CLOUT had the podium, everybody became obsessed with whether or not we are supportive of a homosexual lifestyle.

Dad: What was surprising to me about this whole process is the degree to which our identity is so defined by our sexuality and sexual definitions. During these months, when people would want to know something about what occurred at the conference, I would ask if they would like to listen to the tapes. Not a single person listened to a single tape. Acceptance of a sexual definition different from theirs was allowed at the conference, and therefore it did not matter what else happened. One of the significant leaders of the presbytery said, "I can take communion with a murderer and even one who is a repeated murderer, but I could not sit at communion with a homosexual."

Mom: Throughout this whole process, I was thinking to myself: I'm not sure this is even about Re-Imagining. The question here seems to be whether or not people at the lay level truly understand Presbyterianism. It seemed like people were just against everything that I believe the Presbyterian church stands for. I was even wondering whether these people wanted to be Presbyterian because of the foundations on which we stand or if they wanted to be Presbyterian because (in most rural communities where we've lived) Presbyterian happens to be the upper echelon, socially and financially speaking. Maybe they became Presbyterian because their parents were Presbyterian, without truly understanding that this is a denomination that tends to take on advocacy for people without voice.

Daughter (eight years old): *(She has been unable to speak without crying. She has written a few notes and reads them.)* I felt like telling somebody off or hitting somebody, but I told my family how I felt downstairs with the kids. My feelings were hurt, and I needed to have some faith in me to forget all about it. But I found that faith. I thought the kids were just out of hand at first, but I found out they were doing it on purpose. I think they weren't being fair. And people just have to respect others and help others. And people just don't take families apart. It's not right. And I don't think they should have fired him. I mean, what did he do? People don't think right sometimes. And a lot of people need to be blessed by the Lord so they can have more love in their hearts.

This family requested anonymity. They have traveled from small-town provincialism to cosmopolitan graduate education. They have worked through the cultural shock of returning to a rural town to gain an appreciation of the hospitality in rural, small-town America.

PART FOUR

Rejoicing

The joyful prayers come pouring from the community as well. We celebrate

the community and God's presence among us. We proclaim our gratitude for

the good we have done and the goodness given to us. In each proclamation is a

story

of re-membering . . .

and re-imagining . . .

Treasure Held in a Clay Vessel

ANONYMOUS

I brought many things with me to Re-Imagining, including my frustration with the still-pervasive sexism of the church, my experiences of pain and grief as a feminist clergywoman, and my yearning for a truly Spirit-filled community of the beloved of God. I also brought with me (thanks to a last-minute flash of remembering) a pottery bowl to use in one of the event's rituals. It was richly glazed in tones that evoked the deep blue of the evening sky and the loamy brown of the Midwest prairie fields when they have been plowed but not yet planted. Newly purchased for the occasion, it was consecrated to receive the experiences of the gathering.

A small bowl, about the size of a peach half, it was too little to be useful for ordinary purposes like eating a bowl of cereal or ice cream. It would be no good for holding coffee, or pencils, or candies. But during the closing ritual of the conference, it sat nestled in my cupped hands and received the blessing of the Spirit in the sweetness of milk and honey. In this it served very well.

When the conference ended, I faced the formidable task of packing for my flight home. Where to put all the books I'd bought? And, more important, how could I protect this beautiful yet useless, fragile, utterly holy pottery bowl? I swaddled it in layers of my clothing and planted it deep in the middle of my suitcase like the life-generating stone hidden in the heart of the peach.

Returning to my home and my ministry, I placed this bowl on a table in my office. It reminds me of all that Re-Imagining gave me: affirmation, celebration, new songs to sing, and new friends to sing them with. It reminds me also of the cost of singing a new song. As a Presbyterian pastor, I have felt the furor of the *Presbyterian Layman*—whipped backlash. My pottery bowl now holds bitter memories as well as sweet.

But my bowl is not just a collector of memories. It also is a part of my ongoing ministry, especially when I celebrate a baptism. My Re-Imagining bowl, on those holy occasions, holds the fragrant anointing oil that I use to mark the forehead of the newly baptized. Dipping my finger in the oil and making the sign of the cross, I speak the name of the child, saying, "Child of the covenant, you have been sealed by the Holy Spirit in baptism and grafted into Christ forever." And it holds also my anger at a church that requires that I baptize only "in the name of the Father, and of the Son, and of the Holy

Spirit," a naming of the Holy One so narrow and exclusive that I consider it blasphemous and idolatrous.

I brought back from Re-Imagining far more than I dreamed: new life in the Spirit, renewed strength for ministry, new passion for the gospel. These gifts are present symbolically in my small pottery bowl—a simple clay vessel that shows the extraordinary power of God. Sophia will not be denied, for even the church does not have the power to reject her blessings. She will call whom she chooses, birthing and baptizing them into life and into death, spreading the fragrance of the gospel of life.

The author is a Presbyterian clergywoman in the Midwest.

Subversive Learning

MAY TURNBULL DELLER

Manitoba, Canada
17 January 1994

Dear Sally,

This letter has been written to you in my mind many times since the Re-Imagining Conference in early November. Finally, the polar deep freeze we're experiencing has provided me with the opportunity to put pen to paper.

At the present time, I'm situated in a couple of light-housekeeping rooms above the hospital in the little village I grew up in but left as a very young woman forty-four years ago. My elderly mother (eighty-eight) has been hospitalized here for all but three weeks of the past five months, with one traumatic crisis after another as she struggles to maintain her fragile hold on life. The two-hour drive for me back and forth from where I live becomes quite difficult in such weather, so I'm glad to have this little space for my own without having the added stress of traveling.

There's a beautiful view from my window. The wind is whipping the snow across the prairie landscape into fresh, clean, sparkling drifts, and it is minus thirty-five degrees Celsius, a typical Manitoba January day. Aren't you sorry you're missing such an invigorating climate?

How can I convey to you what I feel about having had the once-in-a-lifetime opportunity to be part of such a conference? I do not have adequate words. I was one of the fortunate people who had scholarship help to attend. Thank you and all who made everything to do with that weekend possible.

I am a retired farmer, and if you know anything about the farm situation in prairie Canada for small family farms, you will understand that many, many things others take for granted in their lifestyle are only dreamed about in ours. So you can imagine how very happy and pleased I was to realize this dream of attending Re-Imagining.

After being very involved in all levels of our church courts (the United Church of Canada) as well as in my local church for over fifty-eight years, and in that journey realizing what a powerful love/hate relationship I have had with the church as an institution, I awoke one morning two years ago and knew my journey had taken a dramatic turn. I no longer attend church services. I am still part of a study group, but my sabbatical is extending for who knows how long or where the journey will take me. It's both very painful and tremendously liberating.

I did not have the opportunity for a university education, so you will know just how much it has meant to me to read, read, read—first male theologians, then female, as our consciousness-raising took place bit by bit. Do all you women writers, leaders, and mentors know how very important it has been (I'm sure to many more women than myself) to have written about your journey, your insights? That for me has been the link between being alive or dead many times, I'll tell you. I'm sure there are thousands of women like myself, fairly isolated from the community and mainstream of women spiritual leaders, who have survived because of the hard work you women of faith are doing which has nurtured us for years.

The Re-Imagining Conference experience was so much more than I had dared hope. Since I was in my early twenties, I have dreamed of such ways of expressing being the church. But as I grew older, I realized that was just a dream, and I probably would have to let it go like many other dreams.

On the Sunday morning of the conference, I could not help but become aware that this was a Pentecost experience. I didn't see any tongues of flames over people's heads, but I heard a new language and felt that all my sisters and brothers there heard the new language in their tongue, too. And, of course, we were drunk—and it was only the middle of the day. Had others peered in on that gathering, would they not have believed that to be true? What a spirit-filled weekend!

My daughter had given me a gift of money to take to the conference, and I was able to purchase the album of cassette tapes. What a treasure! I'm presently listening to them and making notes and becoming excited all over again.

Last summer, the University of Winnipeg asked me and a native woman friend of mine in Brandon to teach a course this spring for their certificate in theology. We plan to do some quite different things, and so much of the material has been very useful. We are quite excited and know we'll be subversive, too! How I long to see the end of patriarchy in our world. Of course, I will not live long enough to see that system gone. I pray that woman spirit, creation, and all that goes with the birthing of god(dess) in our midst may continue and flower.

I am involved with small groups of women who struggle to reclaim themselves and their spirituality. We will spend many great times together, I know, sharing and reflecting and acting upon the word that is present for us in the taped messages of all those marvelous women of faith who presented at the conference.

What's ahead I do not know, but I am learning to "greet the unseen with a cheer."[1] Many thanks again.

Shalom.

May Deller

May Turnbull Deller—born the third of six children at Hamiota, Manitoba, Canada, in 1933—was active in the United Church of Canada all her life until three years ago. She taught school for two years, married a farmer, raised a daughter and two sons, and worked as an active farmer until a few years ago. At the present time, she thoroughly enjoys meeting with various groups who attempt to re-imagine what it means to be fully human as we remember what has shaped us in this century. She now resides in the small city of Brandon, Manitoba, Canada.

LOU SCHOEN

Date: 8 November 1993
Place: Doorway to Sally Hill's office, headquarters of the Re-Imagining Conference

---

Sally

SPECTACULAR STUPENDOUS!

What "church" is s'posed to be!!

Thanks for being the coordinating channel that the Holy Spirit used to bring it to us.

Lou

Lou Schoen, Director of Life and Work for the Minnesota Council of Churches, deeply admired Sally Hill as a prized colleague for the last three and one-half years of her career.

International Friendship

KATHY RODRIGUEZ AND JULIA CAMPOS

Julia Campos from Uruguay and Kathy Rodriguez from Denver, Colorado, have become friends while attending women's conferences around the world. Relationships that span continents are part of the Re-Imagining hope.

The Journey That Flows to Community (Kathy Rodriguez)

Being able to share the Re-Imagining Conference with Julia Campos from Uruguay was one of the highlights of the event for me. Julia and I have been attending women's meetings together for nearly twenty years. We first met at a human-rights preconference meeting called by Sister Luke Tobin before the Church Women United Assembly in Purdue in 1976.

Julia has always had connections with the World Council of Churches through the women's agenda. The last few years, she has been working with women in Uruguay and Argentina, promoting the Decade of the Churches in Solidarity with Women. In the spring of 1994, she spent three months traveling from southern to northern Italy, presenting Decade goals to women's groups.

So much has happened in our lives, personal journeys, and theologies in the last twenty years; through our shared letters, visits, and exchanged books, we each have grown.

The blessing of Re-Imagining was that Julia and I met many of the women who have made the same journey with us: the journey that is celebrated within then flows to the community and into the international community. Both of us were spirit-filled from the sharing and imbibing of this historic gathering of sisters and brothers.

Common Interest (Julia Campos)

Dear Sally:

Back home after the tremendous experience of the Re-Imagining encounter, I think I won't be able to say properly what it meant to me.

Needless to say, I am most thankful for the opportunity all of you provided me to be part of such an event.

I still don't even begin to digest the number of new approaches in our common interest and subject: women. What I dare say is that, together with many other women, we have been deeply touched by the creativity that was present in every aspect of the lectures, workshops, music, liturgy, and practical ways of everyday living. We were very moved by women responsible for the songs and drama.

Now I feel that I have to pass the experience on to our women. I think that in the next year we can have a series of encounters to work on the Re-Imagining experience, as its content was new in many aspects to our work on the Decade issues.

I hope we will keep in touch in a follow-up process, and I am looking forward to hearing from you pretty soon.

In sisterhood,
Julia Campos

Kathy Rodriguez is a United Church of Christ Central American activist and pediatric physician's assistant in inner-city Denver. She started her peace and justice work in south Texas in the mid-1960s with farm workers. It broadened into Central American activism, criminal justice, and feminist issues as she began making the connections.

Julia Campos is a lay minister of the Waldensian Church of Uruguay and of an age to be retired. For many years she has been interested in and committed to women's issues in church and society. Today she is mainly related to an ecumenical program that deals with battered women in Argentina and Uruguay, a concern of the Ecumenical Decade: Churches in Solidarity with Women.

A Gift from the Spirit

MARY KAY SAUTER

Saturday morning. Not too many glitches so far. As a matter of fact, this was proving to be more than any of us had dreamed. We talked about being midwives, having helped birth something that now had its own life.

As I passed Chris Smith, who was scheduled to do the Sunday morning sermon, she said that the lesbian and bisexual women had met the evening before and wanted to talk with Kathi Austin Mahle, my steering committee co-chair, and me. Chris mentioned that they were concerned that Sunday—the time she planned to come out during her sermon—would be too late for many people to process their issues around heterosexism in their talking circles. She said they wanted to talk about doing something today that would be helpful.

I thought to myself: Okay, we can handle this, and I admonished myself to keep calm—and I prayed. I was prepared to experience the sweaty palms, heart-rate increase, and stomach knot that usually occur in a crisis. I kept waiting for these symptoms to begin, but they never did.

I walked to the hallway and was greeted by a large group of women, several of whom became spokespersons for the group. They were worried that their voices were not overtly a part of the conference. They wanted time following the morning plenary speakers to sing a song, make a statement, and invite other lesbian and bisexual women to come forward.

I explained that I affirmed them, but that no one person made a decision for the steering committee and that I would need to process this with the other members. They understood this and were very supportive of our process. I also wanted to find Kathi, so that we could work on this together. I later found out that she was inside the ballroom, taking care of another situation. But she had been alerted to this request. Still no panic, just an incredible sense of calm.

I knew of two people with whom we needed to visit, who might have some problems with this. My first stop was with a table of steering committee members. I explained the request, and the immediate response was solid support. One woman said that, by all means, this conference was about being on the cutting edge and that this was a cutting-edge issue. Another said that, of course, we needed to show this support. No one at the table had a problem with the plan.

I still hadn't found Kathi, but I did find one of the two people I knew we needed to chat with. My sense by this time was that we would do something; but, as always, we needed to try for win/win solutions. For this particular person, it seemed most appropriate to explain what was happening and then just listen to her. She expressed pragmatic, real concerns, but in the end she supported whatever the rest of the committee wanted. Still no panic, just calm.

By this time Kathi and I had found each other and brought each other up to date with what was going on. Karen Dimon, another steering committee member, had joined us. During all this time, the plenary session had been opened with ritual, music, and movement, and the first speaker had been introduced. Kathi, Chris, Karen, and I spoke with the second person. She expressed some deep concerns about politicizing the conference. She was not at ease over breaking into the conference with something unplanned. She was also aware of many women in the room with other issues and pain, who didn't have a voice either. What evolved was a suggestion that the statement speak inclusively of women's pain and those suffering in silence. The calmness, the clarity of thinking, continued.

We gathered in the hallway and shared our suggestion with the lesbian and bisexual women. They had no problem with it, and we discussed wording. We were close to running out of time; the second plenary speaker was almost through. We had been in this process for about three hours, but it seemed so right.

Kathi and I stood at the side of the room, weeping as the Spirit filled the room with compassion and care. As bisexual and lesbian women were invited to come forward, most others stood and applauded. The statement was read, the song was sung; it was a celebration in the presence of God of God's inclusive love and our ability to live out of that love. I was no longer calm. I was exuberant.

Later that day, a lesbian clergywoman I know came to me with tears streaming down her face thanking me for the risk I had been willing to take. It seemed like undeserved praise. We simply did what was right. I tried to explain this to her and let her know that my biggest fear is that at another time I will be a coward and not be open to the Spirit. Others came to me quietly and spoke of their pain because they were not in a safe enough place in their lives, relationships, careers, jobs, or churches that they could come forward, though they had wanted to.

I have thought often about that morning. We had no acrimony among any of the participants in this endeavor. We had an openness to trust the process and a strong desire to find a win/win solution. We had an honoring of one another throughout the morning. But it was more than us: in helping to birth this gathering, God's Spirit was working through us for healing and wholeness and to show how the church can be.

I don't recall ever feeling so empowered and so humbled by God's Spirit. Empowered to be bold, to do what was right, to provide leadership and ideas. Humbled because God was working through me as one of the participants in this process. The calm I felt was amazing. It freed me to think and to devise a strategy, to trust the decision-making process we had been using for four years, to listen and hear what others were saying, to seek a win/win solution, to be open to what was happening around me, and to be in relationship with people. It freed me to be open to the continued guidance of the Spirit. This calm was a gift from the Spirit.

Mary Kay Sauter co-chaired the steering committee for the 1993 Re-Imagining Conference. She was a master of divinity student at United Theological Seminary of the Twin Cities at the time and is currently a United Church of Christ clergywoman in Minnesota. She serves as co-chair of the coordinating council of the Re-Imagining Community.

Dancing in Concentric Circles

TERESA MCCORMICK

I am a woman. I attended the Re-Imagining Conference. I am Catholic.

I can indeed proclaim that I have nectar between my thighs and hot blood in my womb. I have married a man, soaked myself in his strength, celebrated his soul. Together we created four children. I loved. I labored. I cried. I gave birth in wrenching spasms to new life, to new definitions, to new interactions.

Why did I attend the "pagan and idolatrous" Re-Imagining Conference?

To dance! To dance a heartfelt prayer of women's common pain and of women's common hope. Were there tears over Korean government involvement in selling prostituting women as a major source of capital? Was there a gripping ache concerning domestic violence and rape? What about job exploitation, inequality, disparity, and outright abuse? What about child brides in India, child pornography in the United States, and the murder and ridicule of lesbians?

We sat at tables of ten, crayons in hand, coloring our anger, creating cloths full of imagery, full of unspeakable, rainbow-raw color. And then we applauded. We sang of our complete and powerful sensuality. We sang of our sexual vibrancy and creative wisdom, our resiliency, our endurance, a birth energy that could work for land redistribution, redistribution of wealth, global prosperity, and community strength.

Shouldn't we honor a collective wisdom that understands this, that understands that conditions of this present time are due to each individual inside a community, inside a global world? Is it Sophia? Is it God? Honestly!

Our most powerful deity must laugh at our all-consuming struggle to name the divine.

I came to the conference, not to theologize or redefine God—we poured out milk and honey and broke the bread—but to seek the potential of unified cries. I came to immerse myself. I came to rise above pain and create a kingdom of all people.

I came not to create a feminine God or a Sophia but to acknowledge God, Jesus, Spirit, Wisdom, and make a plea for a dying civilization, a dying world.

So I danced the prayer. I sang the praise. With an African scarf high over my head I led others to move into and through and under the prayer. It was my quest, as woman-sinner, for an army of friends to re-create my world. Two thousand of us danced in concentric circles to the beat of many kinds of drums from the global village.

I stood then in a flowing black skirt to praise the conference. I stand now to praise it. I honor the audacious past president of the World Council of Churches. I celebrate theologians and activists alike who reach into the cold dark tomb to find life never died, who examine histories and cultures, who pour out wounded hearts and allow an image to form from pain and promise that rebirths the supreme deity. Redefines. Re-imagines.

Let go of the judgment, of the harshness, of the wrongfulness. Let go.

The Ecumenical Decade of Churches in Solidarity with Women must stand as a beacon to all who cradle hope for a better tomorrow.

Teresa McCormick is an Irish-Catholic, forty-year-old, blue-eyed, black-haired, intense, lustful, breakable, God-centered woman, living in Minnesota. She is a community-service learning specialist with elementary schools of Saint Paul and is a recipient of a 1994 Leadership in Neighborhoods grant. She has been working with the Hubert H. Humphrey Institute at the University of Minnesota on economic-development initiatives to improve credit access for the urban poor, people of color, and women, and helped found an ecumenical organization of urban churches and a $2 million loan fund for entrepreneurs who have difficulty obtaining loans. She prays through dance.

Coming Home

ELISABETH MACK

Theology is for everyone. Of course. My parents have always told me that everyone can have good ideas about God. It was because of Re-Imagining that I began to wonder if it were really true. But Re-Imagining also reassured me and made me finally certain that theology *is* for everyone. Even me.

I had anticipated Re-Imagining for months: finally, a chance to be around people whose religious beliefs might even be wilder than my own. The prospect of meeting people who might see things more my way delighted me. At least, I supposed, they would listen. As a Mennonite teenager, I had seldom been encouraged to doubt the "Sunday school truth." I had always been a closet questioner, never really belonging.

But when the first day of the Re-Imagining Conference arrived, I was scared. I didn't want to go. I decided that I would be intimidated. I would never be brave enough to say a single word. Everyone else there would have degrees and titles. They would think that I was silly to be there. My pastor hadn't even been able to register for the conference. I thought maybe I should give my place to her. After all, I reasoned, I was only seventeen—too young to play a part in such an important event.

I was terrified, but I went.

We introduced ourselves. The rest of the people around my table were pastors and Christian educators and officials from the World Council of Churches. They had come from all over the country to be at Re-Imagining. I was surrounded by amazing people. And then I spoke. "I'm Elisabeth. I'm a high school senior here in Minneapolis. I guess I'm interested in theology, maybe, among other things. . . ." I let my voice trail off shyly and waited for the bemused, knowing smiles that adults like to wear around idealistic children like me.

They did not laugh. Instead they started to tell me about their tangled lives and their jobs in various churches. They described how they had been when they were younger. As it turned out, eight of the ten had undergraduate degrees in science, not religion. Apparently they had broad concerns, too. I was surprised that they cared about my ideas and interests. We began to talk about our images of God, and still they did not laugh at me. We daydreamed about the ideal world and the perfect church, and I was an equal still.

After a while, we all stood up and we sang—all two thousand of us. I'd never heard that many people singing at once. I felt as if, after a lifetime of fitting in nowhere, I had finally come home.

Elisabeth Mack was raised in Minneapolis and baptized in the Mennonite church when she was fourteen. Now she is a student at Grinnell College, planning to major in religion.

Joy Compounded

MERCY AMBA ODUYOYE

November 1993

This is to express my appreciation for including me in the Re-Imagining event. When the conference kept expanding from women theologians (academics) to all women concerned with the churches' theological approach to women, I began to doubt the necessity for having three World Council of Churches women present. As it turned out, each of us had a constructive contribution and has brought back a different perspective of what happened to enrich the Decade focus here. Thank you very much for the event itself and especially for your reception and care of us, the international guests.

In spite of the long waits after the meeting at hotel and airports, we were able to join in the week of meetings on Tuesday and to feed on some of what we had experienced at Minneapolis.

I pray that the energy and commitment you and all in the preparatory team have put into this effort will give a fresh dynamism to the churches' solidarity with women. On our part as the World Council of Churches, we continue the task and the joy of stimulating the churches on this issue.

Many, many thanks for contributing to this joy.

Mercy Amba Oduyoye is a Methodist lay theologian from Ghana. She was serving as deputy general secretary of the World Council of Churches at the time of the Re-Imagining Conference.

Occasional Grace

PAMELA CARTER JOERN

There is an old and well-deserved skepticism about the church among theater artists. When we were rehearsing *Simple Gifts* for the Re-Imagining Conference, this discomfort popped out in lots of places: Could we actually perform in a sanctuary? Would people laugh at these lines? Would they be offended?

For my part, I had to work at not being defensive about my position as a playwright who writes about religious themes. I sometimes found myself apologizing for my religious convictions. My discovery was that my apologetic stance was perceived as condescending toward the diverse spiritualities of the theater artists involved in the production. The more I claimed my personal convictions with authenticity, the more freedom the other artists felt to claim their spiritualities. Locating my convictions in my experience gave others permission to do the same.

I was aware while all of this was happening that the rehearsal process was a microcosm of one of the central themes I had tried to write about in the play: the collision between sacred and secular worlds. The Playwright, who is the narrator of the play, says in the opening monologue, "I can't help it. I'm a religious person. In a secular society, I wear this identity like a confession."[2] The play suggests that this perceived split between sacred and secular is a false dichotomy and that one way to bridge the gap is through the imagination. I thought I knew something about that process when I wrote the play, but I didn't expect to be challenged with the opportunity to test the theory.

On opening night, one of the actors asked me if I would give them a blessing. I was surprised to learn from Julia Carey, the British director, that theaters in England commonly employ chaplains. I shared the Sophia blessing with the cast and crew, and it was a fine and intimate moment.

The audiences on both nights of the conference were a playwright's dream. They were responsive, savvy, and appreciative. They laughed when I hoped they would laugh; they were on their feet before the final lines of the play were spoken.

Even then, life handed us more challenge. When the actors returned to their dressing room after the Saturday night show, they discovered that during the second act they had been robbed. They were missing jewelry, car keys, purses, and clothing. We were all devastated and heartsick. The young woman who lost the most kept saying, "I didn't think this would happen in a church."

These losses were particularly hard to bear because these actors, like many artists, live near poverty in order to do what they love, and their participation in this play paid only a minimal honorarium.

When I reached the convention center on Sunday morning, news of the robbery had preceded me. It seemed to me that the idea for a collection came simultaneously from several different people, and the remarkable thing was that this was done with no fanfare. Of course, it was assumed, people would want to help. The collection was announced, baskets were passed with notes attached, and when all was said and done, strangers had reached into their pockets to gift other strangers with nearly fourteen hundred dollars.

Later that afternoon, I called Julia. She had been talking to the actors all day, scrambling through her closets to find what she could share to make up for their losses. I told her the conference participants had gathered money to help defray expenses. I had to repeat the amount several times because she literally could not believe it.

It's hard to convey the moments when the heart lifts. It's hard not to sound like a sentimental greeting card. The tendency is to want to spill neon ink all over the scene to make sure it is not missed. I don't know how to tell you what grace was in that experience. Except this: later that week Julia told me she had been sharing this story all over town among theater folk. "It's the most remarkable thing," she said, "that has happened to me in years."

Pamela Carter Joern is an ordained member of American Baptist Churches USA. Her play Simple Gifts *was commissioned for the Re-Imagining Conference. She served on the steering and program committees for the 1993 conference and is currently editor of the* Re-Imagining Community Newsletter.

A Revived Soul

KITTREDGE CHERRY

Re-Imagining renewed and strengthened me for the future—particularly for the National Council of Churches (NCC) meeting, which I attended immediately afterward. I went to represent the Universal Fellowship of Metropolitan Community Churches (UFMCC), a Christian denomination of nearly three hundred churches in sixteen countries, with a primary ministry in the lesbian and gay community. Despite more than a decade of dialogue, the NCC has refused to grant even observer status to UFMCC. Debate about UFMCC's role always brings to light the disagreements among the NCC's own members about homosexuality, with the majority voting to choose unity at the expense of all else. This discouraging situation weighed heavily on my heart as I arrived at Re-Imagining.

Anyone who followed the controversy that erupted after Re-Imagining would probably assume that the prolesbian content of the conference was what most inspired me. At the time, I felt that Re-Imagining did very little to address lesbian issues. Among the multitude of activities were only two lesbian-themed workshops, one of which included me as a panelist. We lesbians felt so invisible that we asked for a few minutes during one of the last plenaries to name our existence and invite others to stand in solidarity with us. That action was, indeed, very moving.

For me, the highlight was the first night. I walked into the Minneapolis Convention Center awed by the energy of two thousand women (and "a few good men," as we said). How would I ever find my UFMCC colleagues among them? I needed to speak with our chief ecumenical officer, the Reverend Nancy Wilson. I stood in the crowd, feeling overwhelmed. Then, as if God knew my thoughts and prompted action, Nancy appeared from nowhere and waved. From that moment on, it seemed that divine force guided me to the exact people I needed to encounter. Next, I found my assigned table and was amazed to discover that each of my tablemates had experiences and gifts that corresponded to my needs—such as a woman from South Africa, who gave me information and encouragement that prepared me to attend the World Council of Churches meeting in Johannesburg two months later.

Bernice Johnson Reagon was one of the first speakers. "The storm is the only way I know what an anchor is," she said. "There's no way to know what sheltering is if you don't live in the storm."[3] Tears came to my eyes as she sang a familiar hymn ("There Is a Balm in Gilead"):

> *Sometimes I feel discouraged,*
> *And think my work's in vain.*
> *But then the Holy Spirit*
> *Revives my soul again.*
> *There is a balm in Gilead*
> *To make the wounded whole.*

That night I confessed to Nancy Wilson how hopeless I had felt as I thought of returning to face the NCC delegates who had rejected us the previous year. "It's a cross to bear," she acknowledged. Her words sobered me. Was I strong enough to take up this particular cross and follow Jesus?

When I stepped outside, the world had been transformed; it was snowing. Snow blanketed the earth, beautiful, gentle, and pure. As the snowflakes floated around me, I was reminded again that God is with humankind—with me—to the ends of the earth. I knew without a doubt that, "There is a balm in Gilead, to make the wounded whole."

The Reverend Kittredge Cherry is an executive at the international headquarters of the Universal Fellowship of Metropolitan Community Churches, where her responsibilities include communications and ecumenical relations. She is coeditor of Equal Rites: Lesbian and Gay Worship, Ceremonies and Celebrations *and author of* Hide & Speak: How to Free Ourselves from Our Secrets, *and* Womansword: What Japanese Words Say about Women. *A graduate of the University of Iowa, she studied in Japan and earned a master of divinity degree from the Pacific School of Religion, Berkeley, California. She lives in Los Angeles with her spouse, Audrey E. Lockwood.*

Sunday

CATHERINE MALOTKY

Being at Re-Imagining on Sunday was like getting a massage. It felt decadent and absolutely pivotal at the same time. I gasped when the milk and honey came dancing toward our table, carried by the godmother of one of my daughters. At that moment I knew the richness offered by the One who leads us into our promised land.

This Time

It was a time
a break in time
to breathe
and stretch
to sip sweet nectar
in wicker
on a lovely wooden
porch.
There was the slightest
breeze.
It was a time to talk
and laugh
and cry.
There were no
heresy police
this time.
I danced.

Catherine Malotky is an ordained Lutheran pastor, living in Minneapolis, Minnesota, where she is employed by Augsburg Fortress Publishers as a development editor. She has been a high school teacher, a seminary instructor in homiletics, a parish pastor in rural and inner-city congregations, and a curriculum writer, and she is often called on as a retreat leader and speaker. She and her husband, David Engelstad, are raising two daughters, one dog, two cats, two gerbils, one goldfish, and thirty-seven guppies (at last count).

Laundry Day

BARBARA GARLINGER

It's mid-September, and I'm hanging the clothes on the line. It's usually a joyful prayer time for me. I smell the sheets and towels and clothes. I hear the birds. I smell the grass, cut recently. The sky is almost October blue, with wonderful white clouds. Squirrels are scolding me for being in their territory—until I speak and they recognize my voice. I should be filled with good feeling.

But I feel pressured. I hadn't expected to be called to substitute at school for a while. Then the call came to help my friend in her reading program for three weeks and in a second grade classroom for the rest of the semester. I give thanks that I can help. It's good. It's good to be among friends. It's good to be among the children. (I take down laundry to be ironed, just the right dampness.)

Still, I have that presentation this month. And the program for my women's group next month. And making the decisions to get the carpeting removed and the hardwood floors put down and arranging for the sofas to be delivered and finding someone to take the old ones and, somehow, shopping for my mother-of-the-bride dress and scheduling my perm. Today is my only day to do laundry and clean. (I reach up to unpin towels, and the sun is below my line of vision—a change from this morning.)

Mother seems to enjoy causing trouble. Sarah, who keeps us from being empty-nesters, and I laugh at how quickly Grandma runs upstairs when I vacuum. She is able-bodied. She could dust, or vacuum, or peel potatoes, or just answer the phone. But all she does is watch television and empty the dishwasher. Today I found my favorite mug, a gift from one of the four children years ago, put where no mug has ever been. So much gets rearranged. Why is it always *my* things that are out of order? (I fold sheets, smelling their freshness.) If I show her where things go, she gets angry. If I rush to empty the dishwasher, she gets huffy. She watches to see if I will complain. I can't win. It's not a product of age; it's her lifelong pattern. (I fold my husband's T-shirts, smelling the sun.) God must love Mother a great deal, because I can't. So I feel guilty. I'm being petty, unlovable.

Then I flash back as I have often in the last ten months. I am made in God's image, too. I remember sitting with those wonderful and diverse women. I remember hearing speakers I had longed to hear. I remember dancing and singing and praying and laughing and sharing with those two thousand and more people. I remember being affirmed as we affirmed all those who were with us. I remember hearing that what I had long felt was valued and real and true. I count. I am lovable.

I was on the road to this long ago; but boy (boy?) how I was transported last November!

Barbara Garlinger is a reaching, reading, groping, growing United Methodist laywoman, wife, mother of four adults, daughter of God. She has a degree in philosophy/religion and a graduate degree in education. She substitute teaches in elementary schools. She is a hospice volunteer and works in many activities on the local district and conference levels of the United Methodist Church.

The Nine of Us

BERYL INGRAM-WARD

By January the silence was unbearable. Wasn't some agency or official group within the United Methodist church going to step forward to refute the charges of heresy and goddess-worship related to the Re-Imagining Conference? Instead of remaining frustrated and silent, nine women friends gathered on Saturday, 19 February 1994, to do something.

We began with a ritual, invoking God's presence (shekinah) and wisdom (sophia) in our deliberations. Howling with laughter, awash with tears, we relived the blessing of Re-Imagining. We remembered passionately the goodness of women praying, dancing, singing, creating, and learning together. No one was going to take this away from us.

The frustration in the room exploded into energy and resolve when one of us said that the only thing to do in the face of this awesome disapproval was to stage a second Re-Imagining. While this task was too big for us, we knew that we could at least provide a corrective to the distortions being disseminated by *Good News* and the *Presbyterian Layman*.

We would hold a press conference on 8 March 1994, International Women's Day. It would be a teach-in, addressing criticisms of Re-Imagining and also celebrating the contributions of women in the life of the church. Our excitement pushed the energy level higher and higher.

We decided to write a statement and send it to our women friends in the United Methodist church, giving them the opportunity to add their names with ours in solidarity. The statement and signatures would be presented at the press conference. Our cover letter asked them to respond by 5 March, three days prior to the press conference, so that we could compile the list of names. It was madness to expect that we could accomplish all this in a little over two weeks, but we were too filled with the Spirit to yield to reason.

We began to draft the statement that eventually became "A Time of Hope—A Time of Threat." One woman sat at the computer with pages of notes from our conversations while other women made suggestions over her shoulders until a rough draft emerged. We sharpened sentences for clarity and muted acrid language as our work of revision continued long into the night and fresh with the morning. By Sunday night we were refining the fifth draft over the phone.

While waiting for the final document, each of us in our own daily rounds began working our way through our personal address books, hurriedly addressing envelopes whenever there was a moment: on the phone, on the subway, in the air.

The final draft was faxed or hand-delivered to the nine of us on Monday, 21 February, and naturally it was amended. Back to the computer. "A Time of Hope—A Time of Threat" was finally printed late Tuesday afternoon, 22 February.

A Time of Hope—A Time of Threat

by Ann Craig, Ruth Harris, Peggy Halsey, Beryl Ingram-Ward, Susan M. Morrison, Heather Murray Elkins, Pat Patterson, Jeanne Audrey Powers, and Barbara B. Troxell

This is a time of hope. The partnership of women and men in the United Methodist Church is growing—in the Council of Bishops, in Annual Conferences, in local congregations, and in theological schools. Christian community and sharing of leadership are broadening across racial and ethnic lines. Globally, the voices of women are being heard, and cooperation among Christian women increases denominationally and ecumenically. In theological books, sermons, and liturgies, women are singing a new song.

But this is also a time of threat. Hostility toward outspoken, creative, and courageous women of faith is not new, but it is now more sharply focused. Public attacks on the leadership, theology and funding of a recent conference call us to speak out. We are convinced that people frightened by fresh theological insights and by challenges to narrow orthodoxy are attempting to discredit and malign women. Constructive dialogue is welcome, but irrational and distorted attacks increase an environment of violence against women.

For years the United Methodist Church has been divided by controversy over the leadership of women, reproductive rights, inclusive language, and homosexuality. As women have addressed these issues, the clash of theological perspectives has intensified. At the heart of the conflict are diverse images of God, the meaning of a multi-racial, multi-cultural church, ecumenical commitment, equal participation of women, and the dynamics of control and power. What is at stake is who will name these issues, how the issues will be described, and who will set the agenda for the future of the church.

We are clear that the verbal attacks on the Re-Imagining Conference in Minneapolis (November 1993) are not isolated. While some naysayers

*have rushed to judgment on the basis of hearsay, others appear to be part of
an ongoing design to split and weaken the United Methodist Church:*

- *Criticizing the Women's Division and undermining the effectiveness of local
  units of United Methodist Women are affronts to over a century of faithful
  witness and missionary service.*
- *Refusing to acknowledge the positive relationship between sexuality and
  spirituality, present in both Christian tradition and contemporary
  theological writings, deprives the church of a rich and essential wholeness.*
- *Accusing feminist, womanist, and other women theologians, as well as our
  theological schools, of departing from historic Christian faith is an
  attempt to constrict the work of the Holy Spirit.*
- *Engaging in verbal violence against lesbians reveals the homophobia in the
  church and denigrates the rich contributions that homosexual persons have
  made to the church through the centuries.*
- *Creating a climate of witch-hunting, name-calling, and fear destroys
  Christian community and erodes the church's capacity to proclaim the
  gospel of Jesus Christ.*

The earliest letters went into the mail on Wednesday, 23 February, with
cryptic notes of greeting and encouragement. That same day one of us left for
Japan, taking the statement with her for signatures there. With the impossi-
bly short turnaround time—a maximum of ten days before 5 March—what
response could we realistically expect? After all, mail can take a week to cross
the country.

Our letter included instructions that an answering machine would record names to be included if time was too short to guarantee mail delivery by
the due date. The phone began to ring as early as 27 February. "Please put my
name on." "I'm thrilled to sign my name to 'A Time of Hope.'" "Thank you
for doing this." Clearly the statement met a deep-felt need. The testimonials
were heartening, energizing, and inspirational.

By 2 March the phone was never silent. The answering-machine tape
repeatedly filled up, which necessitated taking the phone off the hook to
transcribe the messages and caused endless frustration to women all over the
United States who were trying to get through. At the same time, the fax
machine began whirring with lists of names and addresses of women who
wanted to be counted. Priority Mail envelopes poured in. The numbers accu-
mulated, and so did the stories. One woman signed on her deathbed, the final
witness of her life committed to justice. A twelve-year-old girl signed as her
first act of witness immediately after her confirmation. From laywomen,
clergywomen, bishops; from active United Methodist Women units and from

retirement centers; from most of the states and around the globe came signatures and shouts of acclamation. We were stunned by the response. Three or
four hundred names would have been miraculous, but three hundred names
had been left on the answering machine alone. "A Time of Hope—A Time of
Threat" received over eight hundred endorsements, and we printed them in
big, bold type, two columns to a page, page after glorious page.

The lists of names went to the printer at ten o'clock the morning of the
press conference. It was literally hot off the press when the two o'clock
conference began in the spacious Sockman Lounge in the Interchurch Center in
New York City.

We had invited the press, prepared press packets, and arranged for
videotaping. The room was filled with people standing in doorways to participate in this historic moment. They were not disappointed. The air was
charged with the snap, crackle, and pop of energy. Someone later remarked
that it was as if God's spirit whirled and danced in our midst, inviting all
present to bear witness to her singing once again, "Behold! I am doing a new
thing!"

The ninety-minute videotape of the press conference proved to be such
an excellent resource that eventually 250 copies were distributed at cost. An
additional twelve hundred signatures of women and men have come in since 8
March 1994.

The nine of us are churchwomen who gathered ourselves together and
pooled our resources so that we could speak with one voice rather than remain
individually silent in the face of injustice and wrongdoing. Our action made a
difference. We're glad we did it, and we continue to go from strength to
strength because of it.

*Beryl Ingram-Ward is a United Methodist clergywoman, working on a Ph.D. at Union
Theological Seminary in New York City. She pastored churches in Bellevue and Tacoma,
Washington, prior to her current appointment to doctoral studies in Christian social ethics and
worship at Union Theological Seminary in New York. Her work focuses on the unacknowledged
dynamics of violence and sacrifice at the heart of Christian narrative and ritual.*

A Thank-You Note to Those Who Signed

"A Time of Hope—A Time of Threat"

DONNA MYHRE

I, who am not a man, have hoped for this time.
I have clung for decades to the fringe of the church,
unwilling to leave,
unwilling to think as The Men think,
unwilling to pray as The Men pray.

I, who am not a man, have waited for this time.
I have thought: they define us as not-them. There are men,
and the rest of us are wo-men. There are males,
and the rest of us are fe-males.
Now I think: there is theological correctness, which can exist only in the
    minds of men.
And there is Her-I-See.

My prose turns to song.
We are singing for our lives, but we are singing.

Those of us who are not men, which is to say,
those of us who know for sure who our children are,
have songs not yet sung.
We do not trace the genealogy of God-on-earth through a step-father;
we do not sing of genealogy at all.
We sing the subversion of Imposed Order, which is to say,
our songs flow from the rhythms and patterns of our lives, which is to say,
some songs can only be sung by those who are not men.

I dream of singing together, with those whose original sin was being born of us
who are not men (or so they have said).

I have dreamed that those who are men listen to our song.
I have dreamed that those who are men learn that after-play is part of the
*   main text, not an epilog.*

I, now, this day, this minute, celebrate your invitation to re-form the fold.

Donna Myhre is a sixty-three-year-old white southern woman, living and working in her adopted home city of New Orleans. She is a woman-loving, piano-playing crone, a mother who doesn't know what is best for other people, and a psychologist who doesn't know why people do what they do. She works and has worked as an advocate for women and children, survivors of rape and battering, people who are not heterosexual, people who are not white, people who are not young, and people with disabilities.

A Grain of Sand

SUE SWANSON

Sophia's Song

Dedicated to Sally Hill

Words and music: Sue Swanson, 1994

with energy

1. In ___ the strug - gle for peace and jus - tice
2. When fear and sor - row are all a - round us,
3. From man - y lands, ___ in man - y voic - es,

we need a ref - uge from ___ the fray. We call So -
teach us to fol - low your gen - tle call. With our So -
man - y tal - ents we ___ will bring. With un - der -

phi - a,   come walk be - side   us.   Give us the
phi - a   to walk be - side   us   we dwell se -
stand - ing,   in - sight and wis - dom   we'll do our

strength   to meet the   day.
cure   and nev - er   fall.
RE -   - i - mag - i - ning.

Last time, end

I think of Sally Hill as a grain of sand inside the oyster shell of the church. She gathered the Re-Imagining resources, and each element—people, words, music, dance, art, and ritual—added its own luster and luminosity. We now have a Re-Imagining pearl inside the church which cannot be ignored. All of us who participated are energized grains of sand who can go out into the world and create strands of pearls miles and miles long; we can encircle the globe. This song is dedicated to Sally Hill.

Sue Swanson lives in Woodbury, Minnesota, with her husband and two sons. She attends Arlington Hills United Methodist Church, where she works with Dayspring choir and chairs the administrative board. She is vice-president of Metro East District United Methodist Women and an account executive for AT&T, where she works with video-conferencing equipment.

Naming God

INGELINE NIELSEN

Never in my life did I experience God's wisdom at work in quite the same way. The conference had been very carefully prepared in the theological sense. In the opening ritual, we began by reaffirming God's many names: the biblical and nonbiblical ones; the names of saints and other holy men and women; then the names of grandmothers, mothers, and friends who had in some way revealed God to us. This continued until we arrived at the point where—would you believe it?—we wrote our own names as those of God.

What a powerful experience it was to write your own name for the first time as one of God's names! And also to read and say your neighbor's name as God's. Try it for a day or for a lifetime. See your wife, your husband, child, servant, adversary, friend, or colleague as God's namebearer, and realize the difference it makes in your relationship.

Precisely because God is higher, deeper, and wider than any single denomination or religion can attempt to fathom, we need to widen the limited and often exclusive image of God that we have learned. If we believe that each person—female or male, non-Christian or Christian, hetero- or homosexual, oppressed or powerful, to name but a few—is made in the image of God, then we have a lot of rethinking and hard work to do in our churches: to dismantle autocratic hierarchies, to take down the walls that separate us, to integrate outcasts, to listen to each other, and then do justice in love—all this because we re-imagine God.

We came together in the Re-Imagining Conference to live without the need to fear and defame the other—whoever that might be—to acknowledge God's power and freedom of revelation to all people and not predominantly to male Christians, and to affirm and celebrate God's presence in us. And that is why we came away from it liberated, with a newfound confidence and assurance, a joyful responsibility, and an acute sense of being in God's good company.

Ingeline Nielsen was born and raised in Germany during the war; acquired a doctor of philosophy degree and an American husband in Austria; and in Hong Kong produced four children and built a pipe organ for the Chinese University, where she was professor of organ. After three years in the United States, she moved to Geneva, Switzerland, where her husband continued with refugee work while she became the resident organist for the Ecumenical Centre and involved herself with feminist theology. In Zimbabwe, Africa, she encounters all sorts of Christian and religious beliefs.

A Voice from Brooklyn

NANCY E. K. SCHAEF

I am a lifelong United Methodist and a pastor's wife, and I attended the Re-Imagining Conference. It is one of those rare events in life that continues to effect change as the months extend long past the event itself. I find it difficult to talk of being born again. That language has been taken from me by those who have brutally abused so many with their terminology. Nonetheless, words and experiences of the conference are still alive and reproducing. I wrote this poem on my fiftieth birthday, New Year's Eve, 1994.

The Affirmation of Faith of a Graying, Overweight Fifty-Year-Old Woman with One Functioning Ovary

I believe the juices that flow from
> *lovemaking*
baptize the earth
with love
and make more love
> *and thus,*
>> *we must follow the motto:*
>> *make love not war.*

I believe tears are necessary for
> *the trees to grow,*
> *birds to sing,*
> *and*
> *hearts to beat.*

I believe the real gatekeepers of the Pearly Gates are
> *Dorothy Parker*
> *Emma Goldman*
> *Nina Simone*
> *and Mae West;*
>> *and that they should all be canonized as saints*
>> *in every religion.*

I believe the passion of revolution is the richest form of devotion.

172

I believe electric lighting is bad for the eyes and that
    all light bulbs stronger than forty watts should be outlawed.

I believe God's only error of creation was creating fish without arms.
    It doesn't seem fair they should be swimming all that time without arms.

I believe saunas are hallowed holy places—
    only if you're naked.

I believe in family—
    —that blood is thicker than water
    —that the links between generations are holy ties
    —that no one dare say anything about my family without fear of death.
      (of course, I'm allowed the privilege to curse any and
      all of them for their mistakes.)

I believe the skyline of New York is an empowering and energizing sight
    and
    that if I didn't see it at least once a day, I would die.

I believe greed is a sin
and an act of conduct that
    guarantees entrance directly to Hell.

I believe in the Sandinistas.

I believe singing is the best form of healing.
    —alone, it is self-affirming,
    —within community,
      it is binding and empowering.

I believe lovers cannot be lovers unless they share
    the same taste in music.

I believe dancing is a holy act.

My sweetest memory was on a warm April day in '86
    when a poor, Nicaraguan campesino
      —who had nothing
      —who lived on borrowed land
      —who heard bombs paid for by my tax dollars
      from his bed every night—
    gave me the only color from his garden—
      a hibiscus flower.

My saddest memory
  was kissing my Cousin Annie's
    dead cold face good-bye—
    and laying her casket in the grave.

I am sorry everyone can't be born on New Year's Eve.

I believe evicting senior citizens is a sin.

I believe that having someone believe in you is the most important
  act of love and friendship
    that can ever happen to you.

My favorite people
  cry,
  demonstrate,
  write poetry
  and
  understand everything I say.

My most unfavorite people
  are Jesse Helms,
  and ministers
    who say "Gawd Allmyyyy—teee"
    and "Jeeeez—suuus Chrrrr—istt!"

I believe in
  Shamans,
  laughter,
  Pro-Choice,
  that alcoholism is hereditary
    and
  that you should give people roses when they're alive . . .
    and when they're dead.

I believe the CIA killed Kennedy
  that Cuba is a special place
  and
  that the Pope should move there.

I believe that if the Pope were a woman,
  there would be no Pope.

I believe the '53 Chevy was the best car ever made.

I believe in hard work
    —that people die without it
    —that people need it to be creative
    —that it is a sin to deprive people of it.

I believe that wisdom comes to us from a Goddess
    and the Goddess' name is Sophia,
    and that Sophia is over fifty!

I am willing to try to believe
    that Kevin Costner was right
    when
    he said he believed in

                "slow
                deep
                soft
                wet
                kisses
                that last three days."[4]

I'd like to try it before I'm sixty.

Nancy E. K. Schaef is a fifty-year-old feminist and lifelong New Yorker and Methodist. After a successful fifteen-year career as a television producer, she attended and graduated from the law school of the City University of New York. She has been the wife of a United Methodist pastor for twenty-one years and believes that re-imagining our faith is the only thing that will restore the church for the next generation. Currently, she works as a legislative aide to an elected official in Brooklyn.

PART FIVE

Going On

Our time together has offered us transformation; it has demanded courage. In

gathering to listen, to search for God, to pray, to be at table with one another,

we have created a community of relationships in which we can feel support as

we do the work we are called to do. As we go about this work, we know that

we will continue to add to our stories

of re-membering . . .

and re-imagining . . .

Between History and Hope

MARY FARRELL BEDNAROWSKI

I was dumbfounded by the widespread negative response to Re-Imagining. I shouldn't have been. The response was exactly what a historian of women and religion in America could have—and should have—predicted. After more than twenty years of teaching courses about women in American religious history, I know some patterns only too well:

1. *That, historically, women's theological work has been looked upon as dissenting rather than participatory in nature. Historian Laurel Thatcher Ulrich remarked, in an article about Puritan women in the seventeenth and eighteenth centuries, that "well-behaved women seldom make history."[1] We should have known that if our theological work attracted the kind of attention of which historians take note, we would no longer be considered well behaved.*

2. *That concerns about women's crossing theological boundaries very often become expressed as sexual in nature. The assumption appears to be that if women are out of control theologically, they are likely to be out of control sexually as well. The fears voiced about the celebration of women's sexuality at the Re-Imagining Conference gave evidence of this pattern.*

3. *That it is easier to arouse anger, fear, and hatred than it is to foster an inclination to listen, an openness to ideas, and a willingness to postpone judgment.*

4. *That no amount of describing, explaining, or interpreting can overcome the appeal of simplistic, sensationalized distortions that confirm already formed suspicions.*

Given my knowledge of these historical patterns, why was I so optimistic about Re-Imagining, so unconcerned about wider consequences? I think, perhaps, it was the company I was keeping. Among my most poignant memories of the Re-Imagining experience are the meetings of what I came to think of as the Breakfast Club. Sally Hill, Pam Joern, later Sue Seid-Martin, and I met for breakfast every few weeks during the three years preceding the conference. We planned and worried and grew to care deeply about each other and our families. In fact, we continue to meet and expect to do so as long as we all shall live. If anything strikes me about those preconference breakfasts, it

179

was our innocence. Our worries were so local, so confined to the conference itself. Would the rituals hold together? Would everyone feel included? Would participants like the food? Would we have enough mittens and scarves for women coming from warm climates?

It was an innocence none of us should have had. As lifelong church members—Presbyterian, American Baptist, Roman Catholic—we all knew too much about the struggles of women in the church not to be aware at some level that we were asking for trouble. But it was an innocence that served us well. Without it we might have been too afraid to undertake the struggle that lay ahead.

In the end, I don't think it was innocence alone that kept us from anticipating what lay ahead. It is also the reality that as women we have had access to a different kind of church history. We have lived the history of women's resourcefulness and creativity and persistence in the churches, and we have benefited from the scholarship of women who are looking for histories that have been hidden. We know the truth of what my colleague Ann Braude at Macalester College has pointed out: that women's history *is* American religious history. "When women are present," she says, "religion flourishes, when they are absent it does not."[2] That is another pattern of American religious history that cannot be denied, but it has only recently been discovered as a new plot in the narrative. It has yet to be widely acknowledged or understood, and much of the publicity following Re-Imagining testified to this lack of understanding.

In *The Christian Century*'s annual article about the top ten religious stories of the year, the religious right was Number 1 and Re-Imagining was Number 2—at least it appeared that way at first. As it turned out, Re-Imagining was interpreted as a major story because conservative Christians responded to it negatively: "Held in November 1993, the meeting attracted little notice until the *Presbyterian Layman* . . . and *Good News,* the journal of an evangelical caucus in the United Methodist Church, charged that the conference had been rife with heresy. . . . "[3] The concluding sentence of the article indicated that the controversy had served to give conservatives "a closer hearing within the church." In other words, the Number 2 story was also, for the most part, about the religious right rather than about Re-Imagining. And the subplot was about women's theological work perceived as dissent.

I would tell the story very differently. I experienced Re-Imagining as a vital, public manifestation of women's theological and communal creativity. In a theological tradition in which women's voices have seldom been heard publicly, it is big news. It is, in fact, historic news, worthy of attention as the main event.

What is it that keeps us innocent and hopeful when the oldest lessons of history would lead us to be otherwise? Perhaps it is the certain knowledge that hope is infinitely preferable to cynicism and despair. Or it may be the ever-increasing knowledge of newer lessons from history—not just of women's oppression and exclusion in the churches but of our persistent, creative, and resilient presence. Or again it may be the company we keep: of those who experienced Re-Imagining as a joyful, faithful, and astonishing event and who have learned over and over how grace makes all things new—even old lessons from history.

Mary Farrell Bednarowski, a Roman Catholic layperson, is professor of religious studies at United Theological Seminary of the Twin Cities, where she has served on the faculty since 1976. Her work focuses on theological creativity in American religious history with an emphasis on women, new religions, and literature. She is the author of American Religion: A Cultural Perspective *and* New Religions and the Theological Imagination in America. *Her book,* Women's Religion in America, *is in progress.*

Electronic Heat

SHAWN VICTORIA MACDONALD

I admit it: I signed onto PresbyNet/Ecunet as a result of Re-Imagining. Someone had suggested it to me in passing, and I had yet to try out the modem on my new laptop computer, so a week after Re-Imagining I was on-line. I saw others talking about Re-Imagining in the big chat meetings.

"I just got back and wondered if there is a meeting anywhere on the Net about Re-Imagining."

"My wife went to Re-Imagining, and I'd love to join a meeting to hear more about it. She can't quit talking."

"I got my registration in too late, but I'd love to hear about Re-Imagining."

It seemed that no one else was starting a meeting, so with about a week's on-line experience under my bra—and a fair amount of technical confidence—I joined the ranks of meeting organizers by starting the meeting, "Reimagining Reflections." For the first month, people checked in to share just what the name called for: their reflections. The meeting notes read like testimonials from summer camp.

Then in mid-December things changed. A "Leadership Alert" from the *Presbyterian Layman* started to arrive in select people's mailboxes, and the accusations started to fly. I was just a regular participant at Re-Imagining, and suddenly I was getting a crash course in crisis management.

I insisted that "Reimagining Reflections" be a place for reflections only. Finally a computer-whiz pastor and true peacemaker from Ohio opened the meeting, "Reimagining Reactions." That meeting generated a thousand notes in just over four weeks in February and March of 1994.

The on-line debate was fast and furious. One pastor read through Elizabeth Johnson's *She Who Is* in about a week and declared he would give her a C in theology. Another maintained that a Re-Imagining participant wouldn't know a heresy if it bit her in the heel. Even the participants discovered amazing things. Those sensual images in the milk and honey ritual were drawn from the Song of Songs, an astute Bible reader informed us.

The same five charges were repeated over and over in the meeting and answered in various ways by participants and nonparticipants alike. In the midst of the whirlwind, a new network was formed. People discovered like-minded people in other parts of the country. News was passed in quieter channels about ways that people were discovering to deal with the controversy within the church as a whole and the Presbyterian church particularly. That network made plans for the Presbyterian General Assembly and for our defense in the midst of raging charges. Letters and petitions were circulated through E-mail.

Once the General Assembly was over in June, contributions to the "Reimagining Reflections" meeting diminished to a trickle; but the quiet, underground network continued to be a place for sharing new ideas and discovering new friends. Re-Imagining has continued on-line with a new network of people—men and women from various denominations throughout North America. And, as with other things surrounding Re-Imagining, if it weren't for the heat we would never have found one another.

Shawn Victoria MacDonald pastors a Presbyterian and United Methodist parish in Minnesota. When she was four years old, her mother decided it was time to take her to Sunday school. Her mother chose the Presbyterian church because, in her opinion, it was the most open to women. That was in Los Angeles in the 1960s.

God Makes the Impossible Possible

CHRIS CHALLENGER

It started at Windsor Castle. She was not in residence, but we were—an assorted job lot of newly appointed English clerics, plus a few from elsewhere, thrown together to sort out ministry in the new millennium. We were attending services in the Saint Georges Chapel (resting place of British monarchs), hearing lectures in a thousand-year-old hall built into the castle wall, and staying in a house built in the time of the first Elizabeth with plumbing of Victorian ilk. There I met a large young American priest from Minneapolis. Discovering that he intended to visit the North, I offered him a lift and hospitality on the way. Paul, with whom I share the bungalow, is used to my arriving with sundry oddbods from abroad and welcomed him.

We had an enjoyable day with the Yankee priest, trying to give him a flavour of the edges of Celtic England, in which the true faith was held and still may be revived if you scrape the surface of the Church of England. We wanted to show him Whitby, or Streanaesalch, where the fatal decision was made to agree with Rome under the motherly eye of Saint Hilda, but we could only tell him the real story. King Oswy of Northumbria was of the Celtic Christianity, but his wife was of the new Roman persuasion. They both religiously kept to the rules of Lenten abstinence, including chastity; but their Lenten periods did not coincide, so for a whole two months or more neither partner got their oats. This would never do! Oswy persuaded the parts of the church to meet to agree on one date for Easter. Points were pleaded passionately; and, in the end, the king went his wife's way. That led us down the Roman path and, incidentally, into the problems of the priesting of women.

We were able to show him Rievaulx Abbey, desecrated at the time of the Reformation as a result of another king's failure to find satisfaction. (How mundane is the way history is made. I wonder if in the future, herstory will be influenced by the same sort of driving force.) The abbey is still exquisite in its ancient ruinous splendour in the peaceful riverside setting. A moment of startling revelation was given to me that day at Rievaulx. I had gone to a little cottage on the grounds of the abbey to inquire after a nun who had been my spiritual advisor. She is a gentle, middle-aged, wise, and deeply spiritual woman, a medical professor, much revered by those who have had the privilege of knowing her. I introduced our tall young visitor to her, and she said, "Good morning, Father." The humble nature of the greeting struck me, as did the pure incongruity of the situation; all the frustration and anger I held that this woman could not be a priest and had to defer to the young man did somersaults inside me. His gentle and respectful reply made me realize his different comprehension of the situation, his understanding of her priesthood and its true nature, setting aside the need for her to be ordained a priest (as she later was). He, a man and a priest, seemed to have no problem with women as priests; whereas I, a woman brought up in the "Thou shalt not" world, did.

Some time later we had a letter from the young priest, saying we must come and stay to go to the Re-Imagining Conference, and he had lots of other things lined up, and he had registered me, and we couldn't say no. Despite no money and little experience of travel, we plucked up courage for the big adventure and flew out to the wonderful city of Minneapolis.

There followed a madly spinning kaleidoscopic three weeks—packed with new noises, new smells, new voices with strangled vowels and crucified vocabulary, new laughter and new tears, new concepts and new quiets, new attitudes and new prayers—describable only in phrase and half-sentence. The candles in the study, lit each morning for worship, with varying icons and strange words for the Office. Red autumn streets, huge vacuums that pushed the leaves into lines and others that swept them up and caged them neatly to protect the roses. Furniture left on the pavement and aeroplanes skimming the city roofs. Twin sets of skyscrapers, tiny cathedrals and a big abbey church. A woman consecrating the communion and the people seeing nothing strange in that. Foods cooked in the style of every nation. The land of Hiawatha, plains and falls and streams, and the great Mississippi. Sleeping in a church vestry with the Amtrak lumbering and mournfully giving voice at regular intervals. American Indian children, stretch limousines, and spectacularly short and to-the-point preparation for baptism. Taking the sacrament to the sick and housebound on foot in full white robes through the street. Hearing the objections of Episcopalians United at the consecration of the bishop, and the polite, controlled reply of the presiding bishop, knowing the deeply cutting pain for objectors and the subjects of their complaint, and wondering why we hurt ourselves. Standing nerve-wracked to read a gospel, give a sermon, distribute the wine, and play the minor roles due to a deacon in many differing places.

Then I met the women. These were priests—they really were! I was meeting the impossible. It was possible.

Back to the school buses and the myriad city lakes, the superb art museums, the endless kindness, service, hospitality. Halloween really celebrated, in Latin American style, a dinner party engulfed by people with different codes and ways of expressing. Orange pumpkin bags for the leaves and pumpkin pie, and the Mall of America, the United States' version of our Metro Centre, but with a hat that actually enhanced my appearance.

The conference. Desperate shyness and inadequacy. The sweatshirt that actually was extra large, with room to spare, so I could be one of the crowd until I found my level. The table, anchor point and home in the sea of strangers, meeting and giving, yet finding our integrity. Learning how to follow the book and relax into the pattern of song, dance, word, and action; but first the drummers, declaring their welcome and triumph in welcome, and the ever-changing paintings, layer on layer of experience through the brush, hand, body, and paint. The noise! Oh, the noise. All those loving and enthusiastic and outgoing and varied American women in one room. My quiet English reserve gobsmacked by it all. Listening to the people whose books I had read in the feminist theology section of the master of arts course at Durham. Then Lois Wilson's stunning but gentle re-imagining for children, and at last a tool to raise awareness, used time and again in sermons and lectures. The growth of the tablecloth and the parallel growth of relationships, the need to ask that it be preserved somewhere, at least until I had worked at or forgotten the feelings stroked, scribbled, and scrubbed into it.

Then back out after good-byes and photos and gifts and unkept promises to keep in touch, to a meal in an Israeli restaurant, surrounded by caring and by normal people, and into the swirl again. Waiting on my own in the dark, moving bus stops to be with others, pursued by mendicants who can spot an easy target, and all the time the traffic driving in the wrong direction. The soup kitchen, where parents first fed the children, then the dogs, and finally themselves. The tearing of partings, the last night on the floor, the long flight home, and insensibility in my own bed.

"Did you have a good time?" the polite inquiry comes. "Oh, yes, thank you," the equally polite reply. It is only a few with whom one can trust such treasures of joy and disturbance, and only because they already know and love you. The resource of memory meant that in the dark days of bitterness and hurt leading to 21 May I was empowered by the knowledge that it is right and just that women should be enabled to have true equality in priesthood as they have before the Lord.

So this part of the story ends as it began, encased in the deep roots of history—one minutely insignificant drama played out where so much had been seen before: in York Minster with the soaring arches, the magnificent warm white stone, the floating music, and the dancing souls. It was my place of birth and schooling and recent chaplaincy, but it is a place steeped in hundreds of years of worship, hundreds of years in the making, and every stone a witness to love. There the succession continued, there the order of

Melchizedek found its latest members, there the grace of orders was given and received, and there the power of the Holy Spirit was confirmed to be the messenger of the living God who is unconditional love. To add joy to joy, one of the white-robed throng of clergy was an American priest who played such a part in freeing my spirit to believe in the strength of my womanhood.

This was the new beginning, women in the Church of England in ministry as priest and woman, different but empowered by God whose plans for the world include using anyone He wants to go on helping to recreate the world in Her image.

The Reverend Chris Challenger was one of the women in the historic first ordination of women to the priesthood of the Church of England in 1994. She now serves as chaplain to a community and mental health trust in Middlesbrough.

Continuing Life in Brazil

LUIZA ETSUKO TOMITA

After the marvelous days we spent at the Re-Imagining Conference, where we had a deep experience of solidarity and creativeness, we came back to our life in Brazil. We got together to evaluate our experience of renaming the Sacred and reconstructing new images of God. We felt absolutely happy and enriched, so we planned to work with the material received with our women's groups, particularly concerning feminist spirituality. This wasn't completely new to us, but it was absolutely new for the majority of the Christian population in our country.

I was invited to write an article about the Re-Imagining Conference and feminist theology for one of our biggest newspapers in São Paulo. That small article was published in March 1994. I would like to comment on the various reactions as this newspaper article reached people who had never heard of feminist theology or any image of God beside the patriarchal image of Male/Father.

Women in general showed interest and expressed hope. Some men seemed surprised with the way women were becoming conscious of our gender. But most of the men were aggressive, mad with my audacity to speak of a new image of God, when I wrote that "women will only get the liberation when God loses the male image." These men could not conceive of a different image of God or of women claiming a better place in church than the place of humble service.

However, two months ago, I was greeted by a feminist militant whose brother had told her about my article and had shown a great interest in the subject. I believe we can change attitudes, hard as it is, probably amidst increasing persecutions and marginalizations.

Our group would like to send all our sympathy to the Re-Imagining Conference planners for the violent attacks the conference has suffered from various conservative churches and organizations. We would like to point out that prophets are never understood in their own country or their own age, because they announce the new.

For the centennial of the Women's Bible in 1995, we greet all women who believe Sophia is calling us to fight for a new world of justice for all women and men, for all classes, nations, and races.

Luiza Etsuko Tomita is a feminist theologian, teaching New Testament and feminist theology at Catholic seminaries in Brazil. She is also coordinating feminist groups such as NETMAL (Nucleum of Theological Studies of Women in Latin America) and CDD (Catholics for a Free Choice) in Brazil.

Another Fine Women's Conference

MARY E. HUNT

When the dust settles after the Re-Imagining controversy, I predict that history will show the event to have been extraordinary in its ordinariness. I do not mean to detract from a certain cachet of being in the media limelight and between the cross hairs of conservatives' theological weapons. But in all candor, my reaction to the conference was to note how much it resembled and built upon so many other such events I have attended in twenty years of feminist conference-going.

This may horrify opponents when they realize that their people, and in some cases their funds, have supported other such events. It may disappoint proponents (especially those who were not there), for whom Minneapolis, to hear it told, sounds like the last stop before heaven. But the wonderful event of November 1993 was, happily, just another in a long line of wonderful women's conferences at which thousands of women are nurtured, challenged, and encouraged to share their wealth of insights and experiences with others when they go home.

I went home from Minneapolis to WATER, the Women's Alliance for Theology, Ethics, and Ritual, a nonprofit educational organization in Silver Spring, Maryland. The next day, three Australians, a WATER intern from Germany, a California student intern, assorted WATER staff and friends, all of whom had been to Re-Imagining, joined me for a debriefing. Two Brazilian participants arrived later in the day. As we all sat down to lunch and gave thanks in our own languages, I was reminded of so many international religious community gatherings where women have hosted and been hosted all over the world. It all felt very familiar, and it felt good—the way life should be and surely what it means to be church.

In essence, Minneapolis built on what works, using the important feminist principles of diversity, participation, and respect for the unique contributions of various women. Although it was brilliantly conceived and executed, despite the glaring shortcoming of not doing the antiracism work necessary in this culture, Minneapolis in 1993 was part of a long and proud tradition of gatherings where women have empowered one another into action. From the early United States feminist theologians' get-togethers at Alverno College, the summer programs for seminarians and women ministers at Grailville, the countless workshops sponsored by the Women's Theological Center, the Resource Center for Women and Ministry in the South, WATER, and many other feminist groups, the road to Minneapolis was a short one; and Minneapolis, with all due respect, was a delightful stop on the road. Other paths have been trod on other continents by women with equal creativity and imagination.

I do not mean to suggest that Minneapolis was the same old-same old. Our debriefing stories were enthusiastic about the fine presentations and innovative modes employed in Minneapolis. Moving whole tables of people to different places in the room was new, as was the Plexiglas podium that speakers so gracefully adapted to as they turned toward everyone at some point in their presentations. But I want to emphasize what few have recognized—namely, from my perspective, that Re-Imagining was part of a long chain of events, both here and abroad, which are remaking the world.

The music, for instance, reminded me of a women's band in Frankfurt, Germany, that played on the high altar of the main cathedral when I lectured there on women-church, a triumph of the local women's ingenuity and resolve. The conference music was linked to Carolyn McDade, Ysaye Barnwell, Marsie Silvestro, and Carole Etzler, who have worked to find our voices over the years. The dance was like many spirals we have danced before, ancient in style but ever renewing our spirits. The many stages around the conference hall reminded me of the satellite stage model we had pioneered at the 1987 gathering in Cincinnati, "Women-Church: Claiming Our Power." The sterling quality of the workshops reminded me of a Swiss women-church gathering in Interlaken three years ago, where serious discussion, widespread participation, and legendary Swiss efficiency made a one-day conference into a life-changing experience.

The meals in Minneapolis were an integral part of the conference. As we ate the traditional Minnesota Thanksgiving dinner, I was returned to the Chicago conference of 1983, "From Generation to Generation: Woman-Church Speaks." That was a sit-down dinner for more than a thousand people, which was for me a eucharist—the first time in my adult life as a Roman Catholic woman that I felt I was celebrating communion as a full person. Such meals have power beyond the bodily sustenance they provide. In Minneapolis, it was as much the wonder of that evening's being together—literally from the far corners of the world—that was eucharistic as the ballyhooed nectar brunch on Sunday, which critics mistakenly took for the only communion. Indeed, in Minneapolis, as so often happens in ecumenical women's groups, eucharist and communion took a range of forms—not from disrespect but creativity, not from defiance but genuine efforts to be in union through table-sharing.

The same thing happens where women gather in Buenos Aires, Montevideo, Santiago, Manila, and Melbourne. There is no magic to it—just plenty of hard work, attention to detail, and boundless hospitality, which create an environment where learning and loving can happen. That was the achievement of Re-Imagining, and happily it has been achieved before and since.

Perhaps I see the big picture this way because I have the privilege of working on feminist issues in religion as my primary job or because I started going to such conferences when I was quite young. (Writer Carol Adams and I chuckle that we were in child care together at our first American Academy of Religion gathering, when, in truth, we were at least able to vote.) Or better, it is because I understand the backlash against Re-Imagining as a cheap shot against an easy target. Let those who decry it take in the fact that such conferences are but the tip of a very big iceberg—intellectual as well as spiritual—that is moving inexorably toward the transformation of patriarchal churches in a patriarchal world. Let them take on a panel of feminist scholars instead of isolating a woman minister struggling to do her job.

The very ordinariness of the gathering is indeed its strongest defense against such backlash. There are dozens more scholars to back up, reinforce, and otherwise fortify those whose reputations have been besmirched (in my circles, enhanced) by out-of-context renderings of our words. There are plenty of musicians, artists, and dancers to carry on the embodied messages of justice, pleasure, and peace in subsequent events. There are children aplenty to grow into the roles of planners and participants. There is imagination unending to continue the process as it builds on the solid foundation of decades of feminist work in religion.

I predict that the ordinariness of the Re-Imagining Conference will eventually become obvious. What happened in 1993, continued in the local Minneapolis meeting in 1994, and goes on in so many other places around the world as the Ecumenical Decade: Churches in Solidarity with Women gives way to a new century, will eventually become a normative theological mode. Then the long chain of events to which Re-Imagining is connected will be called *church history,* and we who have participated will be called *faithful.*

Mary E. Hunt, Ph.D., is a feminist theologian from the Roman Catholic/women-church tradition who cofounded and codirects WATER, the Women's Alliance for Theology, Ethics and Ritual in Silver Spring, Maryland. She teaches women's studies at Georgetown University and is the author of Fierce Tenderness: A Feminist Theology of Friendship.

A Letter of Gracious Dissent

JEAN W. DUMAS

9 February 1994

As of this writing, I am requesting that you not release my name, address, or any other information you may have about me at any time. I attended the event in November and chose not to stay. I could not reconcile the events and lectures against my own Christology. The experience was nonetheless a positive one for me. I learned more about my own faith understanding as a woman. I appreciate the need for women to have this type of experience and respect the right of women to grow and stretch in our journeys of faith. My growing and stretching are simply in a different direction.

Thank you for offering a challenging voice to our often complacent Christian experience. It is good to stir the waters in order to create a healthy conversation. I hope the conversation will remain healthy.

I choose to walk in a different path and find ways to bring change by other approaches. God be with you and me, as we walk together, even as we walk separately.

Yours in Christ,
Jean W. Dumas

The Reverend Jean W. Dumas has withdrawn her request for anonymity. She finds her vocation is to serve God in and through the church. Her life is founded in a traditional family committed to ministry in the United Methodist Church. God's call has not been so much her choice as it has been her response to God's choosing.

A Change of Heart

SALLY L. HILL

It happened during the first months of the backlash. I was drowning in a sea of vicious rhetoric; gathering courage from an ocean of supportive letters; sending out reams of material requested by innumerable unknown people; and most of all hanging onto the phone, listening, interpreting, and rejoicing at stories of renewal, crying with people who were experiencing retaliation.

I am a Presbyterian clergywoman, ordained in 1976. I grew in the faith in this church I called home. I was nurtured, supported, trained, called into leadership, nudged into service, challenged to seek justice, and prayed into being. Yet it was members and organizations within my denomination who were leading the parade of accusers and name-callers. Leaders of my denomination were allowing the church to be torn apart by a mean-spirited segment of the church. They were not only not supporting staff and members who attended Re-Imagining but were finding a scapegoat in one of the church's leaders.

It didn't take long to know I was depressed. I lost my sense of humor. I was in danger of losing my charity toward others. I lost my faith in the denomination in which I had been ordained. Leave it behind, I lectured myself. God and Jesus, friends and family, my congregation, other individual congregations and denominations were sustaining me. I did not need the Presbyterian Church (U.S.A.). And yet, to contemplate letting it go was a deep and painful loss for me.

Late in the spring of 1994, I received a call from an organizer of the national More Light conference, which was to be held in Minneapolis. This network of sixty-seven Presbyterian congregations that declared themselves open to gay and lesbian participation in the life and leadership of their churches is working to change attitudes and policies within the Presbyterian Church (U.S.A.). The organizer asked me to come to breakfast on one of the conference days to visit with people who had attended Re-Imagining and to hear stories of what was happening in their lives because of the conference.

After the breakfast and a conversation full of energy and pain, I drove away remembering the faces and stories of the people I had met there. Many of them—perhaps most of them—were gay or lesbian themselves or were the parents or relatives of homosexuals. While driving along Minnetonka Boulevard, a great clarity washed over me. The people I had met are among the

194

most despised and rejected in the church of Jesus Christ. But they have not given up on the church, for they know themselves as children of God, created in God's image. Through rejection after rejection they have hung in, for they are all called. In turn, they are calling the church to re-imagine itself to include all of its children.

Who was I, when an ill wind blew, to give up?

The Reverend Sally L. Hill is a retired Presbyterian pastor and professional ecumenist. She was ordained in 1976 and served as associate pastor at Saint Luke Presbyterian Church in Wayzata, Minnesota, before becoming director of the Twin Cities Metropolitan Church Commission, a coordinating and program agency of the Greater Minneapolis, Saint Paul Area, and Minnesota Councils of Churches, where she served until her 1994 retirement. In 1993, the Minnesota Women's Press *named her one of ten 1993 Newsmakers of the Year for her work as staff coordinator for the Re-Imagining Conference. She is a weaver, wife, mother, and grandmother of two.*

The Church of Reconciliation

LINDA FICKLIN WEBER

Groups of women and men from the Church of the Brethren gathered informally each evening of the Re-Imagining Conference. Much of the talk centered on issues and concerns related to our church: the moving of our theological seminary and the selling of its property, sexual harassment by men in church leadership positions and how the church deals with it, and the twenty-year struggle to change the name of the church to include women. Out of deep concerns and frustration came the suggestion that we could change the church name for ourselves, since the last five-year effort to proceed through church channels had ended at the 1993 Annual Conference with the standing committee's taking no action.

It was now Saturday evening, and the Re-Imagining Conference would end the next morning. Our dialogue and prayer continued. Several names were suggested and discussed until the name *Church of Reconciliation* emerged and won consensus. Reconciliation has long been a part of the Brethren heritage; based on Matthew 18, it is vital to our faith and speaks to our strong belief in peace with justice.

We wanted to share our excitement with the conference participants the next morning, but we hesitated, struggling with our concern not to cause separation or alienation. This courageous, audacious step could not be taken lightly. As we are all active, committed members of our church, we had no intention of dissociating from our denomination. Yet we all felt we must move. We knew the conference had given us the momentum and the openness to what we believed was the Spirit's leading. When we reached consensus, we had the power and the spirit, and we knew it was important to make our statement at the conference so that we could leave with our vision.

On Sunday morning twenty of us, all women, went to the platform in the center of the room. It was a glorious moment as we joined hands in a circle, facing outward toward all the other women and men, and listened to the words of the statement we had drafted:

> *In light of the challenge to re-imagine and live* into *the vision;*
> *In light of being tired of saying, "Yes, Virginia, there ARE sisters among the Brethren,"*

In light of having worked through the proper channels for over twenty years, trying to achieve a name change that clearly includes women, only to get most recently a committee appointed to study whether the time was right to appoint a committee to consider changing the name of the denomination;

In light of the fact that it has become too painful for some of us to keep "explaining" the many positive aspects of our denomination when the name contradicts our words;

And, in light of the fact that our last name change came from the actions of grassroots groups;

We, therefore, most of the sisters and a brother gathered at Re-Imagining, have decided to stop asking *permission and are pleased to announce that we have taken a step toward a new, inclusive name for our denomination.*

This name was conceived by the Holy Spirit in an incredible meeting last evening,

it reflects our heritage as one of the historic peace churches,

it speaks of an ongoing process which is necessary for justice as well as peace,

and it proclaims the vision toward which men and *women have worked in our denomination since our beginnings in Germany.*

Therefore, we invite all who support this vision and who wish to bring it into reality

to begin to use the name, The Church of Reconciliation,

for that which has been known as the Church of the Brethren.

Thank you for being on the journey with us and for your visible support.

We pray that God will bless our efforts in the struggle to live faithfully within, and to bring new life into, our beloved denomination.

After just a few sentences, applause and cheering burst out. The gathering's spontaneous affirmation continued, ending with a standing ovation and their sung blessing.

Since that morning much has happened. At first, there was much flurry and anxiety in our church office. Officials wanted names of those involved. A statement was issued saying we were not official representatives of the denomination but might speak as individuals. Staff members were told they were not to be initiators or leaders on issues such as the name change. The church moderator then sent a letter to all pastors, district executives, and standing committee members, telling them of our action and suggesting that we look toward 2008—the three hundredth anniversary of the denomination and the one hundredth anniversary of the name *Church of the Brethren*—for a name change.

Nothing further has happened within the denominational structure. The officers have not talked with the women, and we have been told by official persons that the name-change issue is dead. It is not dead for the women who are tired of being ignored, left out, and told to wait fifteen more years. Our church needs real, honest inclusion now as well as the new life that a new name can bring. Although the issue was nowhere on the agenda for this year's Annual Conference, our group, the Womaen's Caucus, brought it to life there. Our booth featured Wittenberg doors, with our resolution on one side and space for response on the other. The Womaen's Caucus had buttons saying "2008 Is Much Too Late." Most important, the tape from the Re-Imagining Conference of our reading of our statement played over and over.

Our church has had several name changes. We have been called *Neue Taufers* (New Baptists), German Baptists, German Baptist Brethren, as well as Church of the Brethren. Changing our name is not an unusual, rare event. Today *brethren* is defined as an archaic term for the plural of *brother*. Our church is not made up of only brothers; over half of us are sisters, and we hope we are not archaic. Names are important. It is by our names that we are known. Even Pope John Paul II, when meeting one of our women, commented, "Church of the Brethren? But you're a sister."

Some of our sisters began this effort to change our name over twenty years ago. Many have struggled in the years since to have our voices heard. Now the women's voices have been heard. Over two thousand people from forty-nine states and twenty-seven countries and many denominations and faith groups heard us in Minneapolis. All our pastors, district executives, standing committee members, Annual Conference officers, denominational staff, and church members have heard the news. Other conferences, meetings, and gatherings now know of the possibilities of the name *Church of Reconciliation*.

Church of Reconciliation is not an official name, nor has it come from an official body. It has come from the hearts of Brethren women, led by the Spirit. As such, it is movement, which we hope will lead to more movement. Those supporting this movement can now live faithfully into the re-imagined vision of a church where all are included, working for peace with justice, a church of reconciliation. The struggle goes on.

Linda Ficklin Weber, D. Min., is a former schoolteacher, Gestalt therapist, and general board staff member for the Church of the Brethren. She has worked for many years on women's issues. Her four children and twelve grandchildren are prime motivators for involvement in local, national, and global political arenas. Her dissertation dealt with women and men transforming patriarchy.

Accepting the Challenge

DEE E. MILLARD

What am I doing attending a theological conference? What am I exposing myself to? Am I going to be involved in a radical feminist organization? What is re-imagining all about anyhow? These questions were in my mind as I got ready to go to Re-Imagining.

It actually began a day early for me. I attended a preconference event focusing on the urban American Indian experience. During that day, our group heard articulate American Indian women discuss the accomplishments of their people and address areas for growth. The day ended with a celebration meal and dancing. It was my introduction to a conference that would hold joy, affirmation, and challenge for me.

Sister José Hobday, one of the presenters who gave me joy and affirmation for my journey, is of Seneca Iroquois decent. She told a Native American creation story and a lesson on greeting morning. At creation, woman's first action was waking up man; since then women have moved forward creatively and need to continue moving forward. When we greet morning, according to Sister José Hobday, first we walk into nature, next we walk into ourselves, and last we walk into the mystery of the unknown.

As I wrote in my journal later, I realized that, amidst the joy and affirmations, strong challenges were issued. A part of me did not want to be a flag-carrying activist, but a larger part of me knew I was already a vocal human-rights advocate. With this new awareness of myself, I wondered how I would meet the challenges of re-imagining in my own life. But then I realized I have an opportunity to challenge the racism and sexism in our world in my own business and in my everyday activities.

My first chance came shortly after the conference when I went to my chiropractor's office. I shared my excitement and enthusiasm about Re-Imagining and told Sister José Hobday's creation story; then I went to an examining room to wait for my chiropractor. Outside the door, I could hear a great discussion between my chiropractor and his wife and daughter who work in the office. When he came into the room, he thanked me for sharing my story. He was pleased I had stimulated a conversation on our creation process. I smiled, thanked him, and knew I had already accepted the challenge of re-imagining.

I recalled Sister José Hobday had urged us to live our lives to the fullest, to search for the ecstasy, and to enjoy. I also remembered how the conference had ended in chaos, with people dancing through the ballroom, laughing and crying, before leaving for home. It was an appropriate way to conclude, because our lives are not always going to be full of the joy and affirmation we experienced there. Instead, our lives will be filled daily with questions and the challenges of racism and sexism in our own lives and in the world.

Dee E. Millard is currently working on her master of arts degree at Saint Mary's College of Winona, Minnesota. She is specializing in human development and apprenticing in sacred storytelling. In her own business, she is a spiritual director and an alternative health consultant. She is employed full time at US West, with twenty-six years of experience.

The Call

CAROLYN HENDRIXSON

*I sensed Her presence in my living room as women from new zealand and
    brazil gathered to discuss dinner choices . . .*
Women from around the world hearing
something . . . knowing . . . coming . . . She had called us.
Who among us really knew?

*I heard Her in the footsteps of the women climbing the steps of the state
    capitol to hear our women leaders. Her footsteps fell among ours as we
    gathered in the governor's reception room to safely talk stories instead of
    politics.*

*She was there in Fullest Presence when the doors of the convention center closed
    and a civic room became a Temple blessed with Holiness and filled with
    women seeking.*

And then there was That Moment.
A woman's voice read, "i found god in myself & i loved her fiercely"[4]
*She rose up powerfully from within me and grabbed my throat, her voice
    screaming so loudly my ears were ringing. Pay attention! Can you hear me
    now? I am calling you!*

I finally heard the call in a woman's voice.
She is with me every day. I turn and listen to Her.
She sends me signs, messengers, words, paths, music, and Great Love.

I sense Her.
I hear Her.
I am coming to know Her . . .

*Carolyn Hendrixson is a midlife, midwestern, United Church of Christ laywoman. She was
born in Wilmington, Delaware, and graduated from Northwestern University. She and her
husband, Peter, chose to raise their children in Minneapolis. Carolyn directs the Congregations
Concerned for Children program at the Greater Minneapolis Council of Churches.*

The Colors of Prophecy

BETSY L. NAGEL

Nice color crayons! Socially sanctioned doodling. I can do this. It certainly is a step up from my usual pen-and-yellow-pad activities at events like this. Bright clear colors. Won't mean a thing when I'm done, but it will keep my hands from being bored.

So I draw on the white paper provided for us that is covering our table. One elaborate doodle a day. Every time our talking circle moves to another table, the women with whom I am sitting carefully roll up the large white sheets of paper and move them to the next table. I tell them they don't need to be so careful, but they seem to think what I am drawing has some value. It doesn't have any meaning to me—just a way to focus on what is being said instead of fidgeting from sitting so long.

When the conference ends, I am going to leave my abstract colorings, but my tablemates are insistent. They think I should take them home and frame them. Nice woman that I am, I wouldn't want to hurt their feelings. So I leave with the drawings carefully rolled up, planning to throw them away at home.

But I can't. They nag at me, sitting on a corner of the table with a stack of books. December comes and I need to mat a picture for a gift. For some reason, I take my drawings along and buy cheap mats from the pile of discards at the frame store. My meaningless pictures sit for another month, leaning up in a corner. Why am I keeping them? I'm not even sure I like them.

It is January and I am writing in my journal. A lot has happened for me in these last months of my spiritual journey, my own internal re-imagining. I sit bolt upright. My pictures! I literally run into the next room.

These pictures depict my spiritual quest these last months. These pictures are prophecies of what was to happen to me after Re-Imagining. They are filled with meaning and symbols. How could I have not seen them?

But of course we generally cannot see prophecy except in retrospect. Just like we could not see the coming controversy over Re-Imagining. It was my hands and my soul that knew what was ahead, not my head. It was reflected in my socially sanctioned doodling.

My pictures have frames now and hang over my desk. I look at them every day and I remember November: women and men gathered together to give permission to the yearnings of our hearts for our spiritual selves and for the church. They are strong, beautiful pictures to me. They are a reminder to me to listen to the inner self, to Wisdom speaking within me.

Betsy L. Nagel is a spiritual director and therapist living in the Twin Cities, Minnesota. She is interested in the weaving of spirituality throughout daily lives, healing from abuse, and the relationship of gender to spirituality. Contemplative and Catholic spirituality inform and nourish her spiritual life and her work.

Finding Friends from Home in Faraway Places

BETTY HOLLOWAY KERSTING AND JACQULYN ROLSTAD

Eight women from Santa Fe attended Re-Imagining. They came as individuals and in most cases did not know the others were planning to attend. Since then they have helped form The Women Who Came, a large ongoing women's worship group. The Santa Fe Six, six women from the First Presbyterian Church of Santa Fe, collected hundreds of names on a petition supporting the right of women to search out their own spirituality. The petition was presented at the General Assembly of the Presbyterian Church (U.S.A.) in June 1994. Two of the women from Santa Fe speak of their personal experience of Re-Imagining.

Feeding My Soul (Betty Holloway Kersting)

For years I have searched for a safe place to speak of my deep thoughts. I have searched for a place where I could share my story. I have wanted to be able to share my response to the divine Spirit with others who were interested and would understand. As a woman who is married to a pastor (recently retired), I had been unable to express my true theological beliefs for fear of shaking the political relationship the pastor has with the congregation. After all, I was to be the model of religious orthodoxy. I trembled with joy and disbelief that the time had come when I attended the Re-Imagining Conference.

Since the conference, I have participated in a women's worship group and a book group that studies female theologians. I have received new energy to be myself. Re-Imagining has given me the courage to speak out about such public pronouncements as " . . . the God of Abraham, Isaac, Peter, and Paul." I shout within myself: What about the God of Sarah, Rebekah, Mary, and Martha? But I not only shout within. I write a note to the pastor of the church I am visiting and express my feelings. When a pastor says, "How disruptive it must have been for Abraham to have a baby at this stage of his life," I shout: What about Sarah? Whose life did this baby change the most? The discussion of this statement at coffee after church facilitated the meeting of a new woman friend who had similar feelings but didn't know anyone at church shared them.

I made another new friend from Santa Fe at the conference. We have become so close that we decided to take a Mediterranean cruise together. We spent time on the cruise searching for the mystery and spirit of the Black

Madonna at Monserrat. We toured Russian and Greek Orthodox churches, taking a new look at icons of Mary of Magdalene and Mary the mother of Jesus. We found a source for an icon of Sophia, which we purchased and which is being shipped to us.

Not only have I found courage to speak my truth, but I now have a cherished friend with whom to share my spiritual search. These experiences are feeding my soul and nurturing my life.

Number Sixty-Eight (Jacqulyn Rolstad)

I was number sixty-eight on the waiting list for the Re-Imagining Conference. I just felt it in my bones; this was the conference I was waiting for. I had no doubt that I would get there some way, and when the conference was opened to admit another hundred or so—I was in!

My only concern about the conference was that it might be the noisy I-hate-men thing. The first speaker, Mary Bednarowski, calmed those fears immediately. I thought after hearing her: This is it; it can't be better than that. The next speaker came on; two dynamic voices in one evening. Can't be anything but downhill from here. After the third speaker, I sat back and thought: How can I be so lucky to be here? It isn't that one speaker was better than another, but that each had a story to tell that was meaningful, helpful, and insightful. I relaxed and let the messages and stories take over. I cried inside at some of the stories, I laughed, I identified, I rejected, but I never felt pressured. I felt good. I was thinking, feeling, searching, and learning.

My table group was not the high point I had hoped for. I so wanted to reach out and share my fears, my joys, my beliefs, and yes, my doubts, but it just didn't happen. After I thought about it, I realized that my table connection was in my own backyard. I had come to the conference with someone from my own church whom I hardly knew. We have become good, deep, soul-searching friends, trusting and loving. We have just returned from a fourteen-day trip to the Mediterranean, and if one new friend isn't enough of a blessing, I discovered another new friend at the conference from my church. She is a friend of great depth, experience, and love. So at the grand ol' age of fifty-nine, I have two new good Christian, caring friends.

I am so much more aware of all oppressed people, especially women, who have had to struggle for justice and equality. I am committed to doing all I can for that which is right and good and fair—inside and outside of the church. I am speaking out where I was silent. It has been an exciting and exhilarating time for me within my church. Because of my report to the elders and deacons of my church (who have been extremely supportive), I was placed on our church's pastor-nominating committee. Then I was made co-chair. I feel empowered. I feel the Holy Spirit within me, as I did at the conference. Lucky number sixty-eight.

Betty Holloway Kersting is a clinical social worker and Christian educator in Santa Fe, New Mexico. She is a team manager in community mental health and psychotherapy private practice in the Denver, Colorado, area, and has been involved with Habitat for Humanity; the Teenage Pregnancy, Drug and Alcohol Task Force; and Juvenile Offenders Alternative Programs.

Jacqulyn Rolstad is a retired kindergarten teacher in Santa Fe, New Mexico, where she has lived for thirty-two years. She is a mother and grandmother, plays the flute, and loves to read and travel.

Stay a Little Longer

JILL HARTWELL GEOFFRION

I turned left out of the Hilton parking lot and cranked up the volume on the tape player. Instinctively, I began singing and swaying along with the music. I was surprised at how loudly and enthusiastically my voice joined those blaring out of the sound system.

I had heard "Stay" for the first time during the Re-Imagining weekend that was now drawing to a close. I can't remember if Sweet Honey in the Rock (an ensemble of African American women who, as the Re-Imagining literature stated, " . . . sing fiercely of being fighters, tenderly of being in love, and knowingly of being women") sang it at their concert on the second night of the conference. Maybe it had become familiar as I'd listened to the "Still on the Journey" cassette as I drove to and from the conference each day.

The clock on the wall, says it's time to go,
But I know my heart really wants you to stay a while.

As I headed west on Highway 394, I glanced up to see if there was a sunset in front of me. It was early afternoon, but it seemed to be much later—a brilliant orange afterglow time, full of the beauty of what had been and the apprehension of what seemed like a descending darkness.

When the song was over, I rewound the tape to its beginning and pushed PLAY. As my voice rejoined the women's voices, it had lost none of its passion. I sang my experience using the words of this song.

Sitting here with you is so sweet, so divine
Like the sound of the wind, whistlin thru the trees . . .

The Re-Imagining experience was a breath of fresh air in my life. After the first evening of shared worship, nourishment, listening, and talking, I barely slept. How could I? In the Re-Imagining Christian community, I had felt so at home—a rare experience for me during church events. All of me—my senses, intellect, hurts, and hopes—had been engaged by the process. I felt very alive and thus awake. I spent most of the night praying, celebrating with God the wonder of this experience. I got up the next morning feeling refreshed, excited, and ready for more.

But now, four days and nights later, the conference was over. As I sang the same words over, I felt water filling my eyes and spilling beyond them.

Wanting to honor the loss that is always a part of good-byes, I rewound the tape and let my singing of the words move me to more tears.

When I'm with you baby, not a word, needs to be said
Tender love, I'm asking you to stay . . .

I hadn't said a lot at the conference. I was surprised that when I did speak, the women around me listened carefully and heard with their ears and their hearts. Receiving understanding in such beautiful ways meant having to speak less. No wonder I was now begging the experience as a whole to stay.

I turned up the volume to its loudest setting and opened the sunroof. I wanted my prayer to be heard, even if it meant the freezing November Minnesota air was pouring in to the car. If singing at the top of my lungs to the God of the universe would make a difference, I was ready and willing.

Why don't you stay a little bit longer?

I pleaded for the conference to stay with me, even though I knew that the last session was over. I couldn't imagine or embody any other response. It seemed both pointless and meaningful. So I kept on singing.

Just to live my life with you would be so sweet, so divine . . .

How would I stay in touch with the Re-Imagining experience? I feared the worst. What if I was never again in such a creative Christian environment? Just the thought of it hurt deep, deep within. Giving voice to my apprehensions somehow moved my singing from being a prayer of lament to one of hope.

Why don't you stay a little bit longer?

In fact it was *I* who was going to stay. I had moved to the Minneapolis/Saint Paul area less than three months before. One of the realizations of the conference was that this metropolitan Minnesota environment allowed Christian women to express their love for God in beautiful, creative ways that nurtured my deep spiritual passions.

I lifted my left hand to my cheek and gently brushed my tears toward the outside of my face. I pushed REWIND and took a deep breath. I moved the fingers of my right hand across my right cheek and then pushed PLAY— again.

I turned down the volume and sang, "I'm asking you to stay with me a little longer."

Stay a little bit longer . . .

This time as the song came to an end I pushed the STOP and EJECT buttons. I was afraid of overheating the tape. I knew I would need to sing along at other times, even though I didn't know when they would be.

How could I have known that Re-Imagining was not only a conference that I had been a part of? How could I have known that as I sunk my life into the Minnesota soil of my childhood I would become part of the Re-Imagining Community of Minnesota, which did not exist yet?

One light, one breath, one spirit, one heart
One love, lives between us
When you drink, my thirst is satisfied
And when I tire I know you'll be there to give me rest . . .

Jill Hartwell Geoffrion is an American Baptist pastor studying women's studies and Christian spiritualities.

An Outsider's View

CATHERINE WESSINGER

When my good friend Mary Farrell Bednarowski told me about the Re-Imagining Conference in Minneapolis, I knew that was the place to be in November 1993. As a historian of religions, it is all I can do to keep up with the historical and anthropological work on women in the world's religions; I seldom have time to read works by feminist theologians. I saw the conference as a way to discern what was current in feminist theology by immersion in the Re-Imagining experience.

I was raised in the southeastern United States in what was then the Lutheran Church of America. A college course on Hinduism and a student trip to India in the early 1970s prompted my conversion from Christianity to Eastern modes of thought in a manner that I have subsequently learned is typically American. I left the church because I no longer believed in its teachings. My religious outlook is a highly personal syncretism not easily identified by any particular label. I have resisted labels—except that of *feminist.*

Quite honestly, I found the Re-Imagining Conference to be an astounding experience because of the nontraditional content that resonated so strongly with my own outlook. I felt very much at home at Re-Imagining and with the Christian women there, and I was amazed that this was so. I loved the boundary crossing and syncretism of Re-Imagining. From the beautiful wall-hangings representing artistic motifs from the Shinto, Chinese, American Indian, and Australian aboriginal traditions, to the American Indian women drumming and singing, I loved the multicultural beauty that was so sensitively conveyed.

After preaching to my students on the need for Christian feminist women to create new liturgies and hymns, I cried at the overwhelming beauty of the feminist hymns and the realization that such have already been created. Since I am not a Christian, I also took note that these hymns and liturgies had little or no traditional Christian content.

I was amazed and thrilled by Mary Farrell Bednarowski's call for women to re-imagine every aspect of the Christian tradition in order to give it continued life and meaning. I was astounded that Re-Imagining provided such a receptive forum for Chung Hyun Kyung's presentation of her own highly personal syncretism, which is authentically Korean and Asian and later was so widely misunderstood and denounced by theologians who did not attend the conference.

In the session on Jesus, I marveled at the statements of Delores Williams and Barbara Lundblad. Delores Williams, recalling African American women's experiences of forced surrogacy, questioned the surrogacy inherent in atonement Christology and emphasized the importance of how Jesus lived rather than how he died. She articulated her view that Jesus was killed because of the lived demonstration of his pastoral vision of what constitutes proper human relationships. Barbara Lundblad, an ordained minister in the Evangelical Lutheran Church of America, said that there are episodes and interpretations in the Judeo-Christian scriptures that cause women to gasp in horror and disbelief—particularly Abraham raising the knife over Isaac in supposed obedience to God's command and the death of Jesus on the cross to appease a vengeful Father God. Barbara openly articulated that feminists and womanists reject belief in a God that demands human sacrifice and are concerned to reinterpret their traditions to make them life-giving. Positioned outside the Christian tradition, I heartily agreed with all these statements, and I was amazed that women inside the Christian tradition would find them to be so obviously true.

Therefore, I was not surprised that conservative Christians severely criticized the Re-Imagining Conference for being heretical. From the view of traditional Christianity, it *was* heretical. I would have been more surprised if there had not been a backlash. The Re-Imagining Conference demonstrated to me that while I have been on my personal journey outside the church for the past twenty years, many women inside North American churches have been making intellectual journeys similar to mine. To my surprise, we have arrived at a similar, if not identical, destination. We have more in common with each other in our appreciation of diversity and wisdom wherever it is found than we do with conservative North Americans, who are concerned to maintain the boundaries around what they believe to be infallible truth.

Since in my work I also study new religious movements, I noted rhetoric in the backlash against Re-Imagining similar to accusations used against alternative religions that are pejoratively stigmatized as cults. Religious conservatives apparently are motivated to maintain boundaries wherever they perceive them as threatened—whether by competition from new religious groups or by feminist theology. I see the United States population becoming increasingly polarized between those who appreciate the diversity, fluidity, and complexities of the world and those who see reality in simplistic, dualist (good versus evil) terms.

I am happy to have participated in Re-Imagining and to be part of the

Re-Imagining network that developed after the conference. I say to Re-Imagining women: You need to realize that you *do* represent radical changes in your churches and theologies as theological conservatives charge. I observe this as an interested and supportive outsider looking at your relationships to your church institutions.

Catherine Wessinger is associate professor of the History of Religions and Women's Studies at Loyola University, New Orleans. She is editor of and contributor to Women's Leadership in Marginal Religions: Explorations Outside the Mainstream *and editor of* Religious Institutions and Women's Leadership: New Roles Inside the Mainstream. *She is currently writing a textbook on women in religions and cultures.*

A Vessel Full of History

HELEN BETENBAUGH

I cannot be in a gathering of Christians without the topic of Re-Imagining arising fairly quickly. What I have said again and again—apart from setting right the press's false witness on many of the specific events and rituals—is that I believe it is the single most historic event in which I will participate. Some day, when the history of the church is rewritten from the twenty-first century's perspective, I believe Re-Imagining and Minneapolis will go down with Nicaea, Chalcedon, Vatican II, and the other great councils of the church. I believe the church can never be the same again after Minneapolis in 1993—and *must* never be the same again. Formerly scattered questions have been raised in one place on the record: named, not whispered in rituals or discussed quietly in safe places. With burning intellect and blazing passions, with love for justice and the energy of feminist community touched by the Holy, a new model has been set forth. And I have discovered that I can use that model in my own life.

A little more than a year after the conference, I was to preside at a ritual for a sister feminist whose husband of twenty-eight years, a priest, had recently left her. We were going to claim her house as a safe place, bless it, and help her rewrite her future story.

As I gathered up materials on the day of the ritual, I put them all into my Re-Imagining tote bag. I called another sister who was to participate and asked her to bring a silver, china, or crystal bowl to use for water for the house blessing. When she unpacked her basket later, she offered me the small pot her daughter had made in a high-school pottery class—the same pot she had given me for the vessel I needed to take to Re-Imagining. Perfect!

Before we began the ritual, I asked everyone to share the special symbols in the clothing they wore, the actions they had taken during the day, and the things they had brought that are part of women's ways of doing things and that we would be likely to overlook if they were not named. Then it was explained that the water container had once contained the now-infamous milk and honey. Oh, the sounds that came from all over the room! Such a symbol of empowerment it became instantly. Such a humble object, infused with the Sacred. We opened with the Sophia blessing, and we were off.

May the Holy Spirit continue to fan the fires of our passion for justice and peace and inspire our work toward that end.

Helen Betenbaugh is a candidate for the Episcopal priesthood and a doctoral student at Perkins School of Theology of Southern Methodist University in Dallas, Texas. She earned a master of divinity degree with honors from Perkins School of Theology in 1993 after a distinguished thirty-year career as a church musician. She writes and lectures widely on issues of theology and disability, having used a wheelchair for eighteen years.

Moving Right Along

DOLORES COSTELLO

"We're not waiting for permission any longer!" was the cry from the podium. I sat and listened to this group of women from the Church of the Brethren, frustrated by the lack of response from their church to requests to change the name of their denomination to a more inclusive one. Their desperation resonated within me. Their struggle touched mine—a Catholic woman struggling for inclusion in a church in which I am called to discipleship by virtue of my baptism.

All the way home those words haunted me. I recalled how I, as well as many other Catholic feminists, had tried to make our voices heard by speaking out to clergy and bishops, writing letters, joining national organizations, signing petitions, and on and on. My anger flared. My mind and heart returned to those words again and again.

Do it! Sophia kept insisting in my prayer time. I argued, Who, me? Why? This is just too bizarre. No, I can't. I don't know where to begin. The idea would not disappear. Sophia/Wisdom would not take "no" for an answer.

Two weeks after the Re-Imagining Conference, I sent out a letter to eight women I sensed would be willing to attempt a Eucharist celebration. My honest assessment was that we had all the resources we needed. All these women have remarkable gifts which have been suppressed in the church's liturgies. What a crime! We needed to celebrate and utilize these gifts of the Holy Spirit. We needed to begin to take care of our own spiritual needs that the church insists on denying us.

We met for the first time in January 1994, and we planned our liturgy to take place on the Feast of the Annunciation. What more appropriate time to announce our new creation? Everything fell into place almost without effort. Because it promised to be such a creative, meaningful celebration of the Divine, we felt it would be selfish to keep it to ourselves. We invited other women to join us. The room was almost overflowing on that day, the day of the Annunciation.

We continue to worship and grow together. This past summer, we went on an overnight retreat and bonded together as a laywomen's spiritual community. We are now the Daughters of Mary Magdalene, who pray together every Monday evening and hold monthly worship services.

Bless Sophia! She has blessed us richly through the Re-Imagining experience.

Dolores Costello is a nonconforming Catholic laywoman, grandmother, and a graduate student in theology at the Saint Paul Seminary in Saint Paul, Minnesota. She is active in women's spirituality and re-visioning the new church. She holds a bachelor of arts degree from the University of Minnesota in anthropology and psychology.

He Doesn't Have to Know

HEIDI HUDNUT-BEUMLER

I almost died last month, the man said
as he stepped to the microphone.
His lips quivered as he struggled to
say with angry, mournful passion what
was on his heart.

The ears of two hundred were his.

I almost died last month,
and nobody ever prayed at my bedside
to Sophia. And I stand before this presbytery
meeting today to say—and he raised his arm
and pointed it at me—
your God is not my God! That "Re-Imagining God"
is not my God! I don't care what you say!

> *(His face grew redder than Georgia clay*
> *and his voice raised a notch.*
> *Our eyes met—held—locked—*
> *he averted his gaze and searched the room for*
> *affirmation.)*

As long as I live and when I die,
no one is ever going to pray to Sophia at my bedside.
No one ever has in all my seventy years.
No one ever will. That's all I have to say.

I rose after taking the blows.
Steadying my voice, I spoke of the many-imaged God
of Abraham, Isaac, Sarah and Rebekah,
Jesus and Mary and John: this Bible God, this Living God,
this female image Sophia-God.
We are together in this, I tried to say, reaching out with words
to clenched minds.
I believe our God is the same God
yearning to be known by you and me.

His eyes said no, and claiming victory
in his walk, he returned to his seat.

But as sure as I felt the babe that moved within me then,
I know that Sophia lives. She pulses through my body and
the world with energy and power I am only beginning to understand.

I made a promise to myself.
When the red-faced man needs Sophia again,
I will pray to her for him.

He doesn't have to know.

Heidi Hudnut-Beumler is a minister in the Presbyterian Church (U.S.A.) living in Decatur, Georgia. She is currently exploring what it means to nurture life with her husband and two young children. Prior to moving to Georgia, she served four congregations in the Northeast and Midwest.

Bane and Blessing

JERIE ROBISON SMITH

Living in Minnesota, it may be no surprise that I am Norwegian and Lutheran by birth and baptism. Because I have never lived anywhere else, at times I have been accused of being parochial. One of the blessings of Re-Imagining was that I was confronted on the issue of privilege. Even our attendance at such an event is evidence of our educational and economic privilege. I heard over and over again messages from women of color, women from other countries, and women of sexual diversity who confronted my parochialism and privilege. I appreciated being exposed to writing, thinking, and theology from sources that seemed more global than what I hear from local pulpits. I appreciated hearing an African woman's observation that North Americans are obsessed with finding community. It's true, I had to admit. We talk about it, search for it, and never seem to be part of it, even when it exists right where we are. I appreciated the voice of lesbian women. I am embarrassed by the way my church deals with sexuality and sexual diversity. Most of all I appreciated hearing and seeing women all day long for all those days. As a woman in ministry, I don't often get to hear women speak, because I am often the woman speaking. I was challenged by every speaker I heard.

At the same time, Re-Imagining was a bane in my life. Why? Because it wasn't enough. It didn't come soon enough. It disappointed me. As I listened to the women at my table and to the speakers, I was involved but almost always close to tears. I was confused by the ritual which sometimes seemed to be a womanized way of doing what we have always done. At times I felt duped. All that energy in one large room was supposed to lull me into the belief in possibilities, but I feel in the depths of my being that denominational church life in its present forms cannot continue. Somehow it seemed this gathering was created to hype me to go back to my job and make creative change happen. Why is it my responsibility to create the necessary interaction? Why were not more men present? Why were lesbians, bisexual and transgender women not more visible? And why if I voice these thoughts do some say that I am ungrateful? Is that not a denial of my experience?

After one of the caucus times for ELCA (Evangelical Lutheran Church in America) women, Elizabeth Bettenhausen was asked: "Why is it so difficult for us as Lutheran women to be able to focus on any means of action?" Elizabeth responded, "You all like your jobs too much." Then she softened it by explaining how few places exist in this culture for women to do the things they are most suited to do as professionals, and one of the few available places is the church. Her answer has stayed with me and continues to give me courage as her example has done for years.

Ivone Gebara, a feminist theologian from Brazil, says of religion, "These old clothes no longer fit. We must look for new clothes, new constructs which we probably won't live to see firmly in place. But we are called to do so by the future, by our grandchildren."[5] Re-Imagining compelled me to recommit to visioning new clothes. I yearn for a way those new clothes could be designed by the institution. I yearn for female and male designers who can experience the full potential of their power without having to worry for their personal safety or professional security. I yearn for a church that has as its basic desire the eradication of racism, sexism, and homophobia. I think that is what Jesus had in mind when he talked of a community of people who care about the extension of justice to all the world—a pluralism that includes the whole of creation.

And by the way, I continue to work on a Re-Imagining committee.

Jerie Robison Smith works on the University of Minnesota campus on behalf of the Evangelical Lutheran Church in America. She is also codirector for Spiritual Growth Retreat House, a small spiritual retreat center in Cambridge, Minnesota. She is an emerging menopausal woman reclaiming her humor and exploring the future, especially of spirituality in the twenty-first century.

weavings

KAROL E. HENDRICKS-MCCRACKEN

we exchanged mantles for a time
one from hot sierra leone, africa
one from cold bemidji, minnesota
both beloved cloths
kente cloth, a shelter, a baby carrier, a sack
grandma's work apron, bibbed, bowed, rose-budded
two nations meet
kente cloth to the at-home mother
grandma's work apron to the woman from africa
oh, not so quick
mammies' apron, servitude realized for first time
slavery never experienced, solidarity with american black women
aha, Sophia teaches
womanist theology comes alive

Karol E. Hendricks-McCracken is a Catholic-at-heart Lutheran serving as a Stephen Ministry Leader and wife and mother in a happy family in Bemidji, Minnesota.

November Easter

ANONYMOUS

Dear sisters of my talking circle,

We might just be fortunate enough to have our first real blizzard to-night. It has been four weeks since we took leave of one another. And for me, those four weeks have been intense.

I was fortunate enough to spend Sunday night after the conference at a friend's home in the Twin Cities. Several people who were at Re-Imagining got together to talk about it. I felt like a blob of Jell-O that day. I had too much to process and deal with at once.

It took me a couple of weeks to begin admitting to myself what I was facing: during our weekend together I began to see that I am not as straight as I thought I was. You, dear women at our table, gave me the freedom to be in touch with myself and open enough to myself that I was able to see myself in new ways. I forgot to hide my true self from myself.

The last several years I have been praying for a family. I've had in mind a man and then the kids, right? The image that has emerged for me from that weekend is of God coming over to me, putting her arm around me saying: Beloved daughter, let me show you something, and then opening the door to my soul so I can look in.

I don't really know who I am yet. The process of dealing with this intellectually and emotionally is long. It's like when I go to the eye doctor and he flips the lenses so quickly my eyes can't focus on either one. My mind is still flipping back and forth too fast to focus. This has been tough and energizing and freeing. I have been filled with the empowering love of God in amazing ways. The care and love of the people I have shared this with has been extraordinary.

Last Wednesday I was to have my third night home alone in a row. I needed to be in touch with a human being, an accepting human being, and lifting the phone or writing a letter wouldn't do. The doorbell rang. I thought it would be the Lions selling Christmas wreaths. No, it was a seventeen-year-old member of one of my congregations with her Bible and a notebook in hand saying, "I have some questions about the Bible."

She came in and she was furious. She had seen a television show where a minister had talked about God as hating homosexuals. "How could anyone think that? God loves everyone equally. God made gays to be gays." She has

223

such a strong belief in God's love and justice that she couldn't believe that even the Leviticus passage condemned homosexuality; God couldn't say that. Then she gave me a lecture: "Why don't we talk about these things in the church? How come people don't speak up when people say such hateful things?"

Now isn't God amazing? I don't think it could be just a coincidence. I don't have members of my congregation at my door very often, especially with their Bibles in hand.

This morning was our first communion since this process began. Somehow I summoned the courage to invite myself to the table as who I am. Actually at the end of the sermon I listed off all sorts of people whom Jesus invites to the table and included gay men and lesbians in the list. Of course no one knew that I was also inviting myself, but it was the first time I've said the *L*-word from the pulpit—and I did it in all three services. As if that weren't enough for one day, the Advent wreath caught on fire at the first service!

The communion at that first service was one of the most moving I have ever served. I'm sure it will be surpassed the day, if it ever comes, that I can serve and receive openly as who I am.

That last Sunday morning of the conference I rose before dawn and returned to the convention center through almost empty, frosty streets. I was eager and fearful but ready to discover what new things were before me. As those women who followed Jesus rose early on a Sunday morning long before to discover that a new thing had been done, I, too, was filled with fear and confusion, yet confident that God was working to bring me a new life different from any I had known before.

As I have dared to ask the question in the weeks following that November Easter morning, the answer has come back clearly: Yes. And with that *yes*, not the fear and confusion I had expected, but a new clarity, a new strength, a new depth of faith. I discovered my true self through a spiritual process, not a sexual one, and with it I have discovered even more gifts for ministry. Unfortunately, like those women who witnessed the resurrection in Mark's gospel, I find I am still unable to proclaim the good news of my new self and have not publicly told anyone anything. Please continue to keep these things within your hearts. May God's abundant blessings fill your days as they have mine.

The writer is a pastor in a denomination that is not yet open to the good news of this Easter story, but she is grateful for the grace God has bestowed on her in this revelation and in the time following it.

A Question

JO RINGGENBERG

Solidarity!
We went re-imagining
Boldly, openly.

Re-Imagining!
How could such great adventure
Become such sorrow!

Friends have argued, cried;
They've grieved and been sacrificed
Re-imagining.

After the grieving
Will solidarity guide
When church meets woman?

Solidarity!
We come re-imagining
Boldly, openly.

Jo Ringgenberg is a Presbyterian laywoman and elder living in Plymouth, Minnesota.

After the Fact

MARTHA D. WARD

Write an article about the Re-Imagining Conference for publication? Oh, I must admit that I was initially hesitant. I did not want to get hate mail or phone calls from people who had been intimidated by the scare tactics of those who thought Re-Imagining was a threat to Christian faith. I was concerned because I was writing for my Iowa United Methodist Conference newspaper, the *Hawkeye*, and I was writing about the *S*-word.

You see, I've been called a few names in my day, but not usually a heretic or a pagan. After attending Re-Imagining, however, people like myself who appreciated the conference were so labeled by *Good News* magazine and its supporters. Why? No doubt the reasons are extremely complex in reality, but in print they often boiled down to one thing: the *S*-word—*Sophia*. Apparently we shouldn't say it aloud in just any circles, and so I was concerned about the response I might get by writing about it.

Maybe if we had used the Hebrew word for God's wisdom, *hokmah*, at Re-Imagining, we would not have gotten such a rise. But *sophia*, the Greek word, is a woman's name in our culture, and in Proverbs 8 God's wisdom is personified as female; I suppose that's the problem. Many of us have no difficulty understanding that God's wisdom could be characterized as feminine, but some folks seem to. To them apparently it's not *TC*—theologically correct.

The two thousand women and men of many traditions who attended were accused of goddess worship because, for a few days at Re-Imagining, we immersed ourselves in an attribute of God that has a feminine name. I later reread my Re-Imagining worship materials to see if somehow I was secretly duped into goddess worship while thinking I was celebrating God's wisdom as part of our Christian tradition. But it was clear to me that when one of our worship leaders would lead us in the beautiful Hawaiian chant before each speaker by singing "Bless Sophia, dream the vision, share the wisdom dwelling deep within,"[6] we weren't conjuring up a goddess. We were praying that God's wisdom might be shared through the person speaking. In fact, it reminded me of an experience common to events like a lay witness mission, when the one about to speak asks someone to pray for her. Usually then the prayer goes something like "O Lord, I ask that you bless this sister with your wisdom and fill her with your power as she shares your message tonight." It's the same thing; they just don't use the *S*-word.

But I felt compelled to write the article, and I got so irritated by the attack on the conference and on women's groups like United Methodist Women that I decided to send it in. After it was printed in the newspaper, I received none of the angry direct response I feared. What I did receive were numerous verbal expressions of appreciation for my article and about ten written responses from women and men, lay and clergy, that were all positive. The responses ranged from simple words of appreciation to thoughtful reflections on the dangers of hate groups in all areas of our lives today. The only unfavorable responses to my article were two letters to the editor in the next issue of the *Hawkeye*.

While attending Re-Imagining, I never dreamed some participants had come as spies to condemn the event. I thought all had come for the fine theological experience. Only later, when there was no opportunity for direct dialogue, did the attack on Re-Imagining occur. So I'm not surprised that I got no direct negative response to my article, although I'm no longer so naive as to believe that means everyone agreed with me. Perhaps those who disagree also do not want the opportunity for direct dialogue.

For me, one of the great strengths of our United Methodist tradition has been that we have been encouraged to use our critical thinking (reason), celebrate our diversity, and grow from exploring one another's different approaches to faith. As John Wesley said, "We think and let think."[7] Let us be cautious of those who would take such liberties away.

Martha Ward was ordained an elder in the Iowa Conference of the United Methodist Church in 1981. Since 1980 she has pastored local churches in Waterloo and Knoxville, Iowa, where she currently serves as full-time copastor with her husband/colleague, Bob Ward. They have served together in team ministry, modeling egalitarian shared leadership since 1983.

Testimony

DONA E. BOLDING

At Re-Imagining I danced with African women from Liberia. I discussed institutional racism with many colors of Christians, understanding anew its pervasive and sinister force in the popular media and in our hearts. Each day I learned and listened until my soul was full. Women weaving the rag rug together, creating something from nothing. Eating the apple with Eve, breaking a taboo a day. We thrilled to Sweet Honey in the Rock. We sang beautiful music and danced exuberantly. We created color and shape. I fought yawns occasionally and at times wished to slow everything down, to reduce the abundance of liturgy to allow more discussion at our table-full of wonderful, wondering women. Milk and honey made a lovely meal, a brilliant communion. Fed with miraculous manna, transported to the mountaintop, I received Her Spirit: wisdom, justice, power, holiness, goodness, truth, and amidst all, love.

Disappointed in the androcentric language of liturgy and in hymnody; in the gaps in the lectionary and Bible studies where women's stories should be; in the missing voices of women biblical scholars and theologians in sermons and lessons; in the patronizing of women, lay and clergy, who serve the church; in the lack of parity in clerical employment; in all these things that keep the community out of balance, I came to Re-Imagining worn out. Amazing Re-Imagining, where disappointment turned to hope, to a promise of a new way within the church, a lifeboat. Beholding the beautiful sound of uninterrupted women, spending a long weekend remembering God without a single sports metaphor, being among faithful, brilliant, searching, thinking, giving, loving women, I was delighted and blessed.

I returned home to enjoy a pleasant holiday season, sharing my tales of Minneapolis with my friends in Houston. I was packing up my Re-Imagining memorabilia when, surprisingly, Re-Imagining became the great new issue—replacing homosexuality as the place where good and bad Christians part ways in the Church Institutional. Vitriolic letters flew to the editor of the *Sun Presbyterian*, like one from a reader in Louisiana who declared that "The 'Re-Imagining 1993' emphasis was largely downward, toward the genitals. Monkeys emulate that point of view."[8] The executive director of Episcopalians United, writing to Episcopal clergy, rang out a warning of "what our church is coming to!" along with an apology for reprinting words we used in prayer (the now-famous nectar stanza) because they were of a "vulgar nature."[9] The *United*

Methodist Reporter published a photograph of a church leader with the caption, "Retired Bishop Earl Hunt Condemns Sophia." Hunt pronounced that "This is material which must be eradicated from Christian thinking now!"[10] Huh? The Re-Imagining Conference I went to? What did he mean? I wanted to ask Bishop Hunt: How shall the church eradicate wisdom from our thinking? Will the remaining elements of the Spirit—power, holiness, justice, goodness, and truth—have to go also?

Suddenly "How I Spent My Fall Vacation" became a theme I was asked to expound upon by a variety of interested parties. I received an invitation in midwinter to appear before the church court of a very large, very wealthy church in the suburbs. The court was instituted to determine whether that church's session should issue a condemnation of what was now called simply "The Conference." Although I'd never heard of a church court, it sounded like a fun thing for an ex-lawyer and once active Presbyterian elder. The convenor of the court was a wonderful person, warm, open, intelligent, and chagrined to inform me that the preliminary questions the court wanted answered were:

1. *What kind of person would go to a conference like that?*
2. *What is your faith?*

I thought both questions were wonderful. On 8 March 1994, I appeared before the panel of twenty or so—five of whom were women. I felt that I had come foremost on the women's behalf, to speak truth where it would be hard for them to do so. I held forth for fifty uninterrupted minutes, witnessing my love for the community of and in Christ; expressing my appreciation for feminist theology; articulating my own experiences, blessed and cursed, in the patriarchal church; telling the stories of women whom I met in Minneapolis whose commitment to ministries difficult and undersupported amazed me; and assuring them that the Presbyterian money had been well spent for a worthy event. Their attention held. I responded to their questions or opinions for fifteen minutes. From a young male lawyer, "One of the speakers said Jesus dying on the cross was a horrible form of child abuse. That offends me." I told him child abuse offended me, too. Another young man (who turned out to be a clergyman) went through a longish discourse wondering if, in concordance with the Gospel of John, the conference glorified Christ. My response was, "Absolutely." I wanted to add: But your court does not. One fellow announced his decision to discontinue his service on this court and asked for a copy of my speech to show his wife. How far-reaching our Minneapolis experience was!

The exchanges among the men and women who had listened to the tapes delighted me. These folks had been forced by the controversy to listen. One man's incomplete reporting about Delores Williams's address on the atonement prompted one of the women to flesh out Williams's argument that our question should be: What are we willing to live for? Greater exposure to feminist thinking brought refreshment and reassurance to many of the women on the panel, several now conversant in God-talk in the new tradition of Chung Hyun Kyung, Rita Nakashima Brock, Virginia Ramey Mollenkott, and the host of shining stars at Re-Imagining. Surely they enlightened a man or two who would never have thought to listen before.

My experience was at the midpoint of the court's deliberations. The majority of the women (excluding one who said during the question-and-answer period that she would go along with whatever the men did) wrote an ancillary opinion expressing differences from the one issued by the committee as a whole. I have not seen the ultimate decree. Though I have heard that it was less than tolerant, this church did not jump on the opportunity to keep their funds local by scapegoating Re-Imagining. They did not withhold from the national church.

I have been riding a Re-Imagining circuit. The *Houston Post* condensed an hour-long interview with me into a declaration that "Houston attorney and mother Dona Bolding, one of the few local women who attended November's Re-Imagining Conference in Minneapolis, said nothing wrong occurred at the meeting which was so controversial that the Presbyterian Church (U.S.A.) lost millions of dollars over it."[11] I have spoken about Re-Imagining to various church groups and a feminist theology group. I declined to give my materials to a caller from another church who seemed intent upon a witch-burning in absentia; she just wanted my stuff, not my voice. I enjoyed a week studying with Rita Nakashima Brock at Ghost Ranch, viewing the United Methodist Women's press conference, and listening again to the Jesus tapes with a new audience.

Re-Imagining has become a part of my identity. I was there. The blessing continues.

Dona E. Bolding is an attorney, currently serving as a performance artist in public-school libraries in Houston, Texas. She is an ecumenist who enjoys the community of Saint Stephen's Episcopal Church. Married for eleven years, she and Roger Hamilton have three children in elementary school.

Hope with a Borrowed Pen

NANCY J. BERNEKING

True confession time. I left Re-Imagining thinking: Nice conference, now what? On my to-do list were choir on Wednesday, write the clerk of session's monthly report to the congregation by Sunday, do the reading for Thursday's antiracism team meeting, and design the family Christmas card. Don't get me wrong. Re-Imagining was fascinating, and it had some real high points for me.

For example, as a northern Presbyterian born and bred on Brueggemann, Buechner, and Brown, I loved listening to famous women I'd never heard of give colorful, passionate, and enormously sensible talks. I whooped and cheered when these women spoke out loud about my Jesus—the one I'd known for some time who was the victim of political murder. I learned more about myself when I stopped resisting Nancy Chinn's coloring instructions and dutifully scribbled my negative feelings; I was stunned to realize I had instinctively picked up the black pastel: the bad-equals-black tapes of my childhood I had been working so long to eradicate lingered in heretofore undiscovered crevices. At table I found the whirl of presenters, ritual, and conversation somehow combined to further enlarge and make more intimate my image of God. So Re-Imagining was a delightful weekend of discovery, but it was also one more checked-off item on my to-do list. I left feeling relieved, tired, and secretly disappointed that it had been rather conservative.

Since I'm already quite conservative in many ways—I pinch pennies, don't use a credit card, wash dishes by hand, and wouldn't dream of owning an air conditioner—I like to be stretched now and then. In a group, I'm always reluctant to drag out my middle-this middle-that married-mother slide show; other people's lives are much more fascinating, and my life is so stable that even my children are not interested in it. Re-Imagining seemed so tame to me that I was dumbstruck by the backlash. But then I've been surprised by people before.

I remember being at dinner one time in the mid-1980s and asking my teenage daughter what her friends and their families were saying about United States aid to the Nicaraguan Contras. "Mom," she said, "most people don't even eat dinner together let alone talk about aid to the Contras." Is that so? Then there was the Sanctuary movement. Our congregation got involved by providing shelter for a refugee from El Salvador. I had some free time, so I agreed to coordinate the committee's work. I was surprised, amazed actually, a few years later to appear on *60 Minutes*, talking about political asylum law. I thought I had only been doing the work of the church and saving a life. The Gulf War was another stunning moment. While babies were being bombed in Baghdad and I was writing letters and carrying a protest sign between crying jags, most of the world around me thought our country was doing the right thing. It's been the times when things were so clear to me that I have been most surprised to find I hold the minority opinion. It's been those same times—when this-is-not-right slaps me in the face—that I have felt most called to do something.

Even after the backlash began, I probably would have brushed it off as a few God-is-a-guy fellows needing to exhibit their manhood again. But it got mean and ugly and hateful. This is not right, I thought. I must do something, fix it, make it right, get some work done. The steering committee of the conference was continuing to meet to tidy up loose ends when discussion turned to going on. I've known for a long time that going on is one of the things women do best: women are the resurrection gender. As meanness intensified and pleas for help mounted, it seemed the only thing to do. Go on. Resist. Incorporate. Consequently, there we were on that warm summer day.

Perhaps it's my penchant for perfection, but I always use a pencil. As a left-handed child, I found fountain pens difficult and messy to use; and by the time ballpoint pens became common, I was firmly committed to change-your-mind, fix-your-mistake, make-it-neater pencils. So it wasn't unusual that I sat at the table that day with my favorite blue mechanical pencil in my hand, ready to jot notes on my meeting agenda.

The catching-up time at the beginning of the meeting went quickly. We were gathering so frequently these days that little had happened since we had met last. Mary Kay Sauter was chairing the meeting in her new role as co-convenor of the Re-Imagining Community Coordinating Council. She reminded us of our long agenda and moved to the first item, saying "I've been working on the incorporation papers for the community, and they're almost ready to mail to the secretary of state. There's room for a couple of us to sign on the form, but I think it would be great if everyone's signature could be part of the document. I'll pass around a piece of paper that we can submit with the form. You need to print your name and address legibly and then sign it." She handed the paper to the person next to her and went on to the next agenda item while the paper circulated.

Three people wrote their names, and then it was my turn. As the paper came to me, I looked at the pencil in my hand. This will never do, I thought. Rather than dig noisily through my big purse, I whispered to Sally Hill who was sitting next to me, "Can I borrow your pen?" She gave it to me, and I held it ready to write. Now, I've always been a sucker for ceremonies. I do all the appropriate things like cry, laugh, and stand up straight, and suddenly I needed a ceremony. Here we were, fifteen or so of us, about to create a legal organization to help carry forward the dreams of millions of women who long to be equal partners in the church, and we were signing our names as easily as if we were making a list of who would bring what to the next potluck. I shook my head, amazed and amused, and smiled as tears came to my eyes.

I considered interrupting. But then I realized that signing this paper was actually no more significant than signing up for a potluck. After all, being sure that someone brings chocolate is very important; and if the Re-Imagining Community succeeds, it will not be because we signed that paper. What's more, should the community last no longer than a speck of dust in the scheme of history, it will have been one more step forward, one more symbol of resistance, for the baby girls yet to be born. So I shrugged my shoulders, said my own silent ceremonial prayer, and signed my name with a flourish. As I passed the paper to Sally, I thanked her for her pen. Then I picked up my pencil and got on with the day's agenda. There was work to be done.

Nancy J. Berneking is a Presbyterian laywoman who served on the steering committee of the Re-Imagining Conference as coordinator of the preconference events committee. She continues to serve as a member of the Re-Imagining Community Coordinating Council. She wishes that acts of kindness would become less random and more institutionalized.

Trail Markings

LOU BENDER

Setting out to hike one of our state's many beautiful trails, I was thinking about what I would say to my presbytery later in the week, when I was to make a statement about Re-Imagining. As I searched for the trailhead, found the markers, opened the guidebook, and went on my way, I found before me a picture of my experience with Re-Imagining.

My friend had told me that the trail would be marked with white blazemarks. I knew this meant I would find occasional brush strokes of paint on trees lining the trail. When I started on the trail, however, the brush strokes were blue, and I was momentarily confused. But then I realized that in the time since my friend had hiked this trail, the way had been marked in a new color. Sometimes a splash of blue accented the older white marking. Sometimes the blue marking covered the white one completely. Sometimes blue and white showed side by side; other times the blue marking was on a different tree and the white marking was left untouched.

Women's voices blaze the theological trail in a new way, and the trail will look different when women as well as men have left their marks. For those who are watching, the experience can be disconcerting—even frightening. But if we are to follow faithfully the trail God has set before us, then we must trust the Spirit to lead the trailblazers and to protect them when the trail leads in new directions. As a member of the reformed and always reforming Presbyterian community, I believe we would do well to take notice, to watch together in love, and to wait in anticipation of what God will do next.

Lou Bender is a God-follower, song-singer, and storyteller who has been re-imagining life as we know it for as long as she can remember. She currently serves as associate pastor for First Presbyterian Church, Bentonville, Arkansas.

Afterword

Euphoria prevailed in the conference office in the days after Re-Imagining. Glowing evaluations coupled with the delightful stories that had started arriving helped organizers get through the hard but necessary cleanup work of archiving files and closing books. The mood changed quickly, however, when extraordinary reports of Christian despising Christian began arriving as well. The horror stories included tales of hate mail, job losses, death threats, charges of heresy, and more. Backlash, the bane of women throughout history, had surfaced again and was being coordinated by a coterie of the religious right. The stories of attack and fear and isolation were accompanied by cries for support, for connection, for community, for help from Minneapolis.

Although there had been some talk of a small newsletter to help participants stay in touch, the conference was over and we needed to let it go. But to do nothing in the midst of the backlash would mean abandoning those who found themselves in precarious circumstances, giving tacit permission to those who would silence women's voices yet again. What could be done?

Re-Imagining supporters from across the country offered advice. Some urged the steering committee to sue to recover damages from the flagrant copyright violations that were occurring in religious-right media. Others suggested holding press conferences, organizing, or hiring public-relations people to tell the real story. By using the slow discernment process that had been successful throughout conference planning, the committee eventually agreed to reject retaliation and retribution and to embrace re-membering and re-imagining.

The committee decided to explore the possibility of becoming an independent organization—and to dream. What about a newsletter in which clergy and lay people are welcomed to write about theological questions? What about small discussion groups to provide support, study, worship, and dialogue? What about developing resource materials? What about multiethnic discussions to learn more about the similarities and differences between feminist, womanist, and *mujerista* theologies and to discover what women of differing experiences can learn from their sisters' stories? What about starting a group to try new forms of ritual? What about organizing more conferences? What about creating a Re-Imagining Center for Theological Exploration, where discussions, seminars, and worship could occur in safety with respect for differences? What about gathering church people into a community that struggles to share leadership, maintain respectful dialogue, acknowledge differences and work to resolve the conflicts they create, encourage storytelling, practice kindness and civility, challenge old notions, and experiment with new ideas?

With encouragement from the three councils of churches that originally sponsored the conference, the Re-Imagining Community became an independent organization. Its existence is a symbol of hope, of resistance, of remembering, and of course, of re-imagining.

The members of the Re-Imagining Community are not seeking a new religion. Most occupy pews every Sunday and have no intention of abandoning the traditions they claim. They serve on committees, sing in choirs, visit the sick, and pray for the community. Yet many feel isolated and undernourished. The three questions printed on the back of each *Re-Imagining Community Newsletter* reflect concerns we've heard voiced again and again: How do we sustain hope? How do we stay connected? How do we nurture our faith in God?

Re-imaginers are devoted Christians who feel exiled from their own tradition and are trying to find a way back home. There are, within the collected wisdom of the church's literature, many similar stories of exile. When Israel is taken into exile in Babylon, the Psalmist writes:

> *By the rivers of Babylon—there we sat down and there we wept when we remembered Zion. On the willows there we hung up our harps. For there our captors asked us for songs, and our tormentors asked for mirth, saying "Sing us one of the songs of Zion!" How could we sing the Lord's song in a foreign land? (Ps. 137:1–4)*

To a people who had understood themselves to be righteous by virtue of their presence in God's land, this was a very poignant question. The answer to the people Israel comes through the prophet Jeremiah: "Build houses and live in them; plant gardens and eat what they produce" (Jer. 29: 5). Plant gardens. God is present anywhere, even in exile.

To the people who feel exiled from the churches they attend, the re-imagining story is an oasis. It is a reminder that God is present to us anywhere, even in exile. It is a witness that God's presence comes to us through the human community, and we are not alone. To tell our stories and speak the truth of our experience is one way to plant a garden. And we will plant them. We will plant gardens of lived truth in our churches, in our communities, and in our homes. We will plant them with our friends, our neighbors, our lovers, our husbands and wives, and above all, we will plant them with our children. We will remember that ferment and discomfort are forerunners of change and that finding a way home from exile requires courage, creativity, and openness to previously unexplored solutions. We will sing the songs of our God. We will sing them with hearts full of love and rage until the land that seems foreign becomes our home.

Nancy J. Berneking and Pamela Carter Joern

Notes

Introduction

1. "The Year's Top Stories: Political Christians, Christian Politics," *The Christian Century* 111 (21–28 Dec. 1994): 1211–1213.

Part One: Gathering

1. *Household* is used here in the sense of Letty M. Russell's *Household of Freedom: Authority in Feminist Theology* (Philadelphia: Westminster Press, 1987), 36–37. That is, household is a metaphor for a community of mutual caring in which personal relationships are in patterns of partnership.

2. This is the text as originally written. The refrain was altered slightly for the Re-Imagining Conference because it was set to music.

3. Rosemary Radford Ruether, "Seeking the Better Part," *Soujourners* 21 (Nov. 1992): 24–25.

Part Two: Finding God

1. The Re-Imagining Community, *Re-Imagining* (Minneapolis: Twin Cities Metropolitan Church Commission, 1993), 2.

2. Letty M. Russell, Kwok Pui-Lan, Ada María Isasi-Díaz, Katie Cannon, eds., *Inheriting Our Mothers' Gardens: Feminist Theology in Third World Perspective* (Philadelphia: Westminster Press, 1988), 70.

3. Pamela Carter Joern, *Simple Gifts* (play commissioned for the Re-Imagining Conference, Minneapolis, Nov. 1993), prologue.

4. Kwok Pui-Lan, *Re-Imagining: Jesus*, session at the Re-Imagining Conference, Minneapolis, Nov. 1993 (Apple Valley, Minn.: Resource Express, 1993), audiocassette.

5. Delores Williams, *Re-Imagining: Jesus*, session at the Re-Imagining Conference, Minneapolis, Nov. 1993 (Apple Valley, Minn.: Resource Express, 1993), audiocassette.

6. Barbara Lundblad, *Re-Imagining: Jesus*, session at the Re-Imagining Conference, Minneapolis, Nov. 1993 (Apple Valley, Minn.: Resource Express, 1993), audiocassette.

7. Martin Buber, *The Eclipse of God: Studies in the Relation between Religion and Philosophy* (New York: Harper and Row, 1952), 17–18.

8. The Re-Imagining Community, *Re-Imagining*, 19.

9. Nancy Chinn, *Even the Stones Cry Out,* a series of art forms created for the Re-Imagining Conference, Minneapolis, Nov. 1993.

10. Ibid.

11. Rita Nakashima Brock, *Re-Imagining: God,* session at the Re-Imagining Conference, Minneapolis, Nov. 1993 (Apple Valley, Minn.: Resource Express, 1993), audiocassette.

12. Mary Daly and June Caputi, *Webster's First New Intergalactic Wickedary of the English Language* (Boston: Beacon Press, 1987), 114.

13. Mary Farrell Bednarowski, *The Spirit of Re-Imagining,* session at the Re-Imagining Conference, Minneapolis, Nov. 1993 (Apple Valley, Minn.: Resource Express, 1993), audiocassette.

14. Bernice Johnson Reagon, *The Spirit of Re-Imagining,* session at the Re-Imagining Conference, Minneapolis, Nov. 1993 (Apple Valley, Minn.: Resource Express, 1993), audiocassette.

15. Delores Williams, *Re-Imagining: Jesus.*

Part Three: Lamenting

1. United Nations, *The State of the World's Women 1985* (Oxford, U.K.: New Internationalist Publications, 1985), 4–18.

2. Mary Daly, *Beyond God the Father: Toward a Philosophy of Women's Liberation* (Boston: Beacon Press, 1973), 19.

3. The VISN Women's Television Project, "Violence against Women and Children: Where Is the Faith Community?" (New York: Vision Interfaith Satellite Network, 1993), 1.

4. Marie Fortune, quoted in *Reducing the Risk: Making Your Child Safe from Child Sexual Abuse* (Matthews, N.C.: Church Law and Tax Report, 1993), videocassette.

5. Letty M. Russell, *Human Liberation in a Feminist Perspective: A Theology* (Philadelphia: Westminster Press, 1974), 43.

6. *Presbyterian Layman*, Jan./Feb. 1994, cover photo.

7. Faye Kommedahl, "Re-Imagining the Church for Women," *Minnesota Women's Press,* 17 Nov. 1993, 13.

8. Thomas C. Oden, "Encountering the Goddess at Church," *Christianity Today* 37 (16 Aug. 1993); reprinted in *Good News: The Bimonthly Magazine for United Methodists* 27 (Nov./Dec. 1993).

9. Bard Thompson, *Liturgies of the Western Church* (Cleveland: Meridian Books, 1961; Philadelphia: Fortress Press, 1980), 22.

10. Elizabeth Dodson Gray, "Women Want Power to Imagine and Name God," *National Catholic Reporter* (1 April 1994): 21.

Part Four: Rejoicing

1. Robert Browning, "Epilogue to Asolando," in *A Treasury of Great Poems English and America*, comp. Louis Untermeyer (New York: Simon and Schuster, 1955), 874.

2. Pamela Carter Joern, *Simple Gifts*, prologue.

3. Bernice Johnson Reagon, *The Spirit of Re-Imagining*.

4. *Bull Durham*, motion picture, Orion Pictures, 1988.

Part Five: Going On

1. Laurel Thatcher Ulrich, "Vertuous Women Found: New England Ministerial Literature, 1668–1735," *American Quarterly* 28:1 (spring 1976): 20–40.

2. Ann Braude, "Women's History *Is* American Religious History" (paper presented at the meeting of the American Academy of Religion, Chicago, Ill., 20 Nov. 1994).

3. "The Year's Top Stories: Political Christians, Christian Politics," *The Christian Century* 111 (21–28 Dec. 1994):1211.

4. Ntozake Shange, *For Colored Girls Who Have Considered Suicide When the Rainbow Is Enuf* (New York: Macmillan, 1975), 63.

5. Ivone Gebara as interviewed by Mary Judith Ress, "Cosmic Theology: Ecofeminism and Panentheism," *Creation Spirituality* (Nov./Dec. 1993): 11.

6. The Re-Imagining Community, *Re-Imagining*, 19.

7. John Wesley, "The Character of a Methodist," in *Works of the Reverend John Wesley, A.M.*, 3d ed., ed. Thomas Jackson (London, 1829–31), 340–47; quoted in Albert C. Outler, ed., *John Wesley* (New York: Oxford University Press, 1964), 92.

8. J. A. James, "Letter to the Editor," *Sun Presbyterian* (Denton, Tex.: Synod of the Sun), March 1994.

9. Todd H. Wetzel, *Episcopalians United* (newsletter of Episcopalians United), 13 June 1994.

10. Stephen L. Swecker, "Bishop Calls 'Sophia' Theology Worst Heresy in 1,500 Years of Christianity," *United Methodist Reporter*, 28 Jan. 1994, 1.

11. Steve Brunsman, "Women's Conference Imagery Causes Bitter Division," *Houston Post*, 4 June 1994.

About the Editors

Nancy J. Berneking is a writer, project manager, curriculum developer, and adult educator with a bachelor of arts degree in mathematics and a master of arts degree in educational psychology. Her volunteer work in the church and community led to her selection as a member of the Twin Citian Volunteer Hall of Fame in 1993. She is married to Bill Berneking, her favorite dance partner, and is mother of Dr. Michael Berneking, a family-practice physician in Indianapolis, Indiana, and Amanda Berneking, a businesswoman in the Twin Cities. She enjoys reading, thinking, singing, working with Girl Scouts, sleuthing for family history, and encouraging kindergartners to love books by reading them stories.

Pamela Carter Joern is an ordained member of American Baptist Churches USA. A graduate of United Theological Seminary in the Twin Cities, she is a freelance writer and educator, and editor of the *Re-Imagining Community Newsletter*. She has also written five plays that have been produced in the Twin Cities, including *Simple Gifts,* which was commissioned for the Re-Imagining Conference. She is mother of two daughters, Shannon and Raegan, and lives with her husband, Brad, in Minneapolis. When she is not reading or writing, she likes long walks, quilting, gardening, and music, and she swears that one day she is going to take a tapdance class.

Index of Contributors